THE ULTIMATE MONEY GUIDE FOR

BUBBLES, BUSTS, RECESSION, AND DEPRESSION

THE ULTIMATE MONEY GUIDE FOR
BUBBLES, BUSTS, RECESSION, AND DEPRESSION

MARTIN D. WEISS, PhD

WILEY

John Wiley & Sons, Inc.

Published by John Wiley & Sons, Inc., Hoboken, New Jersey.
Published simultaneously in Canada.

Substantial portions of this book were taken from an earlier edition, *The Ultimate Depression Survival Guide: Protect Your Savings, Boost Your Income, and Grow Wealthy Even in the Worst of Times,* published by John Wiley & Sons in 2009.

For general information on our other products and services or for technical support, please contact our Customer Care Department within the United States at (800) 762-2974, outside the United States at (317) 572-3993 or fax (317) 572-4002.

Wiley also publishes its books in a variety of electronic formats. Some content that appears in print may not be available in electronic books. For more information about Wiley products, visit our web site at www.wiley.com.

ISBN 978-1-118-01134-8

Printed in the United States of America

10 9 8 7 6 5 4 3 2 1

For my wife and son, Elisabeth and Anthony

CONTENTS

INTRODUCTION

Never before in your lifetime has your money, your home, your retirement, and your entire financial future seen greater turmoil!

You've already witnessed the worst real estate disaster, the largest bank failures, and the biggest losses of wealth since the Great Depression.

You've seen America's most powerful corporate executives forecasting disaster, confessing they're going bankrupt, and begging Congress for massive bailouts.

You've seen our government take gigantic, radical steps to end the crisis and bring about a recovery, only to create new bubbles and risk larger busts.

You've seen the U.S. Federal Reserve do something it had never done before—print massive amounts of paper money to try to pump up the economy.

You must recognize it's high time to *do something* to protect yourself.

In this book, you will learn how. I give you step-by-step instructions to avoid the dangers, get your money to safety, and secure your family's financial well-being. I explain what's likely to happen next, how far real estate and stocks could fall, how long the crisis can last, how much government rescues can or cannot actually achieve, and how to know when a true recovery is about to begin.

Best of all, I show you how to separate the weak from the strong with our Weiss ratings, the only ratings that cover all U.S. financial sectors with no conflicts of interest.

And as a special extra, I show how to turn this massive crisis into an equally massive opportunity. While most people cringe in fear of real estate declines, you can turn them into unprecedented bargains. While most investors run away from stock market crashes, you can transform them into profit opportunities. Instead of the confusion and paralysis that overcomes most Americans, you will have clarity of vision and a solid plan of action. Instead of losing a lot of money, you can grow your wealth significantly.

Surviving—and thriving—during this crisis is not rocket science. You don't have to forecast the future. You don't even need investing experience.

The simple secret is to throw out your prejudices, start with a clean slate, and then follow common sense. Right now, that means taking a cold, hard look at the events around you and recognizing that the value of your home, your 401(k), and even some of your supposedly safe investments *can* continue to run into trouble. You have the power to stop the bloodletting; there's no law, rule, or ethic that requires you to sit there quietly or accept financial punishment passively. You have easy ways to get your money to safety without delay and without remorse. Plus, you have every right to *use* the crisis to grow your wealth—not only for your family, children, and grandchildren—but also to do your part for the future of the U.S. economy.

Our Weiss ratings identified the vulnerable companies most likely to fail—and most likely to thrive. Plus, I warned about this very crisis in my 2003 book, *Crash Profits,* and I have continued to do so in my *Money and Markets* e-letter ever since. I have nagged, cajoled, and shouted this message from the rooftops. But it has given me no pleasure to see my warnings come true. I have dreaded the bubbles and busts as often as I have predicted them. I prayed they would not come to pass. But now that they're here, I have a new prayer:

That you are, or soon will be, out of danger and ready for the worst.

That the worst will strike swiftly and *end* swiftly.

That, when we hit bottom, no matter how ugly the future may appear, you, we, and many others will have the fortitude to reinvest, help get our country back on its feet, and move on to better times.

Just promise me one thing: No matter how dark a tunnel may seem, never forget it is *not the end of the world.* Our country has been through worse before, and we survived. We will survive today's tough times too.

But you cannot stand idly by. At this landmark turning point in our history, the choices you make today could determine your fate—and the destiny of everyone that depends on you—for decades to come. Your decisions now could make the difference between a lifetime of struggle and a successful career; becoming a ward of the state or retiring comfortably; risking poverty-stricken illness or enjoying wealth and health.

Whatever your choices may be, *do not procrastinate.* And whenever you take action, don't do so in haste. Your response to the current crisis—or any new crisis that may ensue—should be both prompt and planned, both bold and prudent.

This book is your action plan.

In Chapters 1 and 2, I show you why tough times are likely to continue, and I walk you through your first and most urgent priority—to reduce debt and build the biggest pile of *cash* possible.

A major continuing source of financial difficulties is Wall Street deceptions, cover-ups, and lies. So before you make one more decision about your investments or your financial future, you must be aware of this hidden danger, the subject of Chapter 3.

Next, in Chapters 4 through 10, I guide you through the many land mines still threatening the average investor—in the housing market, common stocks, banks, and insurance companies—while guiding you to safe alternatives.

Chapter 11 is dedicated to *protection.* You may have real estate you cannot sell or a pension fund beyond your control. You may have bonds that have no market or a business that continues to provide income. All could be assets that you must keep, and yet, at the same time, all are assets that could be vulnerable to losses in any future decline. In this chapter, I give you a practical solution to help untie this knotty dilemma.

Chapter 12 guides you to a major profit opportunity with a plan to make money directly from a market decline; and Chapter 13 shows you how to *continue* making money even with the worst disasters.

But your largest payoff of all will come when the price of many assets hits rock bottom and it's time to buy the bargains of the century. Recognizing that bottom when it comes can open up the opportunity to greatly boost your income, buy some of the best assets in the world for a pittance, and stake out a high ground for yourself, your children, and generations to come. In Chapters 14 through 17, I show you when and how.

Just remember that none of this is predetermined. At times, the tsunami of crisis may seem unstoppable. But ultimately, when the causes of the crisis have finally been largely removed, it will finally open up a window for you, me, and our leaders to choose our own destiny. Chapters 18 and 19 represent my best effort to define what I think our worst and best choices will be.

Last, as a true, enduring recovery gets under way, it will be time to expand your horizons and look for new opportunities to grow wealth. When you read this book, it may still be too soon to buy many of the best investments. But it won't be too soon to cast a glance into the future and see how some of the world's largest fortunes are likely to be made, the subject of Chapter 20.

If you have read my 2009 book, you will see that this book thoroughly updates every chapter and adds several new ones—on the Federal Reserve, on insurance, and on other key topics. So much has changed in just one year. Yet, the broad trends and conclusions have not.

In this volatile new world, the key to your success will be to stay up to date with change. And with so much changing so quickly, I have decided to give you a free service to alert you by e-mail to any upgrades or downgrades in our ratings of *your* company. To sign up, go to www.weisswatchdog.com.

Plus, we promise to keep you up to date daily by our e-letter. At critical turning points, especially in the real estate market or the stock market, these alerts could make the difference between missing an important danger or opportunity . . . and taking appropriate action at the right time.

For your free sign-up, visit www.moneyandmarkets.com/alert. Or send your name and e-mail address directly to me at Martin@ weissinc.com. If you do not have e-mail, and would like to receive one of the free reports mentioned in this book, call 800-814-3029. Or mail your request to Martin D. Weiss, c/o Ultimate Money Guide, 15430 Endeavour Drive, Jupiter, FL 33478.

Good luck and God bless!

Martin D. Weiss
Palm Beach Gardens
November 9, 2010
Martin@weissinc.com

CHAPTER 1

WHY THE TOUGH TIMES ARE JUST BEGINNING!

Despite the greatest government rescue operations of all time, America continues to suffer through the toughest of times.

The place is every home, business, and community. The time is now.

And the pattern is now clear: First a great speculative bubble . . . then a great bust . . . followed by massive government stimulus, bailouts, and money printing . . . and then . . . still another, even greater bubble and bust.

When all is said and done, some people make fortunes. But millions of average hard-working people lose their jobs, get evicted from their homes, sink deeper into debt, and even risk abject poverty.

Wall Street and Washington talk about recovery. But for nearly everyone on Main Street, the bubble-and-bust cycle is a roller coaster that begins to feel more like an on-again-off-again *depression* with each passing day.

No one under the age of 80 has ever had personal experience with a similar episode.

Nor have I. I was born in 1946, just as we were leaving the final vestiges of America's Great Depression behind. I've studied that historic period with books, charts, and numbers, but that's not the same thing. I spent years in Japan before and after their 20-year depression, but that, too, was different.

What truly brings me close to a visceral understanding of bubbles, busts, recessions, and depressions is the half century I shared with my father, J. Irving Weiss, one of the few economists who not only advised investors during the Great Depression, but actually predicted it.

Dad was so proud of that unusual feat that he began telling me stories about it when I was five years old. Vicariously, I lived through the bubble of the Roaring Twenties, the Crash of 1929, the massive bank failures of the 1930s, and the multiple great recessions that ensued. Through Dad's teachings, I felt as though I was there with him when investors lost fortunes, when we hit rock bottom in 1933, when the economy rallied, fell again, and then finally enjoyed a true recovery; when old fortunes were lost and new ones were made.

Dad was not only a loving father, but also my mentor, partner, and best friend. I wish he could be here today to write to you directly and help you get through these tough times personally. But as soon as I was old enough, I helped him write his investment books; and in 1971, soon after I founded my own investment research and ratings company, he helped me write mine. Although he's gone, I can feel his vibrant energy and calming spirit beside me; and in almost every chapter of this book, I will let him speak to you posthumously.[1]

Think of this book as co-authored by the two of us. He will tell you about his experiences and analysis during the 1930s; I will tell you what it means for the crises of today—*and what you can do about it*—based on our objective research and ratings. A lot has changed since then. What hasn't changed is our passionate desire to help you through it.

Dad first went to Wall Street in 1924 to learn everything he could about money. Five years later, when the Great Crash struck, he did not own any stocks. His parents were recent immigrants from Eastern Europe with barely enough to keep food on the table. He had to save everything he earned, bring it home, and give it to his mother. He knew how real estate had collapsed in Florida, and he saw how America's farms were in disarray. He didn't want to gamble his hard-earned savings on another bubble.

The bubble turned to bust when the stock market crashed in 1929. But soon after the crash, the market rallied for almost six months, and nearly everyone on Wall Street was sure the crisis was over. Dad was sure it had barely begun. He persuaded his clients and friends to sell everything, get the heck out of the market, and pile up as much cash as they could. He was so convinced the market would fall again that he even borrowed $500 from his mother to sell short—to profit from the market's decline.

Just as he feared, the Crash of 1929 was just the beginning—the opening act of the greatest decline in modern history. From its peak, the Dow Jones Industrials Average fell 89 percent. Compared to the Dow's peak in 2007, that would be tantamount to a plunge of more than 12,600 points—to a low of approximately 1,500. Dad explains it this way:

> In the 1930s, at each step down the slippery slope of the market's decline, Washington would periodically announce some new initiative to turn things around. President Hoover would give a new pep talk promising "prosperity around the corner." And often, the Dow staged dramatic rallies—up 30 percent on the first round, 48 percent on the second, 23 percent on the third, and more. Each time, I sought to use the rallies as selling opportunities. I persuaded more of my clients to get rid of their stocks and pile up cash. I even told them to take their money out of shaky banks.
>
> On the surface, it might have appeared that just sitting out the crisis got you nowhere. Actually, though, it was a great strategy for building wealth. Prices were falling—on homes, on automobiles, on almost everything. So the more prices fell, the more your money was worth. Just by saving money, stashing the cash, keeping your job, and going about your daily life, you were building wealth. You didn't have to know about investing. All you needed to figure out was how to protect yourself from the bad times. Then, when we hit rock bottom—that was the time to start buying real estate, stocks, or bonds.
>
> You could also profit immensely from the decline itself, with short selling. That's how my friend Bernard Baruch built

a great fortune, and how I did, too. But even if you never sold one share of stock short, just sitting out the crash and building cash opened up great wealth-building opportunities as we approached the end of the decline.

That end came with two events: The inauguration of our new president, Franklin D. Roosevelt, and the national banking holiday he declared on his third day in office. But after three years of panics and crashes, most people greeted those events with dread. They thought it would be the beginning of another, even steeper slide. Some people even said it was the final chapter of capitalism itself. As it turned out, that was precisely the right time to pick up some of the greatest bargains of the century and make a lot of money.

Helping people make money was Dad's profession, but his passion in life went far beyond money; he was a man of deep empathy and feeling for his fellow man. When others suffered, he suffered alongside them. He gave them jobs, bought them meals, and offered an abundance of free advice.

Most of all, he did not want to see the United States go through another depression ever again. His vision for accomplishing that goal, however, was very different from that of most economists in the post-Depression era. Whether Republican or Democrat, their strategy was to yank the economy out of nearly every slump and slumber, forever seeking to keep the economy growing, always bailing out major institutions that failed. His philosophy was non-partisan—he believed excesses in either direction hurt both the rich and the poor. What we needed instead, was *moderation* in *both* directions. "The only way to avoid the pain of a great bust," he wrote, "is to refrain from the excesses of a great boom."

Now, in the twenty-first century, it's clear that you face similar dangers and have similar opportunities. Despite the many historic differences between then and now, the 1930s and the 2010s have some key elements in common: A severe contraction in the economy over multiple years, creating massive unemployment, delivering devastating financial losses to large segments of the population, creating giant federal deficits, and prompting governments to take extraordinary measures.

Plus, we also have modern, contemporary episodes to help us better understand these tough times, which I discuss in a moment.

Always remember, however, that economic declines never were—and never will be—one-way streets. Even the worst crisis is interrupted by intermediate rallies and recoveries, sometimes weak, sometimes stronger.

These recoveries, however, can be highly misleading. They are driven mostly by unprecedented government intervention. At first blush, they *appear* to end the crisis. But in reality, they can actually make it worse by creating massive federal deficits. They rarely create prosperity for the majority of the population.

A Permanent Recession?

Imagine a world in which the economy never really emerges from recession. Imagine a time and place in which economists talk first of a double-dip recession; then about a triple-dip recession; and ultimately admit the dire reality of a long, protracted depression. Imagine chronically high unemployment, overwhelming government indebtedness, shrinking population, deepening poverty—even spreading homelessness among college graduates. Think about a 20-year period in which stock investors continually lose fortunes and retirees get nearly zero income on their savings, with no end in sight.

A future scenario? No! It's a very accurate description of Japan's on-again-off-again depression from 1990 through 2010. I worked as a financial analyst in a major Osaka-Tokyo firm before that period. And I periodically visit my son, Anthony, who lives in Japan today. So I have witnessed the before-and-after of Japan's depression firsthand.

There are important cultural differences between the United States and Japan. But there is one overarching similarity: massive, persistent government attempts to boost the economy, which ultimately failed.[2]

Back in the 1980s, Japan was on its way to becoming the world's number one economy—not necessarily in terms of GDP, but in many other key aspects: It led the world in technology. Its multinational companies and financial institutions were the largest in the world. Its trade surpluses and cash savings exceeded those of any other nation on the planet. But by 2010, Japan had fallen to number three in GDP, surpassed by China and slipping on nearly every front in which it was leading before—technology, trade, and cash.

In normal times, more than 99 percent of college graduates were employed during the critical April hiring season. If significantly more than 1 percent failed to get work, it was considered shocking. Reason: Unlike their counterparts in the United States, once they missed that window, most became unemployable. Companies viewed them as rejects, failures. In the next hiring season, it would be extremely difficult for them to get another interview. But by 2010, approximately 20 percent of recent college graduates were failing to get a job. Many wound up at their parents' home to spend their days playing video games, or worse, on the streets. In the Japanese context, that was *20* times more shocking than anything ever seen in prior generations.

When my wife and I lived in Japan in the early 1980s, homelessness was virtually nonexistent. By 2010, although still small compared to homelessness in the United States and parts of Europe, you could see shanties along Tokyo's river banks, people living under bridges, and the jobless college grads loitering around major train stations.

The crime rate in 2010, also still low by U.S. standards, was dramatically higher than it was years ago. Prostitution among middle-class teens, unheard of before, was a real problem. Teenage suicide soared. Health care, once among the best in the world, deteriorated. Not convinced? Then consider the hard facts:

- *The twenty-year depression.* From 1990 through 2010, Japan's economy has been in a semipermanent catatonic state—wavering from subpar growth to mild recession. An old friend, a former director of a major Japanese economic research institute, called it "the 20-year recession that never really ended and the 20-year recovery that never really began—in other words, a depression."
- *Banking dinosaurs.* Every major bank that collapsed in those two decades was patched up with megamergers and government aid. In 1999, for example, we saw the massive three-way marriage of the Industrial Bank of Japan, Dai-Ichi Kangyo, and Fuji Banks—all weak institutions loaded with toxic assets. Both

previously and subsequently, there were many more bailouts. All failed to revive Japan's banking sector.

- *Twenty-year bear market!* Near the end of 1989, Japan's benchmark Nikkei 225 Index reached an all-time peak of 38,957. But then it promptly crashed by 47 percent in less than nine months. And after 20 years, it still had not recovered those losses. To the contrary, at its lows in 2009, the Nikkei was down to 7,021, a loss of 82 percent from its all-time high. And even after a global stock market recovery that began in March of that year, the Nikkei was still down 76 percent from its highs! Were there intermediate rallies? Of course! After its first bust in late 1989, the Japanese stock market enjoyed *five* major rallies. Each one raised investor hopes for an end to the 20-year bear market, and each one gave way to the dire economic realities, ushering in a new plunge to new all-time lows, plus big *additional* losses for investors.

Where did Japan go wrong? Its chronic malaise was not rooted in its culture or its people. It was primarily caused by misguided government policy driven by political pressure to achieve the impossible.

Japan was the first major industrial nation to drop interest rates to practically zero and keep them there almost indefinitely. Japan was the first to bail out so many large banks so consistently. And Japan was also the leader of fiscal stimulus: Just in its first depression decade, Tokyo launched a stimulus package of 10.7 trillion yen in August 1992, another for 13.2 trillion in April 1993, 6.2 trillion in September 1993, 15.3 trillion in February 1994, 14.2 trillion in September 1995, 16.7 trillion in April 1998, 23.9 trillion in November 1998, and 18 trillion in November 1999. In its second depression decade, it launched many more. Yet after each government-engineered recovery, the economy fell back into recession; and after each government-inspired stock market rally, the Nikkei plunged again, falling to still *lower* lows.

Bottom line: Despite all the banking bailouts, stimulus programs, money printing, and zero interest rates—policies that economists lump under "Keynesian pump-priming"—all the emperor's horses and all the emperor's men could not put the Japanese miracle back together again. The Japanese economy still suffered two lost decades of deflation, lackluster growth, and declining stock prices. Corporate earnings still fell. Consumers were still pinched. Japan's status as a world economic power continued to decline. Investors lost fortunes and then lost still more fortunes—again and again.

The *Wall Street Journal* explained it this way:

> Keynesian "pump-priming" in a recession has often been tried, and as an economic stimulus, it is overrated. The money that the government spends has to come from somewhere, which means from the private economy in higher taxes or borrowing. The public works are usually less productive than the foregone private investment.[3]

Ironically, in the 1990s, the U.S. Treasury Secretary and Fed Chairman periodically flew to Tokyo to lecture the Japanese about the futility and danger of their policies. Yet in the late 2000s, their successors vigorously pursued virtually the same policies: They sought to keep dying companies alive. They wanted to outlaw the business cycle. They chased an elusive dream of creating eternal prosperity and an unending bull market.

Obviously, this didn't work in Japan. It could not work in the United States, either. In the real world, companies are born and companies must die. The economy expands and it must also contract. Investors buy and they must also sell. No government, no matter how powerful, can change this reality. No government can stop the march of time, fool Mother Nature, or repeal the law of gravity. Most people in Japan now saw this clearly. They knew how much they had been lied to—repeatedly, for 20 long years. That helps explain why, by year's end 2010, Japan had been through five prime ministers in four years and was going on a sixth. That's also why voters had permanently kicked the ruling party out of office for the first time in modern history.[4]

A growing minority of Americans also began to see the light: Despite the trillions in bailouts and money printing, despite a constant barrage of happy talk from Washington, and even after a series of rallies on Wall Street, the average American knew that the U.S. economy was not passing even the most basic smell test. Even after two years of recovery, the United States was still suffering from the biggest home foreclosure crisis in history, the most people ever on food stamps, and the worst overall poverty rate in half a century. The entire concept of middle class was being challenged. The entire future of the nation was widely questioned.

Like in Japan, this would also have dramatic political consequences. Nearly anyone in office—whether Democratic or Republican—was vulnerable to severe attacks. A kind of third party was emerging. The entire premise of monetary and fiscal policy—including the powers of Federal Reserve itself—was in great flux.

But not all is lost. As I explain later, there is still hope—for the United States, and even for Japan. But looking at the immediate future, all this raises very serious and urgent questions:

Was the United States truly following a path similar to Japan's? If so, how much longer could its on-again-off-again recession last? How much further might home prices fall? What about the stock market? Would the U.S. government continue to let the federal deficit balloon out of control? Or would it change course and shift from stimulus to austerity? If so, would the Federal Reserve print even more money wantonly to offset the shock. Overall, would the United States replicate the experience of Japan's two lost decades? Or would it experience a crisis more akin to its Great Depression of the 1930s?

You could count on your fingers the number of serious analysts who believed the latter scenario was even a remote possibility. And yet, stranger things had already happened, including the largest bank and insurance company collapses of all time. Before he passed away, Dad wrote:

> Some people of my generation have fond memories of the family togetherness and shared sacrifices of America's Great Depression, and I do, too. But I also cannot forget the numbers I studied or the suffering they implied. In just three short years between the peak of the stock market boom in 1929 and the bottom in 1932, it felt like the entire world was falling apart. The financial bubble burst. Big companies failed. America lost 13 million jobs. Unemployment surged to 25 percent. American industry cut its production nearly in half. Home construction plunged by more than four-fifths. Deflation—falling prices—drove the value of almost every asset into the gutter. Over 5,000 banks failed and ultimately disappeared.
>
> Most Americans—especially the youngsters who manage billions of dollars on Wall Street—have no concept of the power

and speed of a great stock market crash. They've never lived through one. So it's hard for them to visualize it. In 1929, people were jumping out of windows, and once-wealthy people were selling apples on street corners. The shock waves reached into almost every office and every home in the country and in the world. Next time, especially if Washington tries too hard to stop the crisis, it could ultimately be just as bad, or even worse.

I agree. Yes, the government is acting more aggressively this time to prevent the worst-case scenario, but is that truly good or bad? Yes, we have a more modern market system, but we also have new, unprecedented risks and weaknesses that were small or nonexistent in the 1930s.

Unprecedented Risks and Weaknesses

If you're still skeptical about the severity of the most recent crisis, you don't have to believe former Fed chairman Alan Greenspan who, in testimony before Congress, said it was the worst in 100 years.

You need not recall the unforgettable image of former Treasury secretary Henry Paulson literally dropping to his knees before Speaker of the House Nancy Pelosi, begging for the billions he said were needed to prevent "a total Wall Street meltdown."[5]

Nor must you heed the testimony of the president's National Commission on Fiscal Responsibility and Reform, urging drastic and immediate action to reduce the nation's trillion-dollar deficits.

All you have to do is get up from your chair, open the door, and take a walk outside.

Nearly everything you see and hear will clue you in to the true plight of our times—1 out of 7 home owners delinquent or foreclosed on their mortgage; 4 out of 10 owing more than the value of their home; nearly 5 out of 10 among the millions of unemployed, out of work for more than six months; 7 out of 10 Americans fearful of the future, and rightfully so.

Or you could just look at the value of middle-class homes, the largest asset of most Americans—properties bought for $450,000 now selling for $150,000; neighborhoods once the pride of their cities, now virtual ghost towns.

Even as they tried to justify their past actions, our leaders them-selves inadvertently sound the alarm. If they had not acted swiftly to rescue the global markets, they claim, the entire system would have collapsed. Thus, to avert what they feared would be the ulti-mate disaster, the governments of the richest countries embarked on the most expensive financial rescues of all time.

The government bailed out bankrupt banks, broken brokerage firms, insolvent insurers, ailing auto manufacturers and any com-pany they deemed essential to the economy. They pumped money into mortgage markets, consumer credit markets, and even stock markets. They prodded lenders to lend, consumers to consume, investors to invest. And they justified all of these extreme measures as their only hope to prevent "the end of the civilization as we know it."

I am not nearly as pessimistic, and, as I explain later, I see silver linings in this crisis that most others seem to be missing. But for the purpose of this chapter, suffice it to say that the urgent measures that leaders have sought so strenuously to justify now beg equally urgent questions that I challenge them to answer: "What happens when a similar or worse crisis returns? Will you have the political will and the financial resources to save the day again?"

They have done everything in their power to prevent another great depression. But have they truly addressed the cause of the crisis? Or are they merely creating another bubble? Here's Dad's answer to a similar question I asked him before he passed away:

> In the 1930s, I was tracking the facts and the numbers as they were being released—to figure out what might happen next. I was an analyst, and that was my job. So I remember them well.
>
> Years later, economists like Milton Friedman and my young friend Alan Greenspan looked back at those days to deci-pher what went wrong. They concluded that it was mostly the government's fault, especially the Federal Reserve's. They developed the theory that the next time we're on the brink of a depression, the government can nip it in the bud simply by acting sooner and more aggressively.
>
> Bah! Those guys weren't there back then. When I first went to Wall Street, Friedman was in junior high and Greenspan was in diapers.

I saw exactly what the Fed was doing in the 1930s: They did everything in their power to try to stop the panic. They coddled the banks. They pumped in billions of dollars. But it was no use. They eventually figured out they were just throwing good money after bad.

You didn't have to be an economist to understand what the real problem was. It was sinking public confidence, and money didn't buy confidence. To restore confidence would take more than just money. It would also take time.

The true roots of the 1930s bust were in the 1920s boom, the Roaring Twenties. That's when the Fed gave cheap money to the banks like there was no tomorrow. That's why the banks loaned the money to the brokers, the brokers loaned it to speculators, and the speculation created the stock market bubble. That was the real cause of the crash and the depression! Not the government's "inaction" in the 1930s!

By 1929, our economy was a house of cards. It didn't matter which cards the government propped up or which ones we let fall. We obviously couldn't save them all. So no matter what we did, it was going to come down anyway. The longer we denied that reality and tried to fight it, the worse it was for everyone. The sooner we accepted it, the sooner we could get started on a real recovery.

Today, however, it seems the governments of the world have yet to learn this lesson. Again, the big question: Will they succeed?

The quick answer is: yes, temporarily. They can kick the can down the road. They can buy some time and postpone the day of reckoning. They can stimulate a stock market rally and even an economic recovery. They can certainly create new speculative bubbles. But that's not the same as assuming responsibility for our future. It doesn't resolve the next crisis and the one after that. It does little for you and me, and even less for our children or theirs.

The longer-term answer is: *No, they will fail.* Or worse, they will create a new, bigger bubble and a broader crisis affecting a wider segment of the population for a longer time.

The editor of our *Safe Money Report*, Mike Larson, and I documented the reasons in a white paper we submitted to the U.S. Congress on September 25, 2008: *The government bailouts are too little, too late to solve the debt crisis; too much, too soon for those who will have to pay the bill.*[6]

Indeed, even as the government sweeps piles of bad debts under the carpet, it accumulates mountains of *new* debts—with the biggest federal deficits of all time. This is why 2010 delivered a brand new crisis, never before witnessed in modern times: Instead of merely corporations going broke, it was entire countries that faced insolvency. In response, investors—beyond just dumping corporate bonds or stocks—began dumping the *government* bonds issued by each of these countries. Result: It became extremely difficult—if not impossible—for their governments to issue new bonds and raise the funds they desperately needed to stay afloat.

Greece was the first to get hit. Its governmental accounting was a mess; its spending, out of control; its deficits, staggering. Suddenly, global investors dumped old Greek bonds in their portfolios and went on a buyer's strike for any new ones being issued.

Ireland was next—all due to a series of events that were eerily similar to those that had occurred on this side of the Atlantic: a real estate bubble and bust, massive bank failures, and equally massive government bailouts. Again, global investors attacked, dumping Irish bonds and cutting off virtually all sources of new financing. Again, a major European nation was virtually bankrupted.

The European Union (EU) and the International Monetary Fund (IMF) came to the rescue with massive bailouts—first for Greece and then for Ireland. But despite a short reprieve after each major new bailout, the crisis continued to escalate, with Portugal, Spain, and others next in line.

Central bankers, finance ministers, and top economists said they were taken entirely by surprise. But the sequence of events was too clear for anyone to have missed:

- In 2007, banks all over the world, including U.S. companies like Bear Sterns, Lehman Brothers, Citigroup, and Merrill Lynch had accumulated huge amounts of bad mortgages and other "toxic" assets on their books.
- In 2008, when investors realized that the bad assets could sink the companies' finances, they dumped their corporate bonds and stocks in panic.

- Next, in 2009, the governments of the United States and Western Europe rescued the near-bankrupt banking giants, scooped up most of the toxic assets and shifted them to their own books. So . . .
- In 2010, when investors realized how bad the governments' finances really were, they dumped their government bonds in panic.

To better understand why, let's consider how deeply and thoroughly the government has assumed ownership of this entire crisis. . . .

Massive Government Actions to Forestall the Debt Crisis

We saw the first telltale warning of the debt crisis in August 2007. Banks all over the world announced multibillion losses in subprime (high-risk) mortgages. Investors recoiled in horror. And it looked like the world's financial markets were about to collapse.

They didn't—because the U.S. Federal Reserve and European central banks intervened. The authorities injected unprecedented amounts of cash into the world's largest banks. The crisis subsided, and everyone breathed a great sigh of relief. But it was a Pyrrhic victory, because in early 2008, it struck anew, this time in a more virulent and violent form, this time affecting a much wider range of players.

The nation's largest mortgage insurers, responsible for protecting lenders and investors from mortgage defaults on millions of homes, were ravaged by losses. Municipal governments and public hospitals were slammed by the failure of nearly 1,000 auctions for their bonds, causing their borrowing costs to triple and quadruple. Low-rated corporate bonds were being abandoned by investors, their prices plunging to the lowest levels in history. Hedge funds got hit as well, with one fund, CSO Partners, losing so much money and suffering such a massive run on its assets that its manager, Citigroup, was forced to shut it down. And above all, major financial firms, at the epicenter of the crisis, were being struck with losses that would soon exceed $500 billion.

The big question was no longer "Which big Wall Street firm will post the worst losses?"; it was "Which big firm will be the first to go bankrupt?" The answer: Bear Stearns, one of the largest investment banks in the world.

Again, the folks at the Fed intervened. Not only did they finance a giant buyout for Bear Stearns, but, for the first time in history, they also decided to lend hundreds of billions to any *other* major Wall Street firm that needed the money. Again, the crisis subsided temporarily. Again, Wall Street cheered, and the authorities won their battle.

But the war continued. Despite all the Fed's special lending operations, another Wall Street firm—almost three times *larger* than Bear Stearns—was going down. Its name: Lehman Brothers.

How to Reduce Debts in Bad Times

In a depression, families overloaded with debts face the worst of all worlds: They miss out on major opportunities, get trapped making payments that are more onerous than expected, confront increasingly aggressive collection agencies, and must abide by harsher bankruptcy laws. Therefore, if there ever were a time to get rid of debt, *this is it*. Amber Dakar, Weiss Research's personal finance specialist, explains how:

Step 1. Declare your own personal war on debt. If debt has the potential to disrupt your life and cause your family serious grief, we assure you it is *not* your friend. Focus all your energy on killing it.

Step 2. Attack the plastic first. Collect all credit cards in the entire household, including your own, your spouse's, and those of anyone else you're responsible for. Then grab a pair of scissors and cut them up.

Step 3. Attack your credit card statements next. Gather all your recent statements and find the annual percentage

(Continued)

rate (APR). At the top of each statement, write down the APR in large numbers. Then, sort the statements with the highest APR at the top, the lowest at the bottom.

Step 4. Add up your minimum monthly payments. Credit card companies *deliberately* require very small minimum payments. Their agenda is to let you pile up as much debt as possible so they can earn as much interest as possible. How long would it take to pay off a credit card with minimum monthly payments alone? If you owe $2,000 with 17 percent interest, it could take you 24 years. And on some credit cards, the compound interest you're paying could be over 35 percent! Do your best to *pay them all off.* If that's not possible, at least pay off the worst ones first.

Step 5. Shun all new credit cards. Once you've kicked the credit card habit, don't go back. If you need the convenience of a card, get a *debit* card instead. But ask your bank to give you a *true, pure debit card*—not one that comes with a built-in credit card feature. If new, unsolicited credit cards show up in your mailbox, trash them immediately.

Step 6. Start paying down any other personal loans you may have. If you've been able to get along with, say, $600 less per month in spending money until now, and if your circumstances don't change, you should be able to stick with it. Use it to pay down any other personal loans you may have.

Step 7. Pay down your mortgage. This is especially important if you're locked in to a high rate or have an adjustable-rate mortgage (ARM). But in bad times, you must assume that even a lower, fixed-rate mortgage could become a bigger burden. The reason: A depression usually comes with deflation, which means almost everything—including wages—goes down. Unfortunately, one of the few things that does *not* go down is fixed debt payments, and these can strangle borrowers no matter how favorable the loan may have seemed originally. Your goal should be to send the mortgage company a larger monthly check than required. Then, that extra amount should be automatically deducted from your principal. If your regular payment is, say, $2,400, send them $3,100. You'll be surprised how much more quickly your mortgage will be paid off.

Step 8. Build up your cash savings! If you're afraid of losing your job, postpone paying down your fixed-rate mortgages until you have enough cash to cover six months of expenses. Plus, be sure to follow the steps detailed next.

HOW TO PROTECT YOUR JOB IN BAD TIMES

In bad times, job cuts can affect almost *everyone*—regardless of profession, job status, income level, gender, or ethnic origin. In other words, we're all in this together.

Ultimately, layoffs could be across the board—financial, manufacturing, services, even states and municipalities. However, for the most part, you can rely more on jobs with companies that provide debt recovery and bankruptcy services; and with industries that sell or service basic necessities such as those related to health care and food. To help protect your current job, consider these steps:

Step 1. Check the financial prospects of your company. If its shares are listed on a stock exchange, you can get a general idea simply by looking at how the stock has performed compared to the S&P 500 Index. If your company is not listed on an exchange, inquire about its revenues and profits for the last few quarters. If your employer says it is confidential, you should be able to acquire a report from Dun & Bradstreet (www.dnb.com).

Step 2. If your company's prospects are positive, devote more effort to Strategy A. If they are negative, devote more effort to Strategy B.

(Continued)

Step 3. In a depression, pursue both of the following strategies:

Strategy A. Do your utmost to make yourself a valuable employee. Seek company-sponsored opportunities for learning new job skills. And even if none are available, allocate at least an hour per day of your spare time to learn skills of value to the firm. With the Internet, you'd be amazed at how much you can learn for free or at a very low cost. And if you do not have access to the Internet from home, free access is available at most public libraries. The librarian should be able to give you some excellent tips on the latest and best sites.

Strategy B. Stay continually on top of the job market. Visit job web sites to take advantage of a wealth of free information on the most marketable job skills, tips on how to get a job, and updates on what's going on in various industries. Also use these sites to keep your resume posted on the Web as much as possible.

Step 4. Learn more about other income opportunities, such as a home business. It can take time to find the right situation, and many supposedly surefire business schemes can waste your time or, worse, lead you to losses you cannot afford. So start researching soon. Even if your company is currently doing well, that could change as the depression deepens. For more information on some of the most reliable options, visit www.MoneyandMarkets.com/SurvivalGuide/HomeBusiness.

Step 5. Rather than just buying in to someone else's prepackaged opportunity, the single best approach to starting a home business is to leverage any unique skills you may already have. In most cases, though, what could make or break your business will be how you *market* your skills. To learn how to market yourself most effectively in a depression, visit www.MoneyandMarkets.com/SurvivalGuide/Skills.

Over a single weekend in mid-September 2008, the Fed chairman, the Treasury secretary, and other high officials huddled at the New York Fed's offices in downtown Manhattan. They seriously considered bailing out Lehman, but they ran into two hurdles: First, Lehman's assets were too sick—so diseased, in fact, even the federal government didn't want to touch them with a 10-foot pole. Nor were there any private buyers remotely interested in a shotgun marriage. Second, foreshadowing the public rebellion that would later burst onto the scene in the Tea Party movement of 2010, there was a new sentiment on Wall Street that was previously unheard of: A small, but vocal, minority was getting sick and tired of bailouts. "Let them fail," they said. "Teach those bastards a lesson!" was the new rallying cry.

For the Fed chairman and Treasury secretary, it was the long-dreaded day of reckoning. It was the fateful moment in history that demanded a life-or-death decision regarding one of the biggest financial institutions in the world—bigger than General Motors, Ford, and Chrysler put together. Should they save it? Or should they let it fail? Their decision: to do something they had never done before. *They let Lehman fail.*

"Here's what you're going to do," was the basic message from the federal authorities to Lehman's highest officials. "Tomorrow morning, you're going to take a trip downtown to the U.S. Bankruptcy Court at One Bowling Green. You're going to file for Chapter 11. Then you're going to fire your staff. And before the end of the day, you're going to pack up your own boxes and clear out."

In both the Bear Stearns and Lehman failures, America's largest banking conglomerate, JPMorgan Chase, promptly appeared on the scene and swooped up the outstanding trades of the two companies, with the Fed acting as a backstop. In both failures, the authorities played a role. But Lehman's demise was unique because it was thrown into bankruptcy.

It was the financial earthquake that changed the world.

Until that day, nearly everyone assumed that giant firms like Lehman were too big to fail, that the government would always step in to save them. That myth was shattered on the late summer weekend when the U.S. government decided to abandon its long tradition of largesse and let Lehman go under.

All over the world, bank lending froze. Borrowing costs went through the roof. Global stock markets collapsed. Corporate bonds tanked. The entire global banking system seemed like it was coming unglued.

"I guess we goofed!" were, in essence, the words of admission heard at the Fed and Treasury. "Now, instead of just a bailout for Lehman, what we're really going to need is the Mother of All Bailouts—for the entire financial system." The U.S. government promptly complied, delivering precisely what they asked for—a $700 billion Troubled Asset Relief Program (TARP), rushed through Congress and signed into law by President Bush in record time.

The U.S. government also loaned, invested, or committed $300 billion to nationalize the world's two largest mortgage companies, Fannie Mae and Freddie Mac; more than $42 billion for the Big Three auto manufacturers; $29 billion for Bear Stearns, $150 billion for American International Group (AIG), and $350 billion for Citigroup; $300 billion for the Federal Housing Administration Rescue Bill to refinance bad mortgages; $87 billion to pay back JPMorgan Chase for bad Lehman Brothers trades; $200 billion in loans to banks under the Federal Reserve's Term Auction Facility (TAF); $50 billion to support short-term corporate IOUs held by money market mutual funds; $500 billion to rescue various credit markets; $620 billion for industrial nations, including the Bank of Canada, Bank of England, Bank of Japan, National Bank of Denmark, European Central Bank, Bank of Norway, Reserve Bank of Australia, Bank of Sweden, and Swiss National Bank; $120 billion in aid for emerging markets, including the central banks of Brazil, Mexico, South Korea, and Singapore; trillions to guarantee the Federal Deposit Insurance Corporation's (FDIC's) new, expanded bank deposit insurance coverage from $100,000 to $250,000; plus trillions more for other sweeping guarantees. Grand total, according to Bloomberg as of October 2010: $11.6 trillion.

Apologists for this mega-rescue policy argued that the government would get most of the money back and would never have to shell out that much in the form of real dollars. But the government's leading watchdog agency itself made mincemeat of those arguments: Even after subtracting all moneys paid back to the government, the Special Inspector General for the Troubled Asset Relief Program

(SIGTARP) reported that, at June 30, 2010, U.S. federal agencies had provided "financial system support" of $3.7 trillion, including $1.7 trillion in purchases of mortgage bonds, Treasury bonds, and agency bonds by the Federal Reserve.

The FDIC threw in another $300 billion into the pot, shutting down over 150 banks in 2010 alone. The Treasury pumped in a net of $300 billion to rescue big companies as part of its TARP program (after paybacks), plus another $500 billion in money outside of TARP. On top of that, several other government agencies have chipped in *another* $800 billion. No matter how you counted it, these were Herculean government efforts.[7]

Yes, with these trillions, the government was able to calm the waters and restore credit markets. But the government was *not* able dissuade average American families from taking matters into their own hands.

Those families could feel the dead weight of their mortgages and credit cards. They feared for their jobs. And they abhorred piling on more debt. So in the years after the debt crisis, they decided to do precisely the opposite. While most folks in Washington were still spending taxpayer money like drunken sailors, American households were waking up to the real world and starting to *cut their debts*.

It was the natural, rational thing to do. But it was also very unusual. Ever since World War II, the U.S. economy had been consistently fueled and sustained by American households on a nonstop binge of borrowing and spending. Indeed, in almost every year since 1946, consumers had consistently borrowed more than in the prior year. Washington and Wall Street were happy: The more consumers borrowed, the more they spent; and the more they spent, the bigger the revenues at the nation's manufacturers, retailers, and tax collectors.

Beginning in 2009, however, all that began to change. American consumers not only borrowed less, but they also cut back on *prior* borrowings—either because they defaulted or because they *voluntarily* sought to restore their finances to *avoid* default.

Result: We witnessed the deepest decline in consumer credit outstanding since the government began keeping records after World War II.

Was this good or bad? The answer should have been obvious. If too much debt was a major cause of the debt crisis, then it stood to reason that debt *reduction* was one of the best solutions. Nevertheless, Washington and Wall Street didn't see it that way. All they seemed to care about was their own wallets. They knew that less consumer borrowing meant less consumer spending. And they know that less spending meant lower sales, reduced profits for corporations, and a sharp decline in tax revenues for Uncle Sam. So America's corporate and political leaders did everything in their power to get consumers to borrow and spend like they used to.

Moreover, many Federal Reserve and Treasury officials were deathly afraid of another big threat, which, in their view, loomed even larger than debt reduction—*deflation*—declining prices.

If prices go down, they said, consumers will naturally wait for still lower prices before buying homes, automobiles, appliances, and more. They'll spend even less. Worse, they feared, consumers will see, with their own eyes, that the purchasing power of their money is *improving*. So they'll be more inclined to—God forbid!—salt it away. That, in turn, they feared, would reduce demand and cause further price declines, creating a vicious cycle of sinking demand and sinking prices.[8]

The fact that this process could help bring down the cost of living and make life easier for average citizens—especially retirees—was brushed aside. Instead, the authorities decided that this back-to-thrift trend was actually dangerous and must be stopped dead in its tracks.

Ironically, this was also the rationale that the U.S. Federal Reserve used to justify its greatest escapade of all, the subject of the next chapter.

2

THE GOVERNMENT DECLARES WAR ON THE FINANCIAL CRISIS

On November 3, 2010, the Federal Reserve, under Chairman Ben Bernanke, announced a new round of what they called *quantitative easing*.

The terminology fooled some people some of the time. But most knew what it really was—rolling the printing presses to try to pump up the economy with more cheap paper money. And ironically, it was the Fed's second attempt to do so.

The first attempt, launched soon after Lehman Brothers collapsed in 2008, had been even bigger: From September 10, 2008, through March 10, 2010, Fed Chairman Ben Bernanke increased the nation's monetary base (cash and reserves in the banking system) from $850 billion to $2.1 trillion—an astounding increase of 2.5 times in just 18 months. It was, by far, the greatest monetary expansion in U.S. history.

Figure 2.1 illustrates the sheer enormity of the Fed's actions.

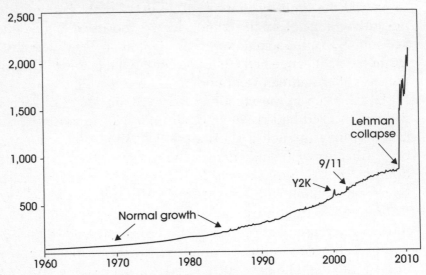

Figure 2.1   U.S. Federal Reserve Runs the Money Printing Presses (monetary base, in billions of dollars)

For 40 years, from 1960 through the year 1999, the nation's monetary base (cash and reserves in the banking system) increased steadily and without sudden changes in the pace of growth. In more recent times, however, the Fed expanded the reserves sharply when it felt a crisis was at hand—first in preparation for the feared Y2K computer problems in the banking system and then again in response to the 9/11 terrorist attacks. Moreover, these two incidents paled in comparison to the Fed's actions in response to the debt crisis that began in 2008: Immediately following the collapse of Lehman Brothers in September of 2008, the Fed printed enough money to double the monetary base in just 112 days. That was 45 times faster than the 5,012 days it took for the monetary base to double before the Lehman collapse. For more details, see Notes, page 269.

Data Source: Federal Reserve.

And to get a sense of its sheer enormity, please consider these facts:

Fact 1. Before the Lehman Brothers collapse, it had taken the Fed a total 5,012 days—13 years and 8 months—to double the monetary base. In contrast, *after* the Lehman Brothers collapse, it took Bernanke's Fed only 112 days to do so. In other words, he accelerated the pace of bank reserve expansion by a factor of 45 to 1.

Imagine a crowded interstate highway with a speed limit of 55 miles per hour and with a long tradition of allowing no one to exceed the limit by more than 10 or 15 mph. Suddenly, a new driver appears on the scene with a jet-powered engine that accelerates to a supersonic speed of 1,350 mph. That's the same magnitude of change Fed Chairman Bernanke presided over in the days after Lehman went under.

Fact 2. Even in the most extreme circumstances of recent history, the Fed had never pumped in anything close to that much money in such a short period of time. For example, before the turn of the millennium, the Fed scrambled to provide liquidity to U.S. banks to ward off a feared Y2K catastrophe, bumping up bank reserves from $557 billion on October 6, 1999, to $630 billion by January 12, 2000. At the time, that sudden increase was considered unprecedented—$73 billion in just three months. In contrast, Mr. Bernanke's money infusion in the 112 days after the Lehman collapse was 14 times larger!

Similarly, in the days following the 9/11 terrorist attacks, the Fed had rushed to flood the banks with liquid funds, adding $40 billion through 9/19/01. But Mr. Bernanke's post-Lehman flood of money was *25* times larger.[1]

Fact 3. After the Y2K and 9/11 crises had passed, the Fed promptly reversed its money infusions and sopped up the extra liquidity in the banking system. But after the Lehman Brothers collapse, Mr. Bernanke did precisely the opposite. He continued to throw even *more* money into the pot

Fact 4. With no past historical precedent, no testing, and no clue regarding the likely financial fallout, Mr. Bernanke invented and deployed more weapons of mass monetary expansion than all prior Fed chairmen combined. The list of new Fed programs boggles the imagination: Term Discount Window Program, Term Auction Facility, Primary Dealer Credit Facility, Transitional Credit Extensions, Term Securities Lending Facility, ABCP Money Market Fund Liquidity Facility, Commercial Paper Funding Facility, Money Market Investing Funding Facility, Term Asset-Backed Securities Loan Facility, and Term Securities Lending Facility Options Program. None of these existed earlier. All were new experiments devised in response to the debt crisis.

Trashing the Past

Back in 1792, with the passage of the Coinage Act, Treasury Secretary Alexander Hamilton established the dollar as the national currency of the United States.

In the 218 years that followed, the United States overcame multiple obstacles, crises and disasters—one pandemic, two great depressions, 11 major wars, and 44 recessions. Four U.S. presidents were assassinated while in office. Hundreds of thousands of businesses went bankrupt; tens of millions of Americans lost their jobs.

Did the U.S. government respond to some of these events with countermeasures? Of course. In the wake of each disaster, there were, to be sure, monetary and fiscal excesses. But never once had the U.S. government resorted to such extreme abuses of its money-printing power as it did from 2008 to 2010. Thus, a long tradition of leadership and discipline was abandoned—all for the sake of perpetuating America's addiction to spending, borrowing, and the wildest speculative bubbles of all time.

I was not the only one who shouted these warnings from the rooftops. Others, more prominent than I, also raised their voices in protest.

Thomas Hoenig, president of the Federal Reserve Bank of Kansas City and one of the lone dissenters in the Fed's Open Market Committee, was among the most prominent.[2] He saw three possible pathways for our nation's fiscal and monetary policy:

Path 1—Monetize. The government runs massive deficits and borrows without restraint. At the same time, the Federal Reserve monetizes the debt—finances it by running the nation's printing presses. This is the path of least resistance for politicians and of greatest danger to the nation. Yet, unfortunately, as evidenced by the explosion in the monetary base described earlier, it was also the speedway down which the Fed was racing.

Path 2—Policy stalemate. As in Path 1, the government runs massive deficits and borrows with little restraint. But the Federal Reserve refuses to finance them. Instead, the Fed lets the natural supply and demand for debt drive interest rates higher. Soon, the government finds it is too expensive—or nearly impossible—to borrow. And ultimately, Washington has no choice but to slash spending despite any near-term consequences. Hard to believe? Perhaps. But this is precisely what happened to many governments around the world in 2010—not only in Greece and Ireland, but also in California, Illinois, New Jersey, New York, and scores of other state and local governments in the United States.

Path 3—Austerity and fiscal discipline. The government takes strong, proactive steps to reduce the deficit. This, of course, is extremely tough politically. But unless pursued promptly and aggressively, the government winds up forced to do it anyway—albeit with more urgency and greater trauma for the country and its people. In the closing days of 2010, however, the U.S. president and Congress agreed to do precisely the opposite—passing a new, grandiose tax-and-spend law that would add another $858 billion to the federal deficit over two years.

These are three stark choices Fed President Hoenig set forth in 2010.

Meanwhile, David Walker, former head of the U.S. Government Accountability Office (GAO) and president of the Peter G. Peterson Foundation, feared a Greece-like Armageddon for the United States by the year 2012. One of his main arguments: The nation's fiscal disaster, no matter how horrible it may be based on the *official* numbers, was actually far *worse* than advertised. His own words:

> The Greeks engaged in a variety of creative accounting practices, and there were a lot of big and bad surprises that caused this situation to arise. The U.S. has [also] been engaged in a lot of creative accounting for years with regard to the Social Security trust funds . . .
>
> [And] now, we've got major creative accounting going on with government-sponsored entities—Fannie Mae and Freddie Mac. We own a super-majority of them, but we're not consolidating them into the financial statements. We don't consolidate the Federal Reserve into the financial statements [either].
>
> The bottom line is: We're not Greece. But we could end with the same problems down the road if we don't get spending under control and start dealing with our structural deficits soon.

How soon? Walker pointed to 2012.

My view is that if you look at total debt to GDP, we're already over 85 percent. We're going to be at 100 percent within two years.[3]

What's even more troubling is that we have to go to foreign lenders to finance our debt. Fifty percent of our public debts are held by foreign lenders, and . . . the Fed has been buying our debt at record rates to hold down interest rates.

J. Irving Weiss, my father, who later founded our Sound Dollar Committee, had probably the greatest impact of all on the public awareness of these dangers. The big difference: That was over half a century ago.

In 1959 he launched a national grassroots campaign that prompted an estimated 11 million Americans to demand an end to federal deficits. And he helped President Eisenhower pass the *last* truly balanced budget—without creative accounting—in our nation's history. In the *New York Times* and *Wall Street Journal* ads that launched our Sound Dollar Committee's campaign in 1959, Dad warned about the future dangers:

Inflation is a narcotic. It soothes and exhilarates while doing its deadly work. Already it has reduced our dollar to half of its purchasing power. It is the killer rampant in our midst, threatening to destroy us as it has other countries whose rulers thought they could have a little bit of controlled spending and inflation; a little cheapening of their money. *Then it was too late.* Deficit spending [and inflation] are the twin poisons which are undermining your future. Some people say we need deficit spending by our governments for prosperity and growth. *But they forget that the means can destroy the end.*

Back in those days, like today, inflation was not perceived to be an imminent threat. But those who ignored it initially later lived to regret their complacency. And like today, Dad was certainly not the only one raising his voice in protest. Also widely quoted in the Sound Dollar Committee's campaign were his associates, supporters, and other contemporaries, including:

■ Bernard Baruch, adviser to U.S. presidents Woodrow Wilson, Franklin D. Roosevelt, and several others, wrote: "Inflation flows from the selfish struggle for social advantage among pressure groups. Each seeks tax cuts or wage raises for itself while urging the others to make the sacrifice and with little regard for the national interest."[4]

- Lyndon B. Johnson, while still a U.S. senator and not yet presiding over the greatest fiscal disaster of that era, said: "We all know that the end of such a spending spree would be fiscal insolvency."[5]
- William M. Martin Jr., then chairman of the Federal Reserve and a supporter of Dad's, declared: "No greater tragedy, short of war, could befall the Free World than to have our country surrender to the easy delusion that a little inflation, year after year, is either inevitable or tolerable. For that way lies ultimate economic chaos."
- Senator J.W. Fulbright, who, thanks to our Sound Dollar Committee campaign, shifted his vote to "yes" in favor of Eisenhower's balanced budget, said: "Excessive inflation in the long run destroys the will to work and the will to save, which are the foundations of our economic system. Inflation is a deadly enemy of a free capitalistic system."[6]

Yet, despite all these voices and despite all this history, our government officials continued to pursue their stimulus, bailouts, guarantees, and money printing. They said it was all for a good cause—to save the world from another Great Depression.

But it was obviously reaching levels that were beyond reason, and it *still* faced serious obstacles to success.

Obstacle 1: Government Debt Too Big and Growing Too Fast

First and foremost, America's burden of government debt was far too big. By mid-year 2010, the U.S. Treasury owed $8.6 trillion, other government agencies owed $7.7 trillion, while municipal and state governments owed another $2.8 trillion.

Moreover, government debt was growing far too quickly—with deficits exceeding $1 trillion—triple the largest deficits in prior history—for *three years in a row* through 2011.

Indeed, the future was so bleak that even the Congressional Budget Office (CBO) issued dire warnings, including:

- *The rising probability of a fiscal crisis!* "In such a crisis," the CBO declared, "investors become unwilling to finance all of a government's borrowing needs unless they are compensated with very high interest rates." The big danger: The more the government borrows, the more interest it would have to pay . . . and the higher the government's interest costs, the more investors would question the government's finances.

- *Fiscal crises and recessions at the same time!* Typically, interest rates go down in a recession and up in a boom. But when deficits are out of control, the opposite can happen. The CBO declared: "Fiscal crises around the world have often begun during recessions and, in turn, have often exacerbated them. Frequently, such a crisis was triggered by news that a government would, for any number of reasons, need to borrow an unexpectedly large amount of money."

- *A disaster potentially worse than Greece's or Ireland's!* Unlike smaller countries that suffered a major sovereign debt crisis like Greece and Ireland, the United States benefited from its status as a safe-haven nation. But, warned the CBO, "the United States may not be able to issue as much debt as the governments of other countries can because the private saving rate has been lower in the United States than in most developed countries, and a significant share of U.S. debt has been sold to foreign investors."[7]

Obstacle 2: Even Larger Nongovernment Debts

In 2010, for every dollar of government debt in the United States, there was close to $3 of nongovernment debt. And overall, including both public and private debts, there were more than $52 trillion in interest-bearing debts in the United States—mortgage loans, credit cards, corporate debt, municipal debt, and federal debt.

Plus, according to the National Center for Policy Analysis (NCPA), the federal government had contingent liabilities of at least $107 trillion in the form of commitments for Social Security, Medicare, veterans benefits, and more.[8]

Plus, U.S. commercial banks held another $223.4 trillion in side bets called *derivatives.*

How big was the overall debt monster? $394 trillion in the United States alone!

The numbers are not directly comparable, but just to give you a sense of the magnitude of the problem, that's 562 times more money than what was budgeted for the highly controversial $700 billion bailout package signed so hurriedly into law by President Bush in late 2008 (see Figure 2.2).

Still, many people believed that if only Washington could avoid the mistakes it made in the 1930s . . . if only Washington could preemptively nip this crisis in the bud . . . if only Washington

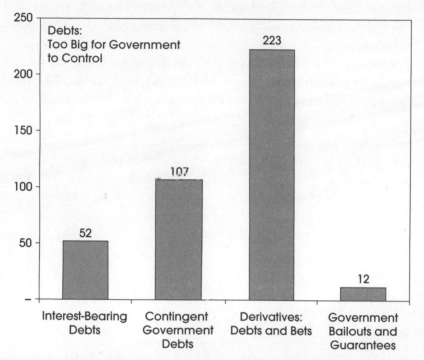

Figure 2.2 Even the Largest Rescue Pales in Comparison to the Buildup of Debts and Bets

A major challenge to governments in dealing with recurring debt crises is the sheer volume of debts outstanding. In the United States, at mid-year 2010, in addition to $52 trillion in interest-bearing debts, the government had an estimated $107 trillion in contingent debts or obligations such as Social Security, Medicare, and veterans' benefits; and U.S. banks were committed to $223 trillion in debts and bets called *derivatives*.

Even the most ambitious of government bailout efforts, which added up to a total of $12 trillion, would be small by comparison.

Data Sources: Interest-bearing debts—Federal Reserve; contingent government debts—Kansas City Federal Reserve and the National Center for Policy Analysis; derivatives debts and bets—U.S. Comptroller of the Currency (OCC); government bailouts and guarantees—Bloomberg and the U.S. Department of Treasury, Special Inspector General, Troubled Assets Relief Program.

could be the world's lender and spender of last resort . . . they could avoid a depression, create millions of new jobs, and get the U.S. economy growing strongly again.

Claus Vogt, editor of *Sicheres Geld* (the German edition of our *Safe Money Report*) and author of *The Global Debt Trap* (John Wiley & Sons), shows how the debt buildup in the United States is far greater than it was on the eve of the 1930s depression: Before the 1930s, the total debt in the United States represented no more than 170 percent of the economy. By 2008, it was close to 350 percent! (See Figure 2.3.)

Moreover, Mr. Vogt reminds us that this does not even include the high stakes gambling arena of big side bets called *derivatives*. Those kinds of bets barely existed in the 1930s. By contrast, in the

Figure 2.3   U.S. Debt Buildup Worse than 1929 (interest-bearing debts as a percentage of GDP)

In 1929, the total buildup of interest-bearing debt in the United States represented no more than 170 percent of gross national product (GNP). Then, in the early 1930s, as the economy contracted, although new debts were not added in significant amounts, the existing debts became far more burdensome in relation to the shrinking economy, exceeding 260 percent of GNP. This continuing burden prolonged the Great Depression; and a meaningful recovery could not begin until a substantial portion of the debts was liquidated through bankruptcies, write-downs, and repayment. In the modern era, U.S. debts have greatly exceeded the peak levels of the 1929–1932 period, reaching 350 percent of gross domestic product (GDP). Moreover, these do not include other forms of debts depicted in Figure 2.2.

Data Source: Federal Reserve.

2000s, they were a major factor behind large bank and insurance company losses and failures.

Obstacle 3: Nobody Wants to Pay the Bill

The second big obstacle the government faces is huge federal deficits and the task of raising the money to fund the bailouts. Apparently, in the rush to spend, lend, or guarantee trillions of dollars, no one in the government bothered to seriously consider the simple question, "Who's going to pay the bill? Where are we going to get all that money?" The government had only one choice: to borrow the money. More big debts!

Sure enough, for fiscal year 2009, the Office of Management and Budget (OMB) reports that the federal deficit was $1.412 trillion, or more than *triple* its largest-ever deficit in history, and in 2010, it was even worse—more than $1.5 trillion. Plus, even after making some very optimistic assumptions, the OMB admitted that it would run up *another* $4.3 trillion in deficits by 2015. And that was *before* the Obama administration and congressional Republicans agreed in December 2010 to renew Bush-era tax cuts, extend unemployment benefits, and cut government revenues with a series of other measures.[9]

As long as foreign money—especially from China—was pouring in to help finance the deficit, even these massive deficits could be swept under the rug as a low priority. But ultimately, to raise the money, the government would have little choice but to shove aside consumers, businesses, and other borrowers; hog most of the available credit for itself; and then, adding insult to injury, bid up interest rates for everyone.

Some people hoped the government's resources, by some feat of magic, might be unlimited. But the reality is that there is no free lunch; someone has to raise the money and pay the bills. And as soon as the bills come due, the consequences could strike swiftly—in the form of steeper mortgage rates, higher credit card rates, or worse, virtually no credit at all.

Obstacle 4: Sinking Public Support

The third obstacle the government ran into was even more daunting. Like in the 1930s, money alone, no matter how lavishly dished out, could not restore public *confidence*.

While the government bought some reprieve for large banks, it could do little to help thousands of smaller banks.

While it could help some percentage of unemployed workers some of the time, it could not help the majority most of the time.

As a result, public support for bailouts and stimulus plunged to the lowest level in recorded history. In a Weiss-Zogby national poll we conducted of likely voters in October 2010, only 6.6 percent were in favor of bank bailouts; 80.4 percent, or 12 times more, said the government should let big banks fail.[10]

Government stimulus and bailouts were a boon for select large corporations, but small and medium-size businesses, who typically hire the bulk of America's workers, remained largely shut out of the credit markets and left out of the recovery. They laid off millions. And even when the economy staged a modest recovery, few were anxious to hire them back. This story Dad told me about 1930 shows some interesting similarities:

> After the crash, President Hoover was worried about the sinking U.S. economy. So he called the leaders of major U.S. corporations down to Washington—auto executives from Detroit, steel executives from Pittsburgh, banking executives from New York. He said, in effect:
>
> "Gentlemen, when you go back home to your factories and your offices, here's what I want you to do. I want you to keep all your workers. Don't lay anyone off! I want you to keep your factories going. Don't shut any down! I want you to invest more, spend more, even borrow more, if you have to. Just don't do any cutting. It's for a good cause—so we can keep this economy going."
>
> That may have sounded like a good idea at first. But then the executives went back to their factories and offices and said to their associates: "If the president himself had to call us down to Washington to lecture us on how to run our business, then the economy must be in even worse shape than we thought it was."
>
> They promptly proceeded to do precisely the opposite of what Hoover had asked: They laid off workers by the thousands. They shut down factories. They slashed spending to the bone. They cut back.

Now, some key aspects of this history are repeating themselves, albeit on a grander scale with a more ambitious government. As before, each new government bailout is initially greeted with enthusiasm. But as more people recognize the danger of swelling federal deficits, or as the fear of inflation and higher interest rates return, the grave danger is that public support and confidence will sink even more.

Washington tries to encourage consumers and businesses to borrow more, spend more, and save less, but they are very reluctant to do so.

Washington prods bankers to dish out more credit, but the Fed's own surveys show that banks all over the United States do precisely the opposite, continuing to maintain tight lending standards.

The government provides cheap money to prod investors to risk more of their money. But that merely creates another speculative bubble.

In each case, government officials instinctively realize that it was too much borrowing, too much spending, and too much risk-taking that got them into so much trouble in the first place. But they ignore their instincts and do everything to encourage more of the same.

The Biggest Obstacle of All:
The Government Rescues Themselves

By year's end 2010, anyone not blinded by greed could plainly see the sick cycle I discussed in Chapter 1. First, the government helped create a great asset bubble. Next, the government-created bubble burst under a dark cloud of hardship for millions of Americans. And third, the government responded by creating still *another* bubble, often far more dangerous than the previous.

A one-time event? Hardly. In 10 short years, we'd already seen three—the tech bubble and wreck of 2000–2002, the housing bubble and bust of 2006–2009, and the sovereign debt explosion and implosion of 2009–2010.

So by this time, most savvy investors—and many average citizens—already knew the drill. What they didn't yet know was the answer to the biggest question of all: *What's the endgame?*

Would the world's money printing presses run amuck, trashing any remaining value in paper currencies? Would major governments ultimately default on their debts, destroying the global credit system? Would our entire civilization crumble?

My answer: Such threats are certainly real. But the final outcome can be very different indeed. In fact, no matter how many tricks governments may play and no matter how wild this twenty-first century roller coaster may get, there is also another possible outcome: *Austerity.*

Austerity can come in many forms: Governments may impose austerity strictly in reaction to market-driven forces. Or they may do so proactively. Austerity may be imposed only after rampant inflation. Or it may come before. It could trigger deep social upheaval. Or the social reaction could be far more limited and less disruptive.[11]

But regardless of how austerity finally arrives, it cannot happen without sacrifice and a reduced standard of living. That's the hard reality. Greece, for example, finally bowed to unrelenting attacks from global investors and slashed 30 billion euros from its budget in three years. Ireland was forced to cut so much so fast, its prime minister resigned and its government collapsed. Spain, also under massive pressure from investors, announced spending cuts of 15 billion euros, plus a 5 percent reduction in public worker wages. Portugal embarked on a program to cut 2 billion euros in 2010 alone. Italy slashed 25 billion euros from its budget over two years. Germany, supposedly the most robust of all eurozone countries, had no choice but to follow a similar path—cutbacks of 85 billion euros by 2014. The United Kingdom implemented the deepest cutbacks of all—slashing its military and social welfare budgets at the same time. Even Japan's newly installed prime minister pulled no punches in declaring that Japan's "outstanding public debt is huge," its "public finances have become the worst of any developed country," and the entire country was at "risk of collapse."

Will politicians in Washington, Tokyo, London, Dublin, or Athens cut enough to restore fiscal balance in the near future? Very doubtful. But even if they didn't cut their spending by a penny—even if they simply failed to *renew* their stimulus programs—the impact could be severe. And any cutbacks in an economy addicted to stimulus will be tantamount to shock treatment.

They won't admit it, of course—much as they wouldn't admit that their earlier policies of spending lavishly were also a shock to the economy. But if you think Washington is guilty of bias, misleading information, and outright cover-ups, wait till you see what Wall Street has done.

CHAPTER 3

WALL STREET DECEPTIONS, COVER-UPS, AND LIES

You put a big chunk of your nest egg in a life insurance policy with an A+ company. You invest another sizable amount in a portfolio of high-rated corporate bonds and tax-free municipal bonds. Then, feeling safe and secure with most of your funds, you take a flyer on a few stocks that a dozen separate research analysts have unanimously rated as a *buy* or at least a *hold*. You assume you've made informed decisions based on the best research the world has to offer.

The reality: Even in the absence of bubbles, busts, recession, or depression, you could suffer wipeout losses.

Hard to believe this could actually happen? Actually, it already *has* happened; and I want to help you make certain you don't get caught in Wall Street deceptions like these in the future. So in this chapter, I tell you what they are, how they emerged, and how to avoid them.

Their primary source: legalized payola and massive conflicts of interest.

The primary result: distorted research and inflated ratings on hundreds of thousands of companies, bonds, stocks, and investments of all kinds.

The threat to you: Far bigger losses in your investments than you would have anticipated otherwise.

Indeed, Wall Street's inflated ratings are, themselves, a kind of bubble, which, when fully exposed, could suffer a great bust of its own—deepening the price decline, hurting the chances of each company's survival, and aggravating any economic crisis.

Wall Street's ratings are the brains and nervous system of the global financial markets, and those markets, in turn, are the heartbeat of the global economy. So when the integrity of the ratings is severely compromised, it places everyone in danger, whether an investor or not, whether rich or poor.

My experience with this sorry saga begins in the late 1980s. I had been rating the financial strength of the nation's banks and S&Ls for more than a decade, and by this time, Dad was already an octogenarian. One afternoon, I told him that Weiss Ratings was going to start rating insurance companies. I can never forget his first words: "Check out First Executive [the parent of Executive Life Insurance]," he said. "Fred Carr's running it—the guy they literally kicked out of Wall Street a few years ago. He's trouble, and he's knee deep in junk bonds. Follow the junk and you will find your answers."[1]

We did, and we found quite a few life insurance companies that were loaded with junk bonds, one of which was First Capital Life, to which we gave a financial strength rating of **D−**. I was generous. The company should have gotten an F. But within days of my widely publicized warnings on First Capital Life, a group of the company's lawyers and top executives flew down to our office. They ranted. They raved. They swore they'd slap me with a massive lawsuit and put me out of business if I didn't give them a better rating. "All the Wall Street ratings agencies give us high grades," they said. "Who the hell do you think *you* are?"

I politely explained that we never let personal threats affect my ratings. And unlike other rating agencies, Weiss Ratings never accepts a dime from the companies we rate. "We work for individuals," I said, "not big corporations. Besides," I continued, opening up the company's most recent quarterly report, "your own financial statements prove your company is in trouble." That's when one of them delivered the ultimate threat: "Weiss better shut the @!%# up," he whispered to my associate, "or get a bodyguard."

We did neither. To the contrary, we intensified our warnings. And within weeks, the company went belly-up, just as Weiss Ratings had warned—still boasting high ratings from major Wall Street firms *on the very day they failed*. In fact, the leading insurance rating agency, A.M. Best, didn't downgrade First Capital Life to a warning level until five days *after* it failed. Needless to say, it was too late for policyholders.

It was a grisly sight—not just for policyholders, but for shareholders as well: The company's stock crashed 99 percent, crucifying millions of unwitting investors. Then the stock died, wiped off the face of the earth. Three of the company's closest competitors also bit the dust. Unwitting investors—who did not have access to my ratings—lost $4 billion, $4.5 billion, and $13 billion, respectively.

Fortunately, those who had seen the Weiss ratings were ready. Nobody who heeded our warning lost a cent. In fact, the contrast between anyone who relied on the Weiss ratings and anyone who didn't was so stark, even the U.S. Congress couldn't help but notice. They asked: How was it possible for Weiss—a small firm in Florida—to identify companies that were about to fail, when Wall Street told us they were still "superior" or "excellent" right up to the day they failed?

To find an answer, Congress called all the rating agencies—Standard & Poor's (S&P), Moody's, A.M. Best, Duff & Phelps, and Weiss—to testify. But we were the only ones among them who showed up. So Congress asked its auditing arm, the U.S. Government Accountability Office (GAO), to conduct a detailed study on the Weiss ratings in comparison to the ratings of the other major rating agencies.

Three years later, after extensive research and review, the GAO published its conclusion: Weiss beat its leading competitor, A.M. Best, by a factor of three to one in forecasting future financial troubles. The three other Wall Street firms weren't even competition.[2]

But the GAO never answered the original question—why? I can assure you it wasn't because of better access to information than our competitors. Nor were we smarter than they were. The real answer was contained in one four-letter word: *bias*. To this day, the other rating agencies are paid large fees by the issuers of bonds, insurance policies, and other investments that you buy.

In other words, *their ratings are literally bought and paid for by the same companies they rate.*

These conflicts and bias in the ratings business are no trivial matter. Consider carefully three of the ratings fiascos of recent times and you'll see what I mean.

Ratings Fiasco 1:
How Deceptive Ratings Entrapped Nearly Two Million Americans in Failed Insurance– and Why It Could Happen to You!

If you have insurance, don't blindly assume it's safe. In a moment, I'll show you how two million others once made that mistake and lived to regret it. And to help you avoid repeating their error, it's vital that you understand their story from start to finish.

The problems began in the early 1980s when insurance companies had guaranteed to pay high yields to investors of 10 percent or more, but the best they could earn on safe bonds was 8, 7, or 6 percent. They had to do something to bridge that gap–and quickly. So how do you deliver high guaranteed yields when interest rates are going down? Their solution: Buy the bonds of financially weaker companies.

Consider what bonds are and you'll understand the situation. When you buy a bond, all you're doing, in essence, is making a loan. If you make the loan to a strong, secure borrower, like the U.S. government or a financially robust corporation, you won't be able to collect a very high rate of interest.

If you want a truly high interest rate, you need to take the risk of lending your money to a less secure borrower–maybe a start-up company or perhaps a company that's had some ups and downs in recent years. And you can earn even more interest from companies that have been having trouble paying their bills lately. (Whether you'll actually be able to collect that interest or get back your principal is another matter entirely.)

What's secure and what's risky? In the corporate bond world, everyone agreed to use the standard rating scales originally established by the two leading bond rating agencies–Moody's and S&P. The two agencies use slightly different letters, but their scale is basically the same: triple-A, double-A, single-A; triple-B, double-B, single-B; and so on.

If a bond is triple-B or better, it's *investment grade.* That's considered relatively secure. If the bond is double-B or lower, it's *speculative grade,* or more simply, junk. It's not garbage you'd necessarily throw into the trashcan, but in the parlance of Wall Street, it's officially known as *junk.* And that's what insurance companies started to buy: junk. They bought double-B bonds. They bought

WITH MOST CORPORATE AND MUNICIPAL BONDS OVERRATED, HERE'S WHAT TO DO WITH THEM . . .

Corporate and municipal bonds can fall dramatically in value because of a series of unusual forces:

■ *Deep and unexpected ratings downgrades.* These may reflect not only deteriorating finances of the bond issuer but also belated attempts by rating agencies to suddenly adjust grades that had been inflated by biased analysis.

■ *Illiquid markets.* Bonds can become very difficult to sell because of (1) a chronic buyer's strike by investors short of cash and fearful of further losses; (2) heavier borrowing by the U.S. government, which pulls away remaining bond investors; or (3) bond dealers short of capital and unable to maintain their traditional market-making role.

■ *Surprise defaults.* Companies, thought to be financially solid, default because of severe losses that are not clearly disclosed in financial statements.

■ *Higher interest rates.* Typically, interest rates decline in a recession. However, in a recession that's driven largely by a severe financial crisis and that creates acute credit shortages, interest rates can spike higher, driving all bond prices lower.

■ *Inflation.* The Federal Reserve may try to push bond prices higher by buying them with printed money. Initially, this tactic can be successful. But if the newly printed money causes inflation or a sharp decline in the value of the U.S. dollar, global investors could dump their U.S. bonds and cause a more enduring bond price decline than any of the preceding factors.

In response, here are the steps to follow:

Step 1. Investors holding corporate and municipal bonds should use any price rally as an opportunity to unload them, regardless of their current rating.

Step 2. If the market is illiquid, give your broker the opportunity to *work the order,* taking advantage of any temporary flurries in trading activity spurred by government rescues and money injections.

Step 3. Also seek to avoid short-term paper issued by corporations and municipalities (often bought by money market funds). Although they are relatively less vulnerable than longer-dated notes and bonds, in a severe financial crisis, significant losses are also possible.

Step 4. Once the economic conditions are in place for an economic recovery (as described in Chapter 14), look to buy deeply discounted, high quality corporate and municipal bonds aiming to lock in high yields and reap major capital gains.

single-B bonds. They even bought unrated bonds that, if rated, would have been classified as junk.

Until this juncture, their high-risk strategy could be explained as a stop-gap solution to falling interest rates. But, unbelievably, a few insurance companies—such as Executive Life of California, Executive Life of New York, Fidelity Bankers Life, and First Capital Life—took the concept one giant step further. These companies weren't just reluctantly forced to buy junk bonds to fulfill old promises. Their *entire* business plan was predicated on the concept of junk bonds from Day One.

The key to their success was to keep the junk bond aspect hush-hush, while exploiting the faith people still had in the inherent safety of insurance. To make the scheme work, they needed two more elements: the blessing of the Wall Street ratings agencies and the cooperation of the state insurance commissioners, many of whom had worked for—or would later join—those same insurance companies.

The blessing of the rating agencies was relatively easy. Indeed, for years, the standard operating procedure of the leading insurance company rating agency, A.M. Best Company, was to work closely with the insurers. If you ran an insurance company and wanted a rating, the deal that Best offered you was very favorable indeed. Best said, in effect: "We give you a rating. If you don't like it, we won't publish it. If you like it, you pay us to print up thousands of rating cards and reports that your salespeople can use to sell insurance. It's a win-win."

The ratings process was stacked in favor of the companies from start to finish. They were empowered to decide when and if they wanted to be rated. They got a sneak preview of their rating before it was revealed to the public. They could appeal the rating if they didn't like it. And if they still didn't get a rating they agreed with, they could take it out of circulation by suppressing its publication.[3]

Three newer entrants to the business of rating insurance companies—Moody's, S&P, and Duff & Phelps (now Fitch)—offered essentially the same deal. But instead of earning their money from reprints of ratings reports, they simply charged the insurance companies a flat fee for each rating—anywhere from $10,000 to $50,000 per insurance company subsidiary, per year. Later, Best decided to change its price structure to match the other three, charging the rated companies similar up-front fees.[4]

Not surprisingly, the rating agencies gave out good grades like candy. At A.M. Best, the grade inflation got so far out of hand that no industry insider would be caught alive buying insurance from a company rated "good" by Best. Nearly everyone (except the customers) knew that Best's "good" was actually bad.

Despite all this, First Executive CEO Fred Carr was not satisfied with his rating from Best and went to S&P to get an even better rating. Typically, S&P charged up to $40,000 to rate an insurance company. And just like the deal with Best, if the insurance company didn't like it, S&P wouldn't publish it. But along with junk bond king Michael Milken, Fred Carr cut an even better deal. Milken paid an extra $1 million under the table and, in exchange, got a guaranteed AAA for his junk bonds and for Fred Carr's insurance company. All this despite a business model that was predicated largely on junk bond investing!

Getting the insurance regulators to cooperate was not quite as easy. In fact, the state insurance commissioners around the country were getting so concerned about the industry's bulging investments in junk and unrated bonds, they decided to set up a special office in New York—the Securities Valuation Office—to monitor the situation.

What's a junk bond? The answer, as I've explained, was undisputed: any bond with a rating from S&P or Moody's of double-B or lower. But the insurance companies didn't like that definition. "You can't do that to us," they told the insurance commissioners. "If you use that definition, everybody will see how much junk we have." The commissioners struggled with this request, but amazingly, they obliged. It was like rewriting history to suit the new king.

This went on for several years. Finally, however, after a few of us screamed and hollered about this sham, the insurance commissioners finally realized they simply could not be a party to the junk bond cover-up any longer. They decided to bite the bullet. They adopted the standard double-B definition, and reclassified over $30 billion in "secure" bonds as junk bonds. It was the beginning of the final act for the giant junk bond insurance companies.

The *New York Times* was one of the first to pick up the story. Newspapers all over the country soon followed. That's when the large life and health insurance companies began to fall like dominoes—Executive Life of California, Executive Life of New York, Fidelity Bankers Life, First Capital Life—each and every one dragged down by large junk bond holdings. And this was just the prelude to the biggest failure of all—Mutual Benefit Life of New Jersey, which fell under the weight of losses in speculative real estate.

What about guarantees? That's the shakiest aspect of all.

Insurance policyholders are given the impression that, in the event of a failure, their state guarantee funds will promptly reimburse them, much like the Federal Deposit Insurance Corporation (FDIC) does for savers in failed banks. But the insurance guarantee funds often have no funds; their standard operating procedure is to raise the money *after* the fact. That works okay when just a few small companies fail. But when the failures are large, where do they get the money? The guarantee system itself fails.

The consequence: After the giant failures of the 1990s, the state insurance commissioners had no choice but to march into the companies' headquarters, take over their operations, and declare a moratorium on all cash withdrawals by policyholders.

How many people were affected? Weiss Ratings checked the records of each failed company: In total, they had exactly 5,950,422 policyholders; and among these, 1.9 million were fixed annuities and other policies with cash value.[5] If you were one of those 1.9 million, your money was frozen. The authorities wouldn't let you cash out your policy. They wouldn't even let you borrow on your policy.

What about the legal mandate for the guarantee funds to reimburse policyholders in failed companies? The authorities put their heads together and came up with a creative solution: To avoid invoking the guarantee system, they simply decided to change the definition of when a failed company fails. Instead of declaring that the bankrupt companies were bankrupt, they decided to call them *financially impaired,* or *in rehabilitation.* Then, after many months, the authorities created new companies with new, reformed annuities yielding far less than the original policies. They gave policyholders two choices.

1. *Opt in* to the new company and accept a loss of yield for years to come.
2. *Opt out* and accept their share of whatever cash was available, often as little as 50 cents on the dollar.

It was the greatest disaster in the history of insurance!

So you'd think that the insurance industry would have learned its lessons. Not so! To this day, the companies are still rated by the same rating agencies, in the same way with the same conflicts of interest.

Like the failed insurers of the 1990s, several large U.S. insurance companies, on the prowl for high yields, invested again in high-risk instruments. Junk bonds were still stigmatized, but a handy substitute for junk was readily available: subprime mortgages. And to make things even more exciting, one giant insurer added a whole new layer of risk: a special kind of insurance known as a *credit default swap* (CDS)—a bet placed on the probability of another company's failure.

Remember, in the earlier episode, the rating agencies collected large fees from the companies for each grade. That, in turn, introduced serious conflicts of interest into the process and often biased the ratings in favor of the companies. This time around, they did precisely the same thing: They collected the same kind of big fees. They gave out the same kind of top-notch ratings. And they covered up the same kind of massive risks.

In addition to this, S&P, Moody's, and Fitch created a whole *new* layer of conflicts and bias: They hired themselves out as consultants to help create newfangled debt-backed securities, giving them a true lock on the industry: They created the securities. They *rated* the securities. And then they rated the companies that *bought* the securities, collecting fat fees at each stage of the process. Not only did that pad the bottom line of the rating agencies, it also gave them stronger reasons to inflate the ratings, ignore warning signs, postpone downgrades, and avoid anything that might bring down the debt pyramid they had helped to create.

The repercussions of this disaster were multiple, and as a part of the Regulatory Reform Act of 2010, Congress sought to address them. But the fundamental business model of the established rating agencies was not changed. They continued to collect large fees from issuers for giving them ratings. And the obvious conflict of interest that naturally flows from that financial relationship continued to persist, leaving the danger of more ratings fiascos to come.

Ratings Fiasco 2:
How Wall Street's "Research" Duped Millions of Investors—and Why You Face Similar Dangers Today

If you think insurance customers got a bad deal in the early 1990s, wait till you see what happened to investors in the early 2000s! And if you think these deceptions are a thing of the past, wait till you read what happened in the 2008 debt crisis and could happen again in the next round of the bubble-and-bust roller coaster.

To be sure, the business of rating stocks is different from the business of rating insurance companies. Instead of just four firms, we counted 47 Wall Street investment banks and brokerage firms that published research and ratings on stocks.

The rating scales were also different and varied. But in essence, they all boiled down to recommendations to *buy*, *sell*, or *hold*.

Unlike the bond and credit ratings, there was ostensibly no charge to the companies for the ratings. But, for reasons that soon became evident, nearly all Wall Street ratings issued on stocks were either *buy* or *hold*. They almost never issued *sell* ratings.[6]

What was most shocking, however, is how common it was for Wall Street analysts to continue to lavish praise on a stock, *even if the company was on the verge of bankruptcy*. To better quantify this phenomenon, Weiss Ratings conducted a study on 19 companies that filed for Chapter 11 bankruptcy in the first four months of 2002 and that were rated by Wall Street firms.

The result: Among these 19 bankrupt companies, 12 received a *buy* or *hold* rating from *all* of the Wall Street firms that rated them. Furthermore, the failed companies *continued* to receive those unanimously positive ratings right up to the day they filed for bankruptcy.

Thus, even diligent investors who sought second or third opinions on these companies would have run into a stone wall of unanimous *don't sell* advice. Furthermore, Weiss Ratings found that, among the 47 Wall Street firms that rated these stocks, virtually all were guilty of the same shenanigans. The Wall Street firms led investors like lemmings to the sea, with rarely *one* dissenting voice in the crowd.

For investors, and for the market as a whole, the consequences were catastrophic.

In April 1999, Morgan Stanley Dean Witter stock analyst Mary Meeker–dubbed "Queen of the Internet" by *Barron's*–issued a buy rating on Priceline.com at $104 per share. Within 21 months, the stock was toast–selling for $1.50. Investors who heeded her recommendation lost up to 98 percent of their money, turning a $10,000 mountain of cash into a $144 molehill.

Undaunted, Ms. Meeker also issued buy ratings on Yahoo!, Amazon.com, Drugstore.com, and Homestore.com. The financial media reported the recommendations with a straight face. Then, Yahoo! crashed 97 percent, Amazon.com 95 percent, Drugstore .com 99 percent, and Homestore.com 95.5 percent.

Why did Ms. Meeker recommend those dogs in the first place? And why did she stubbornly stand by her buy ratings even as they crashed 20, 50, 70 percent, and, finally, as much as 99 percent? One reason was that virtually every one of Ms. Meeker's "strong buys" was paying Ms. Meeker's employer—Morgan Stanley Dean Witter— to promote its shares, and because Morgan Stanley rewarded Ms. Meeker for the effort with a $15 million paycheck. While millions of investors lost their shirts, Morgan Stanley Dean Witter and Mary Meeker, as well as the companies they were promoting, cried all the way to the bank.

An isolated case? Not even close. In 1999, Salomon Smith Barney's top executives received electrifying news: AT&T was planning to take its giant wireless division public, in what would be the largest initial public offering (IPO) in history up to that time. Naturally, every brokerage firm on Wall Street wanted to do the underwriting for this once-in-a-lifetime IPO, and for good reason: The fees would amount to millions of dollars. But Salomon had an issue. One of its chief stock analysts, Jack Grubman, had been saying negative things about AT&T for years. A *major* problem? Not really. By the time Salomon's hotshots made their pitch to pick up AT&T's underwriting business, Grubman had miraculously changed his rating to a *buy*.

What if it was abundantly obvious that a company was going down the tubes? What if an analyst personally turned sour on the company? Would that make a difference? Not really. For the once-superhot Internet stock InfoSpace, Merrill's official advice was *buy*. Privately, however, in e-mails uncovered in a subsequent investigation, Merrill's insiders had a very different opinion, writing that Infospace was a "piece of junk." Result: Investors who trusted Merrill analysts to give them their honest opinion got clobbered, losing up to 93.5 percent of their money when Infospace crashed.

Merrill's official advice on another hot stock, Excite@Home, was *accumulate!* Privately, however, Merrill analysts wrote in e-mails that Excite@Home was a "piece of crap." Result: Investors who trusted Merrill lost up to 99.9 percent of their money when the company went under.

For 24/7 Media, *accumulate!* was also the official Merrill Lynch advice. Merrill's internal comments were that 24/7 Media is a "piece of shit." Result: Investors who relied on Merrill's advice lost 97.6 percent of their money when 24/7 Media crashed.

Subsequently, the Securities and Exchange Commission and other regulators agreed to a global settlement with 12 of the largest Wall Street firms with the aim of encouraging independent research and preventing these issues in the future. *Sell* ratings became a bit more common. But the traps laid for investors changed very little. And independent research never got off the ground. More importantly, the global settlement failed to prevent the *next* ratings fiasco.

Ratings Fiasco 3:
The Giant Debt Crisis of the Late 2000s

Fast forward to March 14, 2008, the day that Bear Stearns collapsed. The Federal Reserve Bank of New York provided a 28-day $29 billion emergency loan and Bear Stearns signed a merger agreement with JPMorgan Chase in a stock swap worth $2 per share, or less than 10 percent of Bear Stearns' most recent market value at the time. The sale price represented a staggering decline from a peak of $172 per share as late as January 2007 and $93 per share just two months earlier.

Wall Street stock analysts, still feeling some of the repercussions of their earlier fiasco, were now a bit more willing to issue negative opinions. But the Wall Street bond rating agencies—Moody's, S&P, and Fitch—persisted in their old ways: On the day of the Bear Stearns failure, Moody's maintained a rating for Bear Stearns of A2; S&P was equally generous, giving the firm an A rating until the day of failure; and Fitch liked Bear Stearns even more, saying it continually merited a solid A+ throughout the 18-year period between February 2, 1990, and March 14, 2008.

Investors lost everything. You must not let the same thing happen to you. Nor can you afford to accept Wall Street's excuses: When Bear Stearns went under, they said it caught them by surprise, and they couldn't be blamed for not foreseeing what no one expected. But 102 days before the failure, based on publicly available data, we warned that Bear Stearns "had sunk its balance sheet even deeper into the hole, with $20.2 billion in dead assets, or 155 percent of its equity; and was threatened with insolvency." Moreover, we were not the only independent analysts issuing such warnings.[7]

Six months later, on September 15, 2008, it was Lehman Brothers' turn to go under, driving down the Dow Jones by over 500 points, the largest single-day drop since the days following the 9/11 attacks.

As you saw in Chapter 1, it was the landmark event that marked a new, more advanced phase of the debt crisis, sending shock waves of panic around the world that have continued to reverberate for many months thereafter. On the morning of its failure, however, Moody's still gave it a rating of A2; S&P gave it an A; and Fitch gave it an A+. As soon as the news hit, the latter two rating agencies promptly downgraded the firm to D. But for investors trapped in Lehman Brothers shares and for lenders stuck with its debt, it was far too late to take protective action.

Again, investors lost everything. Again, I urge you not to let this happen to you. And I repeat my warning about their lame excuses: As with Bear Stearns, analysts said they were caught flatfooted because of circumstances no one could have foreseen. But 182 days before its failure, we warned that Lehman was vulnerable to the same disaster that struck Bear Stearns. Nor was that our first warning. In the prior year, we wrote that Lehman was in a "similar predicament as Bear Stearns" because of an even larger, $34.7 billion pile-up of dead assets, or 160 percent of its equity. Again, we based our opinion on widely available data; and again, we were among several independent analysts that had reached a similar conclusion.[8]

Meanwhile, Fannie Mae and its sister company, Freddie Mac, were placed under conservatorship of the U.S. government on Sunday, September 7, 2008, with the U.S. Treasury committing to bailout funds of $100 billion for each, the largest bailout for any company in history at that time. Common and preferred shareholders were wiped out, and debt holders risked severe losses. But because of Fannie Mae's status as a government-sponsored enterprise, the Wall Street rating agencies completely missed it. S&P first gave the company a triple-A rating nearly seven years earlier and never changed it; Moody's did the same more than 13 years earlier and never changed it; Fitch had continually maintained its triple-A for Fannie Mae for more than 17 years and never changed it.

However, outside, independent observers were as persistent in their warnings as Wall Street rating agencies were consistent in their praise. For example, six years earlier, we wrote "Fannie Mae is already drowning in a sea of debt. It has $34 of debt for every $1 of shareholder equity. That's big leverage and of the wrong kind. Plus, the company has only one one-hundredths of a penny in cash on hand for every $1 of current bills. Think Fannie Mae can't go under? Think again." Other Fannie Mae critics were not quite that blatant, but reading between their lines, it was clear the true rating the company merited was far from triple-A.[9]

We witnessed a similar pattern of Wall Street complacency, bias, and flagrant disregard for investors with the failures of New Century Financial, which filed for Chapter 11 bankruptcy in 2007; Countrywide Financial, which was bought out by Bank of America in 2008; Washington Mutual, which filed for bankruptcy in September of that year; and Wachovia Bank, which signed a deal to be acquired by Wells Fargo by year's end 2008.[10]

And, in the next great recession, brace yourself for similar shocks.

Lessons to Learn and Never Forget

The *New York Times* said Weiss Ratings was "the first to see the dangers and say so unambiguously." But we are rarely the only ones. Other independent analysts also saw the dangers and also issued warnings.

Nor did it take special intelligence or foresight to do so. Again, as in all prior episodes, the most powerful research tool was available to anyone who bothered to use it—*the zealous rejection of payola, conflicts of interest, and bias.*

For investors and savers like you, however, the egregious failure of Wall Street to warn of trouble is an extremely important learning experience:

Lesson 1: You cannot trust the established rating agencies such as S&P, Moody's, Fitch, and A.M. Best. Regardless of regulatory reform, their business models have *not* changed. Until they do, take their ratings with a grain of salt, relying primarily on providers of truly *independent* ratings, such as Bloomberg, Morningstar, TheStreet.com, Value Line, Veribanc, Weiss Ratings, and others.

Lesson 2: Size alone is no assurance of safety. Quite the contrary, often the bigger the companies are . . . the more elaborate the cover-ups . . . the harder they fall and the more difficult it is for authorities to protect consumers or clean up the mess.

Lesson 3: Even in the best of times, large financial failures are possible. In a severe recession or depression, they are inevitable.

Lesson 4: Inflated ratings played a key role in supporting a speculative bubble. Their downfall could play an equally important role in deepening the next recession.

Lesson 5: In the insurance industry, you cannot count on government regulators and guarantees. As you will see in Chapter 6, the FDIC's guarantee of banks is generally stronger. But it also has some similar underlying weaknesses.

These are the lessons that should have been learned by Wall Street–and by Washington–long ago. They should have learned them in the 1980s when hundreds of banks failed, in the 1990s when giant insurers failed, and in the early 2000s when so many tech companies left investors with deep financial wounds. But they didn't learn these lessons of history. And they were destined to repeat it–this time in the greatest bubble and bust of all time.

HOUSING: HOW TO ESCAPE THE GREATEST BUST OF ALL TIME

Dad grew up in Harlem, and his family couldn't afford to buy a home. So most of what he knew about buying and selling real estate was based on his research or on what he discussed with his clients. Here's what he told me:

> One of the greatest blunders people made in the 1930s was to blindly assume that prices were already so low they couldn't possibly go any lower. In reality, the value of their real estate, stocks, commodities, and virtually every other asset didn't stop going down at some particular level that *appeared* to be "cheap." Nor did it stop falling just because it matched some historical price that was considered low. The end of the price declines came only when the natural economic forces driving them down were exhausted; when most of the bad debts were cleaned out and the economy finally stabilized.
>
> This was also true for home prices. But in the Great Depression, none of my clients owed money on their home, and

among my relatives, I cannot remember anyone who took out a mortgage until after World War II.

In the 1920s and 1930s, mortgages were not nearly as common as they were after the war. And I know for a fact that even the people who did take out a mortgage never paid a variable rate. The rate was always fixed. So they could plan on making the same exact monthly payments year after year.

In those days, we had big troubles on the farms. But in the cities, most of the big speculation was tied to Wall Street, and Wall Street firms rarely got involved in housing. We didn't have a secondary mortgage market, either. The big mortgage lenders who created that market, like Fannie Mae, didn't come into existence until years later. The end result is that the housing bust in the 1930s was not nearly as bad as it might have been. While the average stock price fell to a dime on the dollar, the average home price retained 70 percent of its value. And most of that decline came only *after* the economy shrank and *after* millions of people lost their jobs.

Unfortunately, we cannot say the same for home prices in the current era. In the United States before 2010, home prices had already fallen almost as much as in the 1930s. As *Safe Money Report* editor Mike Larson warned in his white paper submitted to the FDIC and the Federal Reserve long before home prices began to fall, what should have been the American dream would turn into the American *nightmare.*

What's most revealing is this: Nearly all of the troubles in the U.S. housing market witnessed in the Great Recession of 2008–2009 were caused by bad mortgages going sour and a massive foreclosure crisis. The more common, traditional cause of housing slumps—high interest rates—had not yet kicked in.

By 2010, even with the lowest interest rates in history, 1 in 7 American homeowners had already defaulted on their mortgage or lost their home in foreclosure. More than 4 out of 10 owed more on their home than it was worth.

Not even in the Great Depression had so much debt been heaped onto the roofs of so many homes! Never before had the terms of that debt been so conducive to defaults! And not even in the least developed countries of the world had we seen sloppier documentation regarding who owed what to whom, opening a Pandora's box of legal challenges to bank foreclosures.

As a result, the American housing nightmare had no precedent, no historical road map to guide you, no proven pathway to follow. With enough government money poured into the U.S. housing market, it was possible to stabilize it for a while and even bring about a weak recovery. But in the long term, no one could tell you how far U.S. home prices would ultimately decline, when they would hit bottom, how many home owners would lose their homes, or when a *sustainable* housing recovery could begin.

To throw some light on the speculative frenzy and panic that swept through the U.S. housing market in the first 11 years of the twenty-first century, the only *approximate* precedents I could find have nothing to do with homes at all. Rather, they are the Dutch Tulip Mania of the 1630s, the South Sea Bubble of the 1700s, and the stock market panics of the early 1900s.

Dutch Tulip Mania. Starting in the early 1630s, investors and speculators drove up the price of tulip bulbs to nosebleed heights. In 1637, at the height of the tulip mania, just one tulip bulb, named *Semper Augustus,* changed hands for 12 acres of land. Another bulb was sold for a massive collection of goods, including 160 bushels of wheat, 160 bushels of rye, 4 oxen, 12 swine, 2 hogsheads of wine, 4 cases of beer, 2 tons of butter, 1,000 pounds of cheese, and more.

South Sea Bubble. The South Sea Company was given a virtual monopoly to trade in the South Atlantic, mostly in slaves from Africa to South America. In 1720, investors drove up shares in the South Sea Company from 125 to 960 pounds in just six months.

Early twentieth-century stock bubbles. Repeatedly in the early 1900s, U.S. stocks were driven higher in speculative frenzies, and the last of these was merely the most extreme of several episodes: The Dow Jones Industrials surged from 213 points in 1928 to 381 in 1929.

Since these historic episodes had nothing to do with home prices, I have no intention of making a direct comparison. But by looking at them side by side with the U.S. housing crisis of the

2000s, you can get a better sense of how utterly serious the housing boom and bust really was—and is.

In those earlier boom-and-bust episodes, the objects of speculation were tulips, slaves, and stocks. This time, it was the American home. But despite that key difference, the powerful forces that helped create the speculative bubbles were similar.

Powerful Force 1: Debt

Debt is the fuel of speculation. Without debt, speculative bubbles cannot emerge. With it, prices can be inflated beyond the wildest imagination.

In seventeenth-century Holland, investors speculated wildly on tulips, putting up as little as 2.5 percent of their own cash. Similarly, in early twentieth-century stock market booms, investors put up as little as 10 percent of their own money, using borrowed funds for up to 90 percent of their purchases.

But in many respects, the borrowing mania that fueled the U.S. housing boom in the first decade of the third millennium makes all previous debt manias pale by comparison. In first phases of the bust, at mid-year 2008, the Federal Reserve reported a grand total of $14.8 trillion in U.S. mortgages outstanding. That was 40 percent more than the entire national debt and triple the total of all the mortgages in the United States just a dozen years earlier.

Sadly, it was not just the super-sized *quantity* of debt that was so dangerous. Even *more* dangerous was the substandard *quality* of the debt. Consider these facts:

- In all prior speculative bubbles of history, investors were required to put up at least *some* of their own money to buy into the boom. Even in the tech stock mania of the late 1990s, investors had to put up a minimum of 50 percent cash for their stock purchases. But in the U.S. housing boom of the 2000s, millions of Americans bought homes with *zero* money down. Lenders and real estate agents didn't merely look the other way while home owners borrowed the down payment; they actively encouraged it. Home buyers without enough cash to buy a $500 TV set were declared the proud new owners of $500,000 luxury homes. Many even took it one step further, with serial purchases of homes, leapfrogging with glee from one free ride to the next.

■ In all prior speculative bubbles, borrowers were invariably required to make payments of interest and principal in full and without fail, with zero tolerance for any other arrangement. In contrast, during the American housing boom of the new millennium, millions of homeowners were allowed to pay strictly interest with no principal payments, or even *less* than full interest. So it should come as no surprise that so many opted to make the smallest payments allowed, while lenders added the unpaid amounts to the loan balance. The more time that elapsed, the deeper into debt the borrowers fell.

■ In prior episodes of rampant speculation, loans were almost invariably held by the lenders, who, in turn, had a vested interest in making sure the borrower's finances were sound and their payments kept current. But in the housing boom of the early 2000s, the mortgages were mostly held by nonlenders—institutions and investors that were far removed from the local scene.

■ In earlier manias, speculators were required to document that they were worthy of the loans. They invariably had to present hard evidence of income, proof of assets, or both. But in the great American housing dream-turned-nightmare, even that was not the case. Millions were allowed to borrow huge sums without a scintilla of proof that they had the wherewithal to make the payments. Many were tacitly encouraged to actually lie on their loan applications, grossly overstating their income. Most shocking of all, it was no secret; industry officials themselves talked frequently about the nationwide boom in *liar loans*.

■ In earlier manias, the bubble was confined primarily to one debt sector. Not this time around! Even after mass foreclosures and write-downs, by mid-year 2010, beyond the $14 trillion in mortgages in the United States, there was *another* $26.6 trillion in consumer and corporate debts. Result: Americans were not only under tremendous pressure to sell their homes due to burdensome mortgages, they were also squeezed by huge credit card balances and by layoffs from employers, many of which were equally entrapped in debt.

■ In prior bubbles, once the big bust occurred, a very large proportion of the outstanding debts were liquidated, and the market found a bottom. Not in this case! Instead, the Federal government did everything in its power to *stop* the debt liquidation process. The nation's two mortgage giants, Fannie Mae and Freddie Mac, now owned by the government, continued to pour money into home mortgages even as most private sector lenders were exiting the market or folding their tent. As if that weren't enough, the U.S. Federal Reserve also poured $1.5 trillion into the market by buying up mortgage-backed securities that few others wanted.

By every measure, the debts piled up on millions of rooftops in the early 2000s were far bigger and shakier than any debt pile-up ever witnessed in history.

Powerful Force 2: Investor Mania

In the Dutch Tulip Mania, the South Sea Bubble, and the stock market booms of the early 1900s, millions of investors and speculators—most with little experience in the market—were caught up in a wild buying frenzy.

Unfortunately, we witnessed a similar pattern in the 2000s, using American homes as the vehicle. As the buying frenzy heated up, houses and condos were flipped faster than hotcakes. Prices were driven through the roof. And even mortgages themselves were transformed into securities that were riskier than some of the riskiest stocks in the world.

At the peak of the housing bubble, the average price of existing homes reached nearly five times the total yearly income of its owners, the highest in history. At the same time, the affordability of each home plunged to its *lowest* level in history.

Once set into motion, the speculative fever spread quickly. From Miami to Phoenix to San Diego to Las Vegas, investors camped outside housing developments to snap up three, four, five, or more units at a time. Condominium developers built gleaming towers in major cities with no evidence of real underlying demand. From coast to coast, investors signed on to millions of preconstruction contracts, only to flip them even before the first shovels touched the ground.

Traditionally in America, this kind of speculation had been just a small niche in the giant housing industry. But at the peak of the housing boom in the mid-2000s, it nearly took over: An astounding 40 percent of houses and condos were bought as second homes or investments. The yearly rate of appreciation on existing homes cata-pulted from 3.6 percent in January 2001 to 16.6 percent in November 2005. On new homes, it surged from 4.8 to 18.1 percent.

Fueling the bubble, government agencies and private invest-ment banks bundled up mortgages and resold them as securities that could be traded as stocks or bonds. These securities, in turn, were bought by investors in the United States, Europe, and Asia. The total amount of mortgages transformed into these securities: $4.8 trillion, 60 percent more than the total value of all the stocks in the Dow Jones Industrial Average. Just in one year—2006—$2.4 trillion in new mortgage-backed securities were created, more than *triple* the amount of six years earlier. And it was this process of trans-forming mortgages into securities—called *securitization*—that played a key role in creating the conditions for a speculative bubble.

Securitization gave lenders the *ability* to make poor lending decisions, but it gave faraway investors the *responsibility* for the con-sequences. It automatically encouraged lenders to maximize the *quantity* of loans while ignoring the *quality* of loans. And it made it extremely profitable for lenders or brokers to lure borrowers into loans that the borrowers had little ability to pay back.

Even in past investment manias, there was no such structure. Even the wild and woolly speculators of the 1600s, 1700s, and the early 1900s did not take the madness to *that* extreme.

Powerful Force 3: Government-Bred Monopolies, Corruption, Fraud, and Cover-Ups

Some of the largest speculative bubbles of all time were born out of government-sponsored monopolies, nurtured by government-bred corruption, and kept alive beyond their time by government-inspired fraud and cover-ups.

In the South Sea Bubble of 1711, the English government needed to find a way to fund the huge debts it had incurred in the course of the War of Spanish Succession. So the Lord Treasurer, Robert Harley, created the South Sea Trading Company to help finance the government's debts. The company got exclusive trading rights in the South Atlantic, plus a perpetual government annuity of more than a half million pounds per year. In exchange, its investors agreed to assume responsibility for about £10 million of the government's debt.

It seemed like a win-win. But the company's managers, thinking they had the government's resources to fall back on, were complacent and ignored signs of economic troubles. They took excessive risk. And ultimately, investigations turned up massive fraud at the company and pervasive corruption in the government. When the entire structure collapsed, there was nothing the government could do except to lamely close the barn door after the fact, passing laws aimed at preventing a future recurrence.

Similarly, in the early 1900s, the panic of 1901 occurred in the wake of a failed attempt to create a massive railroad monopoly; the panic of 1907 followed a failed attempt to corner the copper market; and the Crash of 1929 resulted, to a large degree, from the collusion among brokers, bankers, and tycoons.

In nearly every case, the government gave select companies or individuals special privileges, changed the rules, and encouraged great concentration of wealth or power. And in nearly every case, the government made at least some attempts to salvage the boom long after the bust was evident. But it was ultimately powerless to avert a collapse in the very structures it had helped to create.

Unfortunately, the same, or worse, was true in the American housing nightmare: The U.S. government created two monopolies that made England's eighteenth-century South Sea Company and America's twentieth-century industrial monopolies look small by comparison.

Their names: Fannie Mae (the Federal National Mortgage Association) and Freddie Mac (the Federal Home Loan Mortgage Corporation).

In earlier years, the U.S. government gave these companies monopolistic control over what would become the largest debt market in the United States: mortgages. It later sold the companies to private shareholders. And then, beginning in the 2000s, the government spurred both companies to compete with private lenders, who were making a killing selling teaser mortgages to high-risk borrowers—subprime loans.

Not surprisingly, the results were similar to those of earlier bubbles: extreme complacency, excessive risk taking, and ultimately, fraud.

In September 2004, the U.S. government's Office of Federal Housing Enterprise (OFHE), Fannie's and Freddie's primary regulator, issued a special report revealing massive accounting irregularities. And four years later, in September 2008, the companies had *still* not cleaned up their act, prompting the U.S. Securities and Exchange Commission to launch new investigations into accounting deceptions.

One of the biggest deceptions: In their official filings and public pronouncements, Fannie and Freddie consistently and wildly overstated their capital, while understating their risk. These companies, supposedly built with mortar and steel, were just another papier-mâché edifice in disguise.

Repeatedly, the company executives swore under oath that they had more than enough capital. And even on the eve of their demise, their regulators testified before Congress that the companies were solvent.

True? Based on their smoke-and-mirrors accounting, it seemed to be. But based on the accounting rules you and I must abide by, not even close. For longer than anyone cared to admit, Fannie and Freddie had been insolvent, while their chief executives hid behind their carefully camouflaged façade, marched into riskier corners of the mortgage market, and trashed the trust of millions of Americans—all with no sign of restraint or expression of regret.

Between 2005 and 2008, for example, Fannie Mae purchased or guaranteed at least $270 billion in subprime mortgages—high-fee loans to high-risk borrowers. That was more than *three* times as much as it had bought in *all* its earlier years combined.

Yet no one batted an eyelash.

Rather, Wall Street and Washington cheered loudly, encouraging them to take on even *more* risk. Why such enthusiasm?

Because the rapid growth in fees turbocharged the rapid rise in Fannie's stock price. Because big revenues meant huge bonuses for executives–$90 million for one, $30.8 million for another, and $10 million for a third. And because unlimited money flowing to unqualified borrowers helped buy politicians millions of votes.

Suddenly, however, in September 2008, it was finally recognized that all the financial statements and all the sworn testimony about solvency were worth less than the paper they were printed on. Suddenly, the two largest mortgage lenders on Earth, supposedly rich and prosperous, were thoroughly bankrupt. And suddenly, underscoring the depth of their demise, the two companies needed an unprecedented $200 billion injection of government funds just to keep them alive. But it still was not enough to cover their $5.2 trillion in owned or guaranteed mortgages, $1.5 trillion in debts, and $2 trillion in derivatives.

Powerful Force 4: Consumer Deceptions

The history of speculative bubbles is rife with snake oil salesmen and investor scams. But they were associated with penny stock schemes, hot land deals, fraudulent mining operations, and other so-called investments. They were limited to a niche. And they were usually *illegal.*

The American housing nightmare was unique in that the scams spread nationwide and struck the one asset at the very core of the American dream–the home. Moreover, for the most part, the scams were "perfectly legal." Some prime examples follow.

Deception 1: Predatory Lending
As the value of the average U.S. home soared, the equity in each home grew fat, and this equity attracted predators like flies, including some of America's largest mortgage lenders, such as New Century Financial, Countrywide Financial, and IndyMac Bank.

These mortgage juggernauts then targeted the most vulnerable Americans–the retired, the elderly, and the poor. They charged exorbitant fees. And they spent millions on ads to push mortgages with cryptic, exotic adjustable-rate provisions that snared their victims in some of the worst debt traps ever created.

Even if a home buyer was perfectly qualified for low-risk, less expensive mortgages, salesmen were specifically trained to steer them to high-risk, more expensive mortgages—the primary reason the SEC and attorneys general in multiple states launched major investigations into the kingpin of this scam, Countrywide's CEO, Angelo Mozilo. They didn't nail Mozilo on this particular scam. But they did get him on another, related one—misleading shareholders about the risks associated with his company's loans, for which he agreed to pay $67.5 million in fines.

Even billions in fines, however, would pale in comparison to the money, homes, and lifestyle lost by the millions of his victims.

A typical scenario: A man and wife in their 70s pay off their mortgage. But they live on a fixed income. Inflation drives up the price of everything they need to live and avoid impoverishment—prescription drugs, public transportation, gasoline, and supplemental health insurance. They are forced to use their credit cards to make ends meet. They have to borrow a few thousand more for medical bills.

Along comes a supposedly friendly mortgage broker with a "simple solution" to their problem. He offers a loan against their home for a low initial monthly payment—enough to pay off all their debts and still leave a chunk of change in the bank. But the fine print of the loan agreement contains:

- Outrageous, disguised hidden fees built into the total loan amount, sometimes amounting to 10 percent or more of the loan value, which pad the lender's bottom line.
- Credit and disability insurance. The expensive coverage pays off the loan if the borrower dies or becomes disabled. But all too often, lenders roll the premiums into the loan principal to hide its existence, selling it to customers who already have more than enough coverage from other policies.
- Worst and most common of all: Low teaser rates that soon become sky-high, adjustable rates. Billboards and Internet ads tout "1 Percent Mortgages," but the rate is good for only a month or two. And even the fine print does not clearly disclose that rates could rise to *many* times the teaser rate.

Some real case studies: One Louisiana couple bought a home with a fixed 8.5 percent mortgage in 1994. Seven years later, a lender persuaded them to refinance with a nine-year mortgage at 11.4 percent, *plus* $10,700 in fees (more than 11 percent of the principal), *plus* still another $6,400 in disability and credit life and disability policies they did not need. When they went back to the same lender looking for a way out, they were sucked into yet another loan at 13 percent and with almost $10,000 in *new* fees.

Another couple got snookered into refinancing with a 21 percent loan that doubled their monthly payment to more than $1,200. To help seal the deal, they were told to claim $600 in rental income from the other half of their two-family home. In reality, their unemployed daughter lived there rent-free.[1]

This kind of predatory lending spread like wildfire, corroding the once-healthy American mortgage market, penetrating the broad middle class, even infecting high-end market segments. Not surprisingly, lawsuits alleging lending abuse were rampant. Major, established lenders paid hundreds of millions of dollars in settlements and fines. And even before the contagion reached an advanced stage, the FBI's assistant director for criminal investigations called the predatory lending an "epidemic."

Long before the housing bust, in April 2005, our *Safe Money Report* explained the situation this way: "If it were just a few bad apples and assorted criminal elements, I wouldn't be so concerned. What truly alarms me is the fact that, much as in the tech boom of the 1990s, the most widespread excesses and abuses are condoned or even designed by large, well-established lenders. For many Americans, this implies a triple risk—the risk of overly burdensome mortgages that can strangle even the highest-income households, the risk of sinking investments when the inevitable shake-out strikes, and the risk of falling income when the economy as a whole begins to suffer from the fallout of a housing market debacle."

This is precisely what happened. But the deceptions did not end there.

Deception 2: Inflated Appraisals
In 2005, a group of 8,000 U.S. home appraisers signed a petition to protest a disturbing trend: All over the country, they reported

situations in which appraisers felt they were being pressured to goose up home value estimates to get deals done. Some appraisers even complained of being blacklisted if they refused to play ball. In response, they pleaded—even begged—for relief from lenders who "apply pressure on appraisers to hit or exceed a predetermined value."[2]

At the time, most Americans were already up to their eyeballs in debt. So mortgage lenders, competing for their shrinking business, were having a tougher time making new loans. To keep their revenues flowing, they put the squeeze on appraisers to inflate the value of a home in order to push through mortgages that otherwise would be nixed at the home office.

As an illustration, say a home buyer wanted to close on a house for $310,000 but had only $10,000 in cash. He needed to borrow—and the mortgage broker wanted to lend—the $300,000 balance. But the appraised value was $300,000, and the most the lender would lend was 95 percent of that, or $285,000.

In normal times, the broker would order an objective appraisal to determine the fair market value. If it came back at $315,500 or better, fine. If not, no deal. But in America's great housing bubble, that was not nearly as likely. Instead, the loan officer might send this message to the appraiser: "We need this to come in at $315,500. If you can't come up with that value, we'll find someone else who can."

The mortgage broker got the business and pocketed a big commission. The appraiser got his fee. And the proud new owner, thinking his home was worth more than what he paid for it, was also happy. What he didn't realize was that he had overborrowed on an asset that was overvalued—not only because of the obvious overspeculation in the marketplace, but also because of overzealous officials who routinely resorted to not-so-obvious hanky-panky.

Deception 3: Large Balloon Payments

Home owners could reduce their rates by agreeing to a loan that came with a large balloon payment due in, say, five or seven years. The plan was that, when the fateful day arrived, they'd just refinance or sell the house. In reality, however, even in the best of times, the delinquency rate on mortgages with balloons was 50 percent higher than the delinquency rate on those without balloons.

Some of these deceptions have died out. But, unfortunately, it was rarely because the perpetrators voluntarily changed their ways. By 2008, 297 of the nation's major lenders had been driven into bankruptcy, bought out, or forced to shut down their mortgage lending business. By 2010, most the remaining lenders had failed or exited the business.

Powerful Force 5: Collapse!

How much could home prices ultimately decline in the American housing nightmare? You have no way of knowing with certainty, and neither do I. But we *can* draw some lessons from similar bubbles and crashes throughout history:

- In the Dutch Tulip Mania, investors lost nearly all of their money if they bought for cash; more than all of their money if they bought on the slim margin of just 2.5 percent.
- In the South Sea bubble, the cost of the shares investors bought fell from a peak of 960 to less than 100, a loss of 90 percent or more.
- In the Crash of 1929 and the ensuing three-year bear market, investors lost 89 percent of their money even in America's largest industrial stocks.
- In the tech wreck of 2000–2002, when a myriad of Internet and technology companies collapsed, investors lost 78 percent of their money invested in the average Nasdaq stock, and 100 percent in companies that went under.
- And in the financial crisis of 2008, investors lost 99 percent or more of their money in some of America's most respected financial institutions.

My main point: The speculative bubble in U.S. homes was as extreme as each of these historic examples, and the resulting price collapse could also be extreme, especially in the hardest-hit regions and home categories.

The obvious difference: Most people don't need tulips or stocks. They *do* need a roof over their heads. So demand is not likely to fall to zero. And although wipeout declines are sometimes possible on individual properties, on average, they will not decline *that* far. But even lesser declines will be devastating enough. Indeed, the American housing nightmare seems to be progressing in four phases:

Phase 1: The bust in the subprime mortgage market. By 2007, this had already taken place.

Phase 2: A severe U.S. recession. By 2008, this was already under way.

Phase 3: A temporary stabilization and recovery thanks largely to government intervention. This came in 2009, although the recovery was very weak, driven mostly by a tax incentive for home buyers that backfired, causing sharp declines in sales as soon as it expired.

Phase 4: A second, more severe decline.

The big difference: In Phase 1 of the crisis, it was the housing and real estate bust that sunk the economy. In Phase 4, it could be the sinking economy or rising interest rates that tear a new hole in housing and real estate.

The most critical measure of the crisis: The percentage of home owners who are late in making their mortgage payments, or the mortgage delinquency rate.

In Phase 1, if you asked government officials for an estimate of how much the delinquency rate might rise, their response would go something like this:

"Subprime mortgages? Sure, subprime mortgages will go bad. But prime mortgages? Heck no! They're solid. You'll *never* ever see the prime mortgage market experience similar difficulties." Famous last words!

By 2010, the delinquency rate on all U.S. mortgages, including all *prime* mortgages, had soared to a level that was *higher* than that of subprime mortgages at the time government officials first began making such pronouncements. Indeed, the Mortgage Bankers Association (MBA) reported that the delinquency rate on all U.S. mortgages for one to four family residences *including* mostly prime mortgages—was 9.85 percent of all loans outstanding. In other words, *nearly 1 in 10 mortgages was delinquent—an astronomical level.*

Worse, this figure reflected strictly existing mortgages with payments past due. It did *not* include loans in the process of foreclosure. How bad was that number? The MBA reported that the percentage of loans undergoing foreclosure was an astounding 4.57 percent—more than *triple* the level that would be normal for an economic recovery.

In sum, if you combined the loans in foreclosure with loans past due, the all-inclusive bad mortgage rate was at a Depression-era level of 13.97 percent.

How much money did that involve? According to the Federal Reserve's Flow of Funds, the total amount of home mortgages outstanding in the United States was $10.6 trillion at mid-year 2010. With close to 14 percent of those going bad, that meant nearly $1.5 trillion in U.S. mortgages were still in distress. And that was *after* the Federal Reserve had pumped in a similar sum by buying up mortgage-backed securities!

As more home owners defaulted, more homes were foreclosed and more hit the market, a powerful force that continued to weigh on prices even while the economy was growing. With any new economic decline, that pressure could be overwhelming, again depressing home values.

Bottom line: No matter how far home prices in your area have already fallen and no matter how cheap they may appear, they could fall still further.

In the United States, an individual home that was once priced for $300,000 at its peak fell, on average, by about a third, to $200,000, by the end of Phase 1. But don't blindly assume that's the bottom. Another wave of declines is still possible.

Will the Government Intervene to Support the Housing Market?

Of course. But as thoroughly documented by *Safe Money Report* editor Mike Larson, such interventions have rarely turned the tide.

■ Washington claimed the Home Affordable Modification Program (HAMP) would save nearly 3.3 million home owners by giving them loans with more favorable terms. But less than one-tenth that many—a mere 295,348—were actually helped.

- Officials also swore the government's Home Affordable Modification Program (HAMP) would help up to five million home owners secure new loans owned or guaranteed by Fannie Mae and Freddie Mac. It actually helped less than 5 percent of that number—around 220,000.
- They said the FHASecure program would help 500,000 families refinance—but it was canceled after helping on only 3,900 mortgages.
- Washington's Hope for Home Owners Program, originally billed as the ultimate solution for nearly six million homeowners who may face foreclosure, helped precisely *zero* home owners. There were only 326 applications for the program and not a single one received a new mortgage or even modification of an existing one.
- The HUD Implementation of Recovery Act included $13.6 billion for the Department of Housing and Urban Development. But foreclosures exploded 673 percent after the bill was signed into law by President Obama on February 17, 2009.

All told, the total number of mortgages at risk was estimated to be 6 million. However, the mortgages touched by these multiple government efforts were fewer than 520,000, or less than 9 percent.

Can Washington really be this incompetent? According to the Special Inspector General of the Troubled Asset Relief Program (SIGTARP), the answer is a resounding "yes!" SIGTARP reported that the government's mortgage programs are a disaster. The likelihood of similar programs succeeding in the years ahead is not promising.

And no matter what the future may bring, the recent past has already taught us major lifetime lessons: Never before have we witnessed home price declines of this magnitude! And never before have we seen a bust that reaches so many income groups in so many communities! But that fact alone does not mean it's the end of the American nightmare or that even larger declines are unthinkable. Remember, it's also true that never before in history has so much debt, speculation, government manipulation, fraud, corruption, and consumer abuse been heaped onto any housing market! And if there's one thing that history teaches us, it's that unprecedented causes lead to unprecedented consequences.

Important Lessons to Learn Before It's Too Late

Lesson 1: Don't blame yourself. Virtually every Realtor and expert in America told you that investing in homes was a "sure bet"; and any lender in the country that accepted your loan application was, in effect, telling you that you had the means to make the payments. You could count on your fingers the people in the country who disbelieved real estate experts or second-guessed seasoned bankers. If you weren't among them, it certainly wasn't your fault.

Lesson 2: Don't look back. Forget what your property was worth at its peak, and try to forget what you paid for it as well. That's water under the bridge. Instead, look at what's happening *today*—in the headlines, in your neighborhood, at companies in your area. Is there still an abundance of homes for sale? Are most people under financial stress? Is it still difficult for them to qualify for new mortgages? Is unemployment still unusually high? If the answer to any of these questions is "yes," it's probably *not* too late to sell, and it may also be too soon to buy.

Lesson 3: Don't count on the government to save the day. As you've seen, there have been a whole series of public programs to help some people, some of the time. But they have invariably been spotty, and even the most powerful of those programs are not likely to bring about a lasting recovery in the housing market.

In the earlier stages of the bust, they are available if you qualify. In the later stages, as the economic decline deepens and government resources are stretched thinner, they are destined to be overwhelmed by the tide of foreclosures. Or they will simply fizzle amidst ever-changing government priorities.

The most important lesson of all: Don't overestimate the depth, speed, and duration of the decline.

Bottom line: If you need or want to sell, don't wait! The following section provides step-by-step instructions. Alternatively, if you are unable or unwilling to sell, follow the steps on pages 165 and 173.

10 Steps for Selling Your Home in a Weak Market

If you own investment property in a falling real estate market, I think your choice is clear: Sell!

If you own your own home in a falling market, however, it's primarily a personal choice—not just an investment decision. In that example, I cannot tell you what to decide. Suffice it to say that, if you and your family are comfortable with the idea of moving—and fully committed to the goal of selling—you should not hesitate to sell. The best time to do so will be when the economy is enjoying a temporary recovery. But a home is not a stock. Timing the market is more difficult and should not be your more primary concern.

First and foremost, make sure you are prepared to accept far less for your property than you think it may be worth. If you cannot get over this hurdle, reread this chapter and recognize the utter gravity of the boom and bust in housing. Then follow these steps:

Step 1. Choose a Realtor with a *recent* track record of selling many properties in the same general category as yours and a strong marketing savvy.

Step 2. Work with your agent to review comps—recent sales of comparable homes in your neighborhood. Make sure they are (a) truly recent, (b) actual sales, and (c) really comparable.

Step 3. Calculate an average on the comps and mark it down as much as 10 percent. If market conditions are deteriorating rapidly or you're in a particular hurry or both, mark it down by more.

Step 4. Work with your Realtor to estimate the final proceeds of the sale—the amount you're likely to receive after negotiations, commissions, and costs. If you've priced your property aggressively, the final sale price should *not* be significantly lower than your asking price.

Step 5. When you're ready to list the property, do not mark the price down incrementally. Some people think, "I'll try listing my home at a higher price first. If it doesn't sell, *then* I'll mark it down some more." But that approach is asking for failure because the best time to attract buyers is within a short time window after your initial launch.

Step 6. Consider offering a special commission bonus to Realtors. Typically, commissions are 6 percent, give or take a point in special situations. I highly recommend that you offer a two-point, extra commission bonus, bringing the total commission to 8 percent. Then tell your agent to make sure the extra commission is clearly stated in the MLS listing.

Step 7. Make sure your house is clean! If that means repainting, new carpets, and a lawn makeover, it will be worth every penny of cost and every minute of your time.

Step 8. Develop a carefully crafted, multichannel marketing plan. That can include (1) the single most important, outstanding feature that makes your property different from others; (2) a virtual tour online, with the listing on as many web sites as possible; and (3) creating a special launch e-mail to send to all Realtors in the area. Do not underestimate the importance of *all* of these efforts.

Step 9. When you get bids for your property, never say "no," regardless of how ridiculously low you may think they are. Your agent will have the opportunity to nurse the negotiations along and possibly warm the buyer up to a price that you may be able to live with. And it will give you a sense of what a buyer's typical objections may be to help you overcome the next buyer's objections.

(Continued)

Step 10. Don't do this initially, but if you have to, consider offering special incentives to the buyer. For example, you could offer (1) an allowance for closing costs; (2) a decorating allowance worth some small fraction of the sale price; or (3) if absolutely necessary, even a buy-down of the buyer's mortgage. In each case, your Realtor should seek to get a sense of what the buyer's objections are or what special extras the buyer is looking for. Then, customize your incentives to meet each buyer's individual needs and tastes.

For more detailed instructions and resources for selling your home in tough times visit www.MoneyandMarkets .com/realestate.

WANT TO KEEP YOUR HOUSE, COME HELL OR HIGH WATER? THEN HERE'S HOW TO CUT EXPENSES OR GET ASSISTANCE

You realize how deep and steep future home price declines could be, even after the declines that have already occurred. You know how shaky the stock market and the economy may become, and how that might affect your income. If, despite these dangers, you feel that your financial condition can easily withstand the downside, or you have decided to keep your home for other personal reasons, that's understandable. There are millions of Americans who do not want or need to sell their own home. But there are still some basic steps you can take to reduce your costs:

Step 1. Cut your property taxes. Determine if the residences in your neighborhood have been falling in value, and by how much. For a quick estimate go to http://realestate .yahoo.com/Homevalues and enter your address and zip code. If you see from the web site a significant price decline in your area (say, 10 percent or more from the peak), ask your Realtor to help you gather evidence of the decline and to file the needed forms with your county or town's property assessor's office or treasurer's office.

Step 2. Shop around for home owner's insurance. In tough times, it's not unusual for insurers to compete aggressively for your business. They want your business because they hope you'll buy other insurance products. And in areas where home owner's insurance is harder to get, you can take steps to cut your insurance costs by installing hurricane shutters, adding a burglar alarm system, getting a special roof inspection, and more.

Step 3. Consider a mitigation inspection. If you live in an area considered prone to natural disasters, the moderate fee may be money well spent.

Step 4. Refinance, if possible. If you're stuck in an ARM with rising payments, get help from a mortgage broker to compare your current mortgage with a fixed-rate loan. In tight credit markets, it's harder to qualify.

Step 5. If you have a high net worth, consider hedging vehicles available to help protect you against real estate price declines. The premise is that you own real estate you're unwilling or unable to sell. And, at the same time, you are concerned about deep price declines that could inflict damage to your net worth. In this example, hedging may be a viable choice. (See Chapter 11 for more on hedging.)

Step 6. If you're falling behind on your mortgage payments, contact the Federal Housing Administration (FHA). Starting in 2007, the FHA introduced the FHASecure program, designed to help home owners meet otherwise burdensome mortgage payments. Moreover, in 2008, the FHA expanded the program to also help refinance more loans. In a bust, recession, or depression, there's no assurance

(Continued)

the government will be able to continue to provide these kinds of programs, but as long as it does, you should not hesitate to take advantage of them.

Step 7. If you're near foreclosure, consider Project Lifeline. This government program will freeze the foreclosure process for 30 days, giving you the opportunity to renegotiate your mortgage or get refinancing. For more information, visit www.hopenow.com; or call 888-995-4673. Just bear in mind that, for the most part, this is not *free* money; the government does require a repayment plan.

Step 8. For information on new government programs, visit www.moneyandmarkets.com/homehelp.

CHAPTER 5

COMMON STOCKS: HOW TO AVOID BIG RISKS AND BOOST RETURNS

You've seen how many banks and insurance companies—supposedly the safest places for your money—have taken unprecedented risks that could put your entire financial future in jeopardy.

And in the last chapter, you've just seen how the dearest, largest, supposedly most reliable asset of millions of average Americans—their own home—was the object of speculation, deception, and a gut-wrenching bust.

So ask yourself: If this is what happened with an asset that should rarely be the realm of roller coaster thrill seekers, what about common stocks, which are *normally* subject to sharp ups and downs?

How much will the average stock be worth if the United States suffers a couple of lost decades like Japan did between 1990 and 2010? Or if we see a decline similar to the 1930s?

Conversely, suppose the Fed continues to print excessive amounts of paper money to drive asset prices higher? Will U.S. stocks truly benefit? Or will most of the money go overseas, driving *foreign* asset values higher instead?

If you have an investment portfolio or 401(k) in stocks and stock mutual funds, you don't have the luxury of sticking around for the answer. Yet, that's what most Wall Street experts are telling you to do. Even after the worst financial crisis since the Great Depression, the weakest economic recovery in a century, and massive money printing by the Federal Reserve in a desperate attempt to offset the crisis, most people who give advice about investing are still in denial.

Throughout the housing bust, Wall Street cheerleaders refused to admit that an obviously massive collapse in the nation's real estate industry would inevitably lead to an equally massive collapse in the nation's economy. They repeatedly swore on a stack of bibles that housing would "soon hit bottom," the crisis would be "contained," everything would be "just fine." Then they made equally bold promises about the wonders of government stimulus and the Fed money printing.

They continually tried to persuade nearly every investor to stay the course, keep their money in the stock market, or even buy more.

What they seemed to forget is that buy-and-hold approaches only work during long periods of growth and prosperity. Today, that approach is dead, and we must confront the reality that, if you always hold on despite the risks, or if you always wait until the final bottom, it could take a generation or more to recoup from stock market losses.

No one could possibly deny that the U.S. economy suffered a massive crisis. Anyone can see the evidence—the sharpest declines in the economy since the 1970s, the worst debt crisis in a lifetime, the largest financial failures and bailouts in history, followed by the highest-risk Fed actions of all time. Everyone can also agree on the likely causes—the economic blunders of Washington, the financial greed of Wall Street, the big debts and risky bets by the biggest players. And no one could dispute the consequences: at best, an anemic recovery with chronic high unemployment and burdensome huge debts; at worst, another collapse.

Yet, despite this widespread agreement, nearly everyone you count on for advice and leadership *still* tries to persuade you to keep your money in the stock market. Financial experts on *NBC Nightly*

News tell millions of viewers that, as long as they've got plenty of years to live and recoup losses, they should continue investing most of their 401(k) or individual retirement account (IRA) in stocks. Financial gurus on *Oprah* advise millions more to continue socking away their retirement money in stocks whether the market goes up or down. In *Time* magazine, the *New York Times,* the *Wall Street Journal,* and virtually every newspaper in the country, similar advice is liberally dispensed.

Their unwavering message: Don't sell. Stick with it. Buy more.

It's not a symptom of conspiracy, and in most cases, it's not a sign of intellectual dishonesty. The majority of pundits sincerely believe in what they are advising you, and many follow the same strategy with their own money. But that does not make it good advice. Consider Dad's tale of the average investor's woes in the Great Depression, and you'll understand what I mean:

> I was a young broker in 1930, and the advice my senior colleagues gave out used to make me cry inside. "Just hang on to your stocks for the long term and ride out the storm," they said. The results were devastating for their clients.
>
> If you bought the average stock in 1929 and held on until 1932, you wound up with about 10 cents on the dollar. And that's if you bought the *good* stocks—the ones that survived. If you bought the bad stocks—in bankrupt companies—you'd be left with nothing, a big fat zero.
>
> Then, even if all of your companies survived, it wasn't until 1954—25 years later—that you could finally recoup your original investment, provided you could stick it out that long. Unfortunately, most people couldn't. They lost their jobs. They risked losing their house and home. So they were forced to cash in their stocks with huge losses. The idea of "holding on for the long term" was a joke, an insult, or both. They didn't have that choice. Later, when the market eventually recovered, they never got the chance to recoup their losses.

Even if you don't believe that the late 2000s are comparable to the early 1930s, there is ample reason to exit the stock market. Just consider these facts from *recent* times and connect the dots:

■ Investors who bought Japan's blue chip stocks in late 1989 lost over three-fourths of their money in Japan's "lost decade" of the 1990s. Commercial real estate collapsed. And like in the United States of more recent times, the Japanese government lowered interest rates to near zero and spent enormous sums to stimulate its economy. But despite massive government intervention, investors suffered through a series of bear markets that continued for nearly two decades. And despite many sharp rallies, Japan's Nikkei average still wound up with a devastating 82 percent decline.

Worse, by 2010, after 20 years of excessive public spending, Japan's government has accumulated a mountain of debt, representing close to 200 percent of its Gross Domestic Product, or over *double* the estimated public debt burdens of the United States (98 percent of GDP) and the United Kingdom (96 percent). And still, investors in Japan's blue chip stocks were years–possibly decades–away from recovering their original investment made in 1990.

■ The financial crisis and economic malaise that has struck the United States is similar to, or possibly worse than, what Japan experienced during its two lost decades: By any measure, the financial collapses or near collapses in the United States– Fannie Mae, Freddie Mac, American International Group, Lehman Brothers, Citigroup, Merrill Lynch, and others– were far bigger than the worst and largest financial collapses in Japan. And the bust in U.S. residential real estate was far broader than Japan's bust in commercial real estate. Thus, it's reasonable to assume that the experience of investors could be as bad as Japan's experience of the 1990s and 2000s.

Yes, the U.S. Federal Reserve has run the money printing presses to try to boost inflation and avert these scenarios. But their policies have not been substantially different from Japan's.

Moreover, to the degree that the Fed actually achieves its goal and gives us more inflation, that success will, by definition, reduce the purchasing power of your money and the real value of common stocks.

What we do not yet know is the answer to this question: After it's all over and we can look back at these years from the vantage point of 2020, will we see a crisis that was similar to Japan's lost decade, worse, or not as bad? And the bigger question: Will we see a decline that's shorter than that of the 1930s, longer, or similar in duration?

If you're an armchair historian and your sole goal is to record the consequences or opine on the causes, you can afford to wait for the answer. But if you're trying to provide security for your family, you don't have that luxury. You cannot predict how deep or long-lasting this crisis will be, and neither can I. You have to prepare for the worst. Then, if it's not as bad, all the better.

I repeat: No one knows with certainty how long a stock market rally can endure, how far stocks can fall, how long they will stay down, or how many years it will be before they enjoy a true recovery. No one knows when a new financial crisis will strike or how many banks, insurance companies, brokerage firms, and manufacturing corporations will ultimately go bankrupt. No one can say for sure if the government bailouts and the Fed's money printing will ultimately make things better, just keep things from getting worse, or cause even more serious troubles.

We do know, however, that governments have frequently been unable to prevent booms, busts, recessions, depressions, currency collapses, or run-away inflation; and these crises invariably damage the financial future of millions of citizens.

Bottom line: We know that, in turbulent times like these, regardless of what form they take, *the risk of buying and holding common stocks can greatly exceed the reward!*

So, should you simply cross the stock market off your list of investment opportunities? Absolutely not! There are at least five ways to use global stock markets to build wealth.

Five Ways to Use Global Stock Markets to Build Wealth

We begin with the premise that the traditional strategy of buying and holding U.S. stocks is asking for trouble. Instead, consider one or more of these approaches:

First, minimize your risk and maximize your potential return by using independent ratings. It's with this goal in mind that, a decade ago, we expanded Weiss Ratings to cover not only banks and insurance companies but also every listed common stock, mutual fund, and exchange-traded fund (ETF) in the United States. And that's why we continue to distribute those ratings today. (To get up to five free ratings on your stocks, mutual funds, or ETFs, go to www .weisswatchdog.com.) Key factors to consider:

- In 2005, the *Wall Street Journal* reported that the Weiss stock ratings outperformed those issued by all brokers and independent research firms they covered, including JPMorgan Chase, Merrill Lynch, Goldman Sachs, Piper Jaffray, Credit Suisse First Boston, Smith Barney, S&P Equity Research, Morgan Stanley, and 14 others. And the same ratings, now provided by TheStreet.com and distributed by Weiss Ratings, have continued to earn awards for their accuracy.

- The reason: Most other stock ratings focus primarily on *performance* with, at best, a nod to *risk*. These, in contrast, are completely balanced between those two critical considerations. They measure risk by studying the stock's volatility and valuation, plus the risk the company itself may be taking in its operations and its balance sheet. We believe it is just as important to *protect* your money as it is to grow your money, and we insist that each and every rating we produce or distribute respects this fundamental principle. (Important clarification: These are *stock* ratings, designed to help you decide whether to buy, sell, or hold the stocks. They are entirely separate from the Financial Strength ratings that we issue on the nation's banks and insurance companies discussed in earlier chapters.)

- The key point to remember: *Ratings change*–the thousands of stocks covered are frequently upgraded or downgraded. So to use the ratings properly, you must *monitor them regularly*. Go to Weiss Ratings' www.Weiss Watchdog.com, sign up for the free service, and enter your short list of stocks, mutual funds, or ETFs you would like to monitor. You will instantly get their current rating and, more importantly, whenever the rating changes, you will get an e-mail alert with specific instructions on what to do.

Second, do not restrict your stock investing to the United States. Yes, in years past, it was difficult to venture overseas. But today, there are hundreds of ETFs that invest in foreign markets for you.

There are individual ETFs for each and every major foreign stock market–Brazil, Chile, Mexico, Singapore, China, Indonesia, Japan, and many more. There are ETFs that let you invest in broad regions–Asia, Western Europe, Latin America. And there are ETFs that give you a stake in specific global sectors.

Simply going global does not necessarily reduce your risk. But it does open up the opportunity to invest in countries that have not suffered a housing bust, do not have burdensome debts, and have better prospects for sustainable growth.

Third, focus on companies–whether domestic or foreign–that have a long track record of generating steady income, the subject of Chapter 16.

Fourth, there are specialized exchange-traded funds, called inverse ETFs, that are designed to go up when the market goes down. Use them to help protect your portfolio from broad stock market declines (Chapter 11).

Fifth, if you have speculative funds you can afford to risk, consider using those same inverse ETFs as a vehicle for building wealth in a market decline. As I explain in Chapter 12, the great up-and-down volatility of stocks in times of crisis actually provide some of the greatest profit opportunities.

But no matter when and where you invest, never ignore the risks! Certainly, you are well aware of the catastrophic events that have already happened. You must realize that similar disasters *can* happen again. And if they arrive unexpectedly, as they typically do, it should be clear that nearly all of us–including you–will be affected in some way.

You also must know by now that the same old assurances from Washington and Wall Street–that "all is fine"; that they will soon "lick the problem"; that the latest, biggest bailout is "finally working"–have been proven wrong over and over again. You must be able to conclude, without my help or anyone else's, that, if ever there was a time when stock market investing is risky, this is it.

If you accept that risk and can learn how to control it, then you can consider the alternative approaches to investing cited in the coming chapters.

But if your goal is to save money for the future purchase of a home, to give your children and grandchildren educational opportunities, or to have enough money to cover your long-term health care, and you're loaded with stocks or stock market mutual funds, then use major stock market rallies to greatly reduce your exposure.

Naturally, precisely when and how much you should sell will depend on actual market conditions. But as a rule of thumb:

- The best time to sell is when the stock market is enjoying a big, government-inspired rally.
- If the stock market is falling and already down sharply, tell your broker to sell only *half.* Then sell the balance on a major rally.
- If the market is in a panicked frenzy, overrun by an uncontrollable crowd of sellers and virtually devoid of all buyers, wait. *Don't* sell immediately. As soon as the panic subsides, *then* sell half. And as soon as there's a major rally, *then* sell the balance.

Does the Stock Market Fall in a Straight Line?

No. Sometimes it may look that way, but history shows that, no matter how gloomy the news may be, the stock market can often stage vigorous, medium-term rallies.

In the three years following the crash of 1929, for example, precisely when most people feared the market's fall could only accelerate, the Dow enjoyed *seven* major intermediate rallies before it touched bottom in 1932. After the terrorist attacks of 9/11, when the entire world was still trembling, the market had a similar surge. And starting in March of 2009, when it seemed as though the financial system was collapsing, the Dow began a vigorous rally which lasted for many months. Even in the worst of times, it is almost inevitable that you will see intermediate rallies.

These rallies are routinely portrayed as the "end of the decline." But they can often be traps. Typically, the government steps in aggressively with bailouts, a stimulus, or Fed money printing. The news is greeted with great fanfare and Wall Street hype. Bargain hunters jump back into the market. And stock prices rise.

These rallies can be explosive. They can take stocks 50 percent higher, sometimes more. And they can give the illusion of a "bull market."

Just remember—if the fundamental causes of the crisis have not been resolved, the dangers of investing in stocks do not disappear. As long as the economy's still in trouble, don't be fooled. The rallies could be false starts based on false hopes. Seriously consider using them as opportunities to reduce your exposure and risk.

Warning: Don't Let Your Broker Talk You Out of Doing What's Right for You

Remember what brokers, financial planners, and even government officials told you: to ignore the declines and keep adding more shares to your stock portfolio or more stock mutual funds to your 401(k). They told you "investing in stocks for the long term is prudent," which, broken down to its simplest elements, was conveying the underlying message that "stocks are safe."

Wherever—or whenever—you are reading this book, be it in a falling market or a rising market, nothing could be further from the truth. Most stocks are not safety investments—never were, never will be. They are risk investments. They can deliver losses as well as profits, shrink your wealth as well as grow it.

You probably know that by now. All I'm asking is that you never forget it. Never let anyone disabuse you of the fact that most stocks and stock mutual funds involve risk. If the risk-reward for specific stocks is favorable, there is a time and place to invest in them. But if safety and saving is all that you want, you need to move your money *away* from risk, and that means mostly *out* of stocks.

Unfortunately, however, no matter how prudent and timely it may be to sell, most brokers are in business to make you buy. They have an agenda. They want to keep you as a customer; and they know that, once customers sell their stocks, they often close their brokerage accounts.

With this in mind, many brokers have been trained with up to eight sales pitches designed to keep you in the market, come hell or high water. Here's what they're likely to say—and why you should make up your own mind.

HOW TO GET YOUR 401(K) OUT OF DANGER

Many people confuse two separate questions:

1. The first and more urgent question is: What *investments* do you own?
2. The second question is: What kind of *account* are you using to buy those investments?

Let's begin with the investments: With the exception of certain kinds of accounts guaranteed by insurers or others, if your investments are going *down* in value, you risk losing money regardless of what kind of account you have them in.

And, depending on what investment choices investors have made, they have seen their retirement fall by 50 percent or more in bear markets. Therefore, I disagree with those who recommend you hold the stock mutual funds in your 401(k) and just keep buying more on the way down. Instead, if safety is your primary goal, follow these steps:

Step 1. Get from your employer or 401(k) manager the list of options available in your 401(k).

Step 2. Pick out the safest one, as follows:

First choice: Treasury-only money market fund, as described in Chapter 10. (Unfortunately, these are rarely offered in 401(k)s.)

Second choice: A government-only money market fund, if your 401(k) has one. If not . . .

Third choice: A standard money market fund.

Fourth choice: An income or bond fund that invests exclusively in U.S. government notes and bonds and nothing in corporate bonds.

Fifth choice: An income or bond fund that invests mostly in U.S. government notes and bonds and corporate bonds.

In sum, favor government paper over corporate or bank paper, and favor short term over long term.

Step 3. In bad times, shift most of your money to the safest fund. If you're concerned that the market has just plunged and you are selling at the wrong time, shift half immediately and the balance when the stock market enjoys a major rally.

This is not a solution for everyone. As described on pages 81–83, if you are willing to take risk, there are five other alternative approaches. But if safety is your primary goal, stocks should not be your primary vehicle.

Now, let's turn to the second question—what kind of account you are using.

Step 4. If you have a 401(k) or other retirement account, there is no reason to close the account. The 401(k) account itself is not where the risk is coming from. It's coming strictly from the kind of investments you may have chosen to put in that account. So, unless you feel you may be short of cash, *continue adding to your 401(k) normally.* Just make sure all new funds are invested in the safer choices. In this way, you can continue to take advantage of your company's matching program and your money can continue to grow without the drag of taxes.

Follow the same general approach with IRAs, 529 college savings plans, and other tax-protected plans. These offer the additional advantage of allowing you to buy a wider range of investments, including ETFs and short-term Treasuries or a Treasury-only money market fund.

Trouble is, no matter how prudent and timely it may be to sell, most brokers are in business to make you buy. They have an agenda. They want to keep you as a customer; and they know that, once customers sell their stocks, they often close their brokerage accounts.

With this in mind, many brokers have been trained with up to nine sales pitches designed to keep you in the market, come hell or high water. Here's what they're likely to say . . . and why you should make up your own mind despite even the best of pitches.

Broker Pitch 1: "Buy More"

"What? You want to sell?" exclaims your broker. "But your stock is now trading at a bargain price. So if you didn't already own 100 shares, you'd probably be thinking about *buying*–not selling. Instead of selling, why not double down and buy 100 *more* shares? Then you'll be much better off than you are today. It's called 'dollar cost averaging.' The more the stock falls and the more you buy, the lower the average cost of the shares you own."

The truth: The more stocks you own, the greater your risk of loss. If you own 100 shares, you lose $100 for every $1 decline in their price. If you own 200 shares, you lose $200 for each $1 decline. Double your stake, double your risk of loss. It's that simple.

Broker Pitch 2: "Always Invest for the Long Term"

"The market will inevitably recover sooner or later, right? And history proves that recoveries are always bigger and longer lasting than any intermediate decline. So all you have to do is *always invest for the long term.* Then you'll do well no matter what twists and turns the market may suffer in the near term."

The reality: As we saw earlier, market declines can last for many years. And it could take many years *more* for stock averages to recover to peak levels. During all those intervening years, your money is, at best, dead in the water. Worse, if the companies you own go out of business, your stock will be worthless and will *never* recover. Or, if you need the money because of other financial impacts of a bad economy, you may be forced to sell your shares at lower prices and you won't be able to recoup your losses even in the best of market recoveries.

Broker Pitch 3: "Don't Sell Now! You Can't Afford to Take the Loss"

"Your losses are just on paper right now," goes the argument. "So if you sell, all you'll be doing is locking in your losses. You can't afford to do that."

What they don't tell you: There is no fundamental difference between a paper loss and a realized loss. In fact, the Securities and Exchange Commission (SEC) requires brokers themselves to value the securities they hold in their own portfolio at the current market price—to recognize the losses as *real* whether they've sold the securities or not. A loss is a loss. Period.

Broker Pitch 4: "Don't Sell Now! You Can't Afford to Take the Profit"

"If you take a profit now," they say, "all you'll be doing is writing a fat check to Uncle Sam. You can't afford to do that."

The reality: Although it's not shown on your brokerage statement, the true value of your portfolio is *net* of taxes. So whether you or your heirs pay those taxes now or in the future is mostly a difference of timing. Besides, which would you prefer—paying some taxes on profits or paying no taxes on losses?

Broker Pitch 5: "Don't Be a Fool"

"Stocks look very cheap now and we're very close to rock bottom," goes the script. "We may even be right *at* the bottom. If you sell now, then, three months from today, you'll be kicking yourself. Don't be a fool."

The truth: Brokers don't have the faintest idea where the bottom is. Nor does anyone at their firm. And they know darn well that stocks do not hit bottom just because they *look* cheap. Worse, for their own accounts, brokers and their affiliates may be selling precisely the same shares they're telling you to buy.

Broker Pitch 6: "You're the Only One"

"Look around you. Do you see other people selling? No! They're buying! And that's why the market is rallying right now. So what are you so worried about? If there were something to be afraid of, all these smart investors would be selling too, wouldn't they? But they're not. *You're the only one.*"

The truth: The crowd is rarely right, and often the best time to sell is when most others are seeking to buy. You can get a better price for your shares. And you can do so in an orderly fashion.

Broker Pitch 7: "Don't Be Like Them"

"Look around you," they say again. "All the people selling right now are just running like scared chickens. That's why the market is going down. Don't be like them."

The truth: He doesn't know who's selling or why. But if the economy is sinking and corporate profits are fading, maybe investing like a chicken isn't such a bad idea. As the Wall Street jingle goes, "Bulls make money, bears make money, pigs get slaughtered." To that, I add: Chickens cross the road and come back another day.

Broker Pitch 8: "Be Responsible!"

"Do you realize what would happen if *everyone* does what you're thinking of doing—if everyone just takes their money and runs for the hills? That's when the market would *really* nosedive. But if you and other investors like you would just have a bit more faith in our economy—in our country—then the market will recover and everyone will come out ahead. Be responsible!"

The truth: Losing your nest egg in the stock market and jeopardizing your family's entire future is not exactly responsible. Nor does it make sense to lock up precious capital in sinking enterprises. Better to safeguard your funds and reinvest them in better opportunities at a better time. That's not only good for you, it's good for the future of the country as well.

Bottom line: Follow your own instincts. Don't let anyone in the financial industry entrap you. It's your safety and well-being that's at stake—not theirs.

CHAPTER 6

HOW SAFE IS YOUR BANK?

After reducing your exposure to real estate, selling risky stocks, cashing out unneeded insurance policies, getting rid of low quality bonds, and selling any other assets that may be vulnerable, I hope you have built up a nice little bundle of cash.

If not, there *is* another way to build wealth: *Don't spend it!* Cut your expenditures as much as possible. Follow the instructions on pages 92–93 to save like never before!

Where should you put the money? Your first instinct might be to deposit it in your bank. But recent bank failures prove that *not all banks are equally strong*. Some are strong and merit your trust. Some are at risk and should be avoided.

You ask: "Why worry? Doesn't the FDIC insurance cover me?"

The answer: There are other risks even if a bank is bailed out or taken over by the FDIC and sold to another institution:

- You could miss out on interest income you were promised.
- You could lose access to lines of credit.
- And you could suffer other inconveniences, including some delays in regaining access to your funds or disruptions in your business.

How to Save in Tough Times

In Chapter 1, you saw how families overloaded with debts face the worst of all worlds in a bust, recession, or depression. The flip side is that families free of debts and with solid cash savings face the best of all worlds: They can be among the first to take advantage of major opportunities to boost their income significantly, grow their wealth, and reap the following benefits for generations to come:

■ In a bust or deflation, the cost of nearly everything could go down. So your savings will buy a lot more.

■ At the right time, you will be able to buy great investment bargains. The financial markets will feel like a major department store with storewide markdowns of 50, 75, or even 90 percent.

■ Right now, interest rates are low. But even low interest returns are better than high interest expenses. Moreover, if you wait for a time when yields spike higher, you could lock in a relatively high rate for as long as 30 years.

■ Even if the crisis ends sooner than expected, you will sleep nights in the knowledge that you have a cushion to fall back on in any crisis.

To reap these benefits, follow these steps:

Step 1. Determine how much you can comfortably save each month. Many people aim too high, fail, and then give up. Better to aim low and then stick with it religiously.

Step 2. Resolve to never spend a dime until after your monthly savings have been set aside. There is absolutely no expenditure (except emergencies and basic necessities, of course) that is more important than savings. This is true in good times; in a depression, it's even more so.

Step 3. Start immediately. If you do not have a savings plan in place, the sooner you begin one, the better. Even assuming just 2 percent interest, Saver A, who puts away $10,000 per year beginning at age 25, will have $604,020 at age 65. Saver B, who puts away $10,000 per year beginning at age 35, will have $405,680 at age 65. If you can lock in higher yields as outlined in Chapters 15 and 16, the power of saving earlier will be greatly magnified.

Step 4. Don't confuse savings with investments. Be sure to maintain a clear separation between the two:

- Investments inevitably expose your capital to some risk; savings are designed to protect your capital.

- Investments can be in stocks, stock mutual funds, or real estate, which can go up or down. Savings should be limited to vehicles that rarely, if ever, go down in value. They prioritize the return *of* your money rather than the return *on* your money.

- With investments, it often makes sense to time the market. With savings, it does not, although key strategic changes may be needed to adapt to a major, cyclical, or historical change in the economy, such as a depression.

This is why we recommend you seriously consider avoiding banks with a Weiss Rating of D+ or lower, while seeking to do most of their business with banks meriting a rating of B+ or higher.

Now, on to the next big issue: What are the *future* risks you might face? Will government guarantees protect you in any scenario? What might happen if the world's largest banks fail?

These questions might seem extreme in normal times. But in the depth of the 2008 debt crisis, when many of the world's largest financial institutions came close to the brink, they were precisely the questions being asked by millions of citizens, including many in the highest echelons of government.

The answer: No one can predict the ultimate outcome of a global banking crisis. Therefore, it follows that *no one can guarantee you won't lose money in some way.* It is *possible* that you will lose some portion of your principal value *even if* it is covered by federal deposit insurance.

Finding it hard to believe? If so, you're not the only one. Nor is this the first time bank safety warnings issued by my family have been questioned, as illustrated in this passage from one of Dad's old manuscripts:

In 1930, while I was analyzing factors that might drive the stock market lower, I studied reports issued by the Federal Reserve Bank of New York on bank loans to brokers. In the process, I could not help but notice that too many banks were overly exposed to the stock market overall.

Sure enough, in the early 1930s, some banks began to fail. But still, most people believed in them. It was assumed that, if your money was in a bank, especially a large, well-known bank, it was safe, no matter what. So I had a hard time convincing people to get out of the banks, even close friends.

Mrs. Wallman, my best friend's mother, was particularly hard to persuade. After the market crashed, she asked me what she should do with her money. She had it in the New York Bank of the United States. It was a huge bank, but according to my analysis, it was very weak. I told her to take her money out and exchange it for $20 gold coins.

After much effort, I persuaded her. She went to the bank to withdraw her money. But the teller called over the vice-president, who then proceeded to talk her out of it: "Look," he said, pointing to the others in the bank lobby. "Do you see any of these people taking their money out? You're the only one!"

She put every dime back in.

Later, the New York Bank of the United States went bust, thousands of others followed, and Mrs. Wallman's life savings were frozen for years with no interest. But that was just the beginning. In 1930 alone, 744 U.S. banks failed. By 1932, the total number of bank failures was about 5,000, with more than $100 billion in deposits lost. By the end of the decade, the crisis had claimed 9,000 banks in all.

Fortunately, I was able to get a handful of my other friends out. But they were the only ones. Many others whom I could not convince got caught in failed banks.

Today, seven decades later, my own efforts to persuade people about banking risks are running into similar resistance. I'm not surprised. Only folks 90 or older remember the banking nightmares of the Great Depression. And even they trust the safety of their bank, thanks to insurance provided by the U.S. government agency, the Federal Deposit Insurance Corporation (FDIC). But most observers, including the banking authorities themselves, seem to be missing two pivotal issues:

1. Although government guarantees and depositor insurance can cover a large number of small bank failures, it is uncertain whether they would be able to cover a small number of large bank failures.
2. Despite a government's apparent authority to provide unlimited back-up funding to banks, in practice, it cannot finance thousands of banks without massive, unacceptable consequences.

In August 2008, to make this case more convincingly, we undertook a broad survey of virtually every banking institution in the United States. We produced the Weiss "X" List of institutions vulnerable to failure or likely to require a federal bailout. And, as a pro bono public service, we created a one-hour video, also named *The "X" List,* which was viewed by more than 100,000 consumers.[1]

Most prominent on our "X" List of large banks at risk: Citigroup.

Wall Street types were flabbergasted. Their most common reaction was either utter disbelief or sheer anger. "Impossible!" they exclaimed. "Take Citi off that damn list!" they bellowed.

Meanwhile, I told my nephew, who has most of his savings in Citi. He didn't believe me. I showed the list to another analyst. He laughed at me. I helped a prominent reporter file a balanced, factual story on Citi based largely on our material. Her editor nixed it.

Yes, this was America's largest banking conglomerate with more than $2 trillion in total assets. Yes, this bank had a global workforce of 350,000 with 1,400 offices in 100 countries. But "the numbers are the numbers," we said simply.

Later, when Citigroup came close to the brink of bankruptcy, we were praised for our foresight. And later still, when Congress bailed out banks like Citigroup with its Troubled Asset Relief Program (TARP), that praise faded. Some said we were right because

Citigroup came so close the brink and investors lost fortunes; others said we were wrong because the government came to the rescue and Citigroup depositors didn't lose a dime.

But it's a moot point: Our ratings and analysis are not forecasts of the future. They are current evaluations of actual risk. Moreover, investors and savers have a choice: They can invest or do business with low-risk companies, or they can take their chances with high-risk companies. Our view: Regardless of what the future may bring, risk avoidance is always a worthy goal.

Plus, there are broader risks that you must be aware of. . . .

Dangerous Derivatives

You've probably heard about derivatives lately, and you're likely to hear a lot more about them in the future. So let me explain exactly what they are and why they can be so dangerous.

Derivatives are side bets made mostly with borrowed money. They are bets on interest rates, bets on foreign currencies, bets on stocks, bets on corporate failures, even bets on bets. The bets are placed by banks with one another, banks with brokerage firms, brokers with hedge funds, hedge funds with banks, and more.

They are often high risk. And they can be huge. As I told you in Chapter 1, according to the Office of the Comptroller of the Currency (OCC), on June 30, 2010, U.S. commercial banks held $223.4 trillion in notional value (face value) derivatives.[2]

In addition, according to the Bank for International Settlements (BIS), which produces a tally every six months for the entire world, the global pile-up of derivatives at year-end 2009, including institutions in the United States, Europe, and Asia, was almost three times larger—$614.7 trillion.

That was 10 times the gross domestic product of the entire planet, more than 40 times the total amount of mortgages outstanding in the United States, and nearly 60 times greater than the already-huge U.S. national debt.

Defenders of derivatives claimed that these giant numbers overstated the risk. And indeed, most players hedge their bets. The problem: The risk does not stem strictly from *what* they are betting on. It also stems from the question of *whom* they're betting with.

To better understand how this works, consider a gambler who goes to Las Vegas. He wants to try his luck on the roulette wheel, but he also wants to play it safe. So, instead of betting on a few random numbers, he places some bets on red, some on black, or some on even and some on odd. He rarely wins more than a fraction of what he's betting, but he rarely loses more than a fraction either. That's similar to what big banks have done with derivatives, except for three key differences:

1. They don't bet against the house. In fact, there *is* no house to bet against. Instead, they bet against the equivalent of other players around the table.
2. Although they do balance their bets, they do not necessarily do so with the same player. So back to the roulette metaphor, if a major bank bets on red against one player, it may bet on black against another player. Overall, its bets may be balanced and hedged. But with each individual player, they're not balanced at all.
3. The amounts are huge—thousands of times larger than all the casinos of the world put together.

Plus there's one similarity with the roulette wheel that implies the greatest risk of all. What if the ball falls on green—the zero or double zero? Or, in the parlance of financial risk analysis, what if financial institutions are confronted with a "Black Swan" event—one that strikes from out of the blue, that no one could have possibly anticipated?

In sum, here are the urgent questions that, despite much debate, remain unanswered:

- What happens if there is an unexpected collapse?
- What happens if that collapse is so severe it drives some of the key players into bankruptcy?
- Most important, what happens if these bankrupt players can't pay up on their gambling debts?

These are the kinds of questions we ask when we analyze banks, insurance companies, or any institution. And they are the questions you should be aware of as well. The authorities often say that these questions are merely hypothetical and should never be considered seriously. Yet each of the supposedly hypothetical events I cited in the preceding three questions actually took place in 2007, 2008, and 2009.

First, we witnessed the unexpected collapse of the biggest credit market in the world's largest economy—the U.S. mortgage market.

Second, we witnessed the bankruptcy or near-bankruptcy of five key players in the derivatives market—Bear Stearns, Lehman Brothers, Merrill Lynch, Wachovia Bank, and Citigroup.

Third, we also got the first answers to the last question in the form of a single statement that hit the international wire services on October 11, 2008:

> Intensifying solvency concerns about a number of the largest U.S.-based and European financial institutions have pushed the global financial system to the brink of systemic meltdown.

This statement was not the random rant of a gloom-and-doomer on the fringe of society. Nor was it excerpted from a twentieth-century history book about the Great Depression. It was the serious, objective assessment announced at a Washington, D.C., press conference by the managing director of the International Monetary Fund (IMF).

He was the highest-ranking world authority on this matter. He saw the dangers. And he was *not* joking. But neither he nor anyone else seemed ready to *answer* the most burning, urgent questions it raised for millions of savers:

What the Heck Is a *Systemic Meltdown* Anyhow? And Why Is It Possible?

Here are the answers in a nutshell:

Definition: A systemic meltdown is a chain reaction of failures, forcing a temporary global shutdown of virtually every bank, insurance company, brokerage firm, and financial market in the world. Essentially, the planet's entire economy comes to a screeching halt, hopefully for just a short period of time.

Likelihood: Unknown. However, the unmistakable implication of the IMF's statement is that, by October 2008, so many of the world's largest banks were so close to bankruptcy, the entire banking system was vulnerable to this kind of massive collapse. *The most immediate cause:* Derivatives.

Dad and I studied many of the derivatives from the time they were invented. Weiss Ratings has created one of the largest databases in the country on financial institutions that play the derivatives market. And I can tell you flatly: It is often little more than *a massively large, global gambling network without the structure or organization typically needed by modern society to maintain order or handle contingencies.*

Ironically, even the Mafia knows how to better handle gambling networks to avert systemic meltdowns.

In the numbers racket, for example, players place their bets through a bookie, who in turn is part of an intricate network of bookies. Most of the time, the system works. But if just one big player fails to pay bookie A, that bookie might be forced to renege on bookie B, who, in turn, stiffs bookie C, causing a chain reaction of payment failures.

The bookies go bankrupt. The losers lose. And even the winners get nothing. Worst of all, players counting on winnings from one side of their bets to cover losses in offsetting bets are also wiped out. The whole network crumbles—a systemic meltdown.

To avert this kind of a disaster, the Mafia henchmen know exactly what they have to do, and they do it swiftly: If a gambler fails to pay once, he could find himself with broken bones in a dark alley; twice, and he could wind up in cement boots at the bottom of the East River.

Established stock and commodity exchanges, like the New York Stock Exchange and the Chicago Board of Trade, also have strong enforcement mechanisms. Unlike the Mafia, of course, the trading is entirely legal. But, like the Mafia, they fully recognize the dangers of a meltdown and have strict procedures to counter them.

When you want to purchase 100 shares of Microsoft, for example, you never buy directly from the seller. You must always go through a brokerage firm, which, in turn, is a member in good standing of the exchange. The brokerage firm must keep close tabs on all of its customers, and the exchange keeps close track of all its member firms. So if you can't come up with the money to pay for your shares or put up the needed collateral for broker loans, the broker is required to promptly liquidate your securities, literally kicking you out of the game. And if the brokerage firm as a whole runs into financial trouble, it meets a similar fate with the exchange–very, very swiftly!

Here's the key: For the most part, the global derivatives market has no brokerage, no exchange, and no equivalent enforcement mechanism. In fact, among the $223.4 trillion in derivative bets held by U.S. banks, only $9.8 trillion, or 4.4 percent was regulated by an exchange as of mid-year 2010. The balance–$213.6 trillion, or more than 95.5 percent–were bets placed directly between buyer and seller (called *over the counter*). And among the $614.7 trillion in global derivatives I cited earlier that are tabulated by the BIS, 100 percent were over the counter. No exchanges. No overarching enforcement mechanism.

With regulatory reforms enacted in the wake of the 2008 debt crisis, there was a lot of talk about moving some of the derivatives to regulated exchanges or equivalent; and some initial steps were taken in that direction. But the proportion of regulated derivatives had actually gone *down* when compared to the period before the debt crisis: According to the U.S. Comptroller of the Currency (OCC), on June 30, 2007, 6.5 percent of derivatives held by U.S. banks were traded under regulated exchanges. But as I cited earlier, three years later, on June 30, 2010, only 4.4 percent were regulated. Regulatory reform was obviously not making much headway.

This is not the same kind of regulation that liberals and conservatives throw bricks at each other about. It's not about government interference in the internal structure or decision making of individual banks. Rather, the goal should be to set standards so that everyone can compete *more* freely.

Nor does the current system suffer merely from weak rules. It's far worse. It's the equivalent of an undisciplined conglomeration of players gambling on the streets without even a casino to maintain order. Moreover, the data compiled by the OCC and BIS indicate that the bets were so large and the gambling so far beyond the reach of regulators, all it would take was the bankruptcy of *one* of the second-tier derivatives players–such as Lehman Brothers–to throw the world's credit markets into paralysis.

That's why the world's top banking officials were so panicked when Lehman Brothers failed in the fall of 2008. And that's why the U.S. government rushed to bail out Citigroup two months later, regardless of cost. As the IMF managing director himself admitted, the threat was not stemming from just *one* bank in trouble; it was from *many.* And those banks weren't lesser players; they were among the *largest* in the world. Which U.S. banks placed the biggest bets? Based on mid-year 2010 data submitted by the banks to the FDIC, the OCC provided some answers (see Figure 6.1).

Figure 6.1   Large U.S. Banks Most Likely to Get Caught in a Financial Meltdown (exposure to credit risk of derivatives as a percentage of risk-based capital)

Despite regulatory reform, America's largest banks continued to take serious risks by placing side bets on interest rates, foreign currencies, stocks, and the failure of other major corporations. These side bets, called *derivatives,* not only exposed the bank to the risk of unexpected market moves, but also to the risk that their trading partners could default on their payments. At mid-year 2010, Bank of America's exposure to this form of risk represented 162 percent of its capital. In other words, for each dollar of capital, BofA had $1.62 in gross credit exposure related to derivatives. Citibank's exposure was similar—171 percent of capital. And the exposure of two other major banks was far larger— JPMorgan Chase was exposed to the tune of 257 percent of capital, and Goldman Sachs Bank, supposedly one of the most astute players, had exposure of 690 percent (not included in the above chart.) As a rule, Weiss Ratings believes that any risk exposure on a gross basis (before subtracting offsetting protections) greater than 50 percent is probably excessive.

Data Source: U.S. Comptroller of the Currency.

Citibank NA, the primary banking unit of Citigroup, held $46 trillion in derivative bets. However, only 3.3 percent of those bets were under the purview of any exchange. The balance—96.7 percent—were direct, one-on-one bets with Citibank's trading partners outside of any exchange.

Bank of America was a somewhat bigger player, holding $48.5 trillion in derivative bets, with 93.2 percent traded outside of any exchange.

JPMorgan Chase was, by far, the biggest of them all, towering over the U.S. derivatives market with nearly double Citibank's book of bets—$75.2 trillion worth, with 95.8 percent traded outside of any exchange.

And Goldman Sachs Bank was even less interested, it seemed, in exchange-regulated trading. It held $42.1 trillion in derivatives, of which 97.9 percent was traded outside of the exchanges.

This also meant that these top four derivatives players—JPMorgan, BofA, Citi, and Goldman—controlled nearly $212 trillion, or 91 percent of all derivatives held in the U.S. banking system. This is an oligopoly that ties the fate of the U.S. economy to these firms' stability far beyond anything ever witnessed in previous history.

Just four banks! Making bets of unknown nature and risk! Involving a notional dollar amount equivalent to 14 years of the total production of the entire U.S. economy! In contrast, Lehman Brothers, whose failure caused such a large earthquake in the global financial system, was actually smaller by comparison—with *only* $7.1 trillion in derivatives.

The potential havoc that might be caused by a Citigroup failure, with bets that involve *six times* more money than Lehman's—and the financial holocaust that might be caused by a JPMorgan Chase failure with over 10 times more than Lehman's—boggles the imagination! How bad could it actually be? No one knows, and therein lies one of the primary dangers. In the absence of oversight, the regulators simply do not collect the needed who-what-when information on these bets.

In an attempt to throw some light on this dark but explosive scene, the OCC uses a formula for estimating how much risk each major bank is exposed to in the one particular aspect I highlighted earlier—the risk that some of its trading partners might default and fail to pay up on their gambling debts. Keep in mind: We still don't know how much they are risking on the possibility of market moves against them. All the OCC is estimating is how much they're risking by making bets with potentially shaky betting partners, regardless of the outcome on each bet—win, lose, or draw.

At Citibank, the OCC calculated that the bank was exposed to the tune of 171 percent of its capital at mid-year 2010. In other words, for every $1 of capital in the kitty, Bank of America was risking $1.71 strictly on the promises made by its betting partners.

What is an appropriate risk level? No one knows. But I'd say that the gross exposure (before subtracting offsetting protections) beyond 50 percent of capital is excessive.

And remember: All this was *in addition* to the risk that the market might go the wrong way, and *on top of* the risk it was taking with its other investments and loans.

At Bank of America, the exposure was similar: $1.62 in exposure per dollar of capital. But if you think that's risky, consider JPMorgan Chase. Not only was it the largest player, but, among the four largest U.S. derivatives players, it also had the second largest default exposure: For every dollar of capital, the bank was risking $2.57 on the credit of its betting partners.

Now you can see why JPMorgan Chase was so anxious to step in and grab up outstanding trades left hanging after the fall of Bear Stearns and Lehman Brothers! It could not afford to let those trades turn to dust. If it did, it would probably be the first and biggest victim of a chain reaction of failures.

This is why super-investor Warren Buffett called derivatives "financial weapons of mass destruction." This is why the top leaders of the world's richest countries panicked after Lehman Brothers failed, dumping their time-honored, hands-off policy like a hot potato, jumping in to buy up shares in the world's largest banks, and transforming the world of banking literally overnight. And this is why the U.S. government bailed out Citigroup in November 2008.

Goldman Sachs was also taking similar risks. But it wasn't until this Wall Street giant transformed itself into a bank that the OCC reported on its derivatives exposure: At mid-year 2009, Goldman had $6.90 in exposure to the credit risk of derivatives for each dollar of capital—far more than any other U.S. bank.

Didn't They Bail Out All the Big Banks in Trouble? Why Can't They Continue Doing the Same Thing Forever?

True, the government has already arranged bailouts or buyouts for all the large banks that have failed, and, like Citigroup, *all* of these were on our August 2008 "X" List.

That included Wachovia Bank (with $666 billion in assets), which had made the fatal mistake of buying the nation's largest and most aggressive mortgage lenders at the worst possible time: Washington Mutual ($319 billion assets), the nation's largest savings and loan, loaded with one of the largest piles of bad mortgages in the world; plus National City Bank, one of several large regional banks, loaded with bad commercial mortgages.

However, there are multiple reasons why bank bailouts are ultimately futile, or worse, could backfire.

Reason 1: The Government Is Not Addressing the Underlying Causes

The two underlying causes of the large bank failures are obvious: (1) too much risk taking, and (2) too many bad assets.

But government bailouts fail to address either. Instead, it has precisely the opposite effect, encouraging banks to resume taking risks and trying to shuffle around the bad assets from one bank to another, or from banks to a government agency.

It goes without saying that, until and unless the government deals directly and forcefully with the cause of the problem, it will have to continue to deal with its consequences: more failures.

Reason 2: There Are Many More Banks at Risk

The FDIC maintains its own list of endangered banks. It does not reveal their names, but before the debt crisis struck, it did provide a count: 117 institutions with $78 billion in assets, as of March 31, 2008. The problem: *Most of the banks that failed in 2008 were never on the FDIC's list.* Evidently, the FDIC's criteria are not adequate; they don't flag some of the most important institutions on the verge of extinction.

In response, our team used what we believe to be a more accurate set of parameters. We scanned over 9,000 banks and thrifts for

WHAT HAPPENS TO YOUR MONEY IF YOUR BANK FAILS

Typically, the FDIC steps in, finds a merger partner or takes it over. This can be a quick process. But sometimes it may not be quick enough. I see three possible situations:

1. You are a shareholder in a bank that's failing.

   Likely impact: You will lose all or most of your money whether the government tries to bail out the bank or allows it to fail.

2. You are an insured depositor with savings or checking accounts that are under the FDIC insurance limit.

   Likely impact: In normal times, your savings should be secure and available soon after the failure. However, in a broader banking crisis, if the FDIC is overwhelmed with too many failures at the same time, you may have to wait longer. Worse, in the event of a national bank holiday, even if your bank has not failed, you may be denied access to most or all of your funds for an unknown period of time.

3. You have deposits with a bank that are over and beyond the FDIC insurance limits. Or you have bought bank bonds or bank debentures.

   Likely impact: In most bank failures, you will suffer losses; and with so-called too-big-to-fail banks, you could suffer severe losses as well. Even in the best of times, do not count on the government to cover uninsured bank deposits, debentures, or other bank obligations.

For more instructions plus the latest list of the weakest and strongest banks in America, visit www.moneyandmarkets.com/banks.

risks such as inadequate capital, sinking earnings, bad loans, and overreliance on unstable deposits. We discovered that, based on March 2008 data, rather than 117, there were actually 1,673 banking institutions at risk; and rather than just $78 billion in assets, these institutions had $3.2 trillion in assets, or 41 times the assets of the banks on the FDIC's list.

Reason 3: The Continuing Danger of Bank Runs

Bank runs—depositors rushing to pull their money out of a bank—could be the final trigger of a systemic meltdown. But most observers assume such runs are very unlikely or even impossible. "If deposits are insured," they ask, "why would anyone want to pull them out?"

The reason: Most bank runs are not caused by insured depositors. They're caused by the exodus of large, uninsured institutions that are usually the first to run for cover at the earliest hint of trouble. That's the main reason Washington Mutual, America's largest savings and loan, lost over $16 billion in deposits in its final eight days in 2008. That's also a major reason Wachovia Bank was forced to agree to a shotgun merger soon thereafter.

During the many financial failures of the 1980s and 1990s, the story was similar: We rarely saw a run on the bank by individuals. Rather, it was uninsured institutional investors—pension funds and others—that jumped ship long before most people even realized the ship was sinking. They're the ones who hammered the last nail in the coffin of big savings and loans, banks, and insurance companies that failed.

Reason 4: The Government Cannot Control a Panic by Shareholders

Although the government can do a lot to calm nervous bank depositors, it has no control over bank shareholders, who have shown they can swiftly drive a company's stock into the gutter. This is what happened in 2008: Falling bank stocks were critical factors in precipitating the withdrawals and the subsequent need for big bank bailouts in almost every case. When the stock of a big bank crashed, it sent the signal to depositors that trouble was brewing, and it ripped through the bank's capital, as measured by its total value on the stock market.

In the 1930s, few banks had to deal with this particular problem. Yes, they had to worry about a run by their depositors, but they were privately owned. So shareholders could typically be gathered in a small room and persuaded to hold tight. Even if they were still unhappy, the most they could do was fire management. They had no one to sell their shares to, except themselves.

Today, banking regulators may have tools to stop a bank panic that their 1930s predecessors did not have. But they have no mechanism for stopping a twenty-first-century panic—prompted by investors who run from the bank's shares, which *then* fans the fears of the bank's uninsured depositors, and vice versa.

Biggest Reason of All: America's Next Great Recession

Never forget: All the risks and weaknesses I have cited so far were present *before* the arrival of another bubble, bust, or economic recession plays itself out. This begs the urgent question: If many banks did not get their house in order despite the economic recovery of 2009–2010, what will happen if the United States suffers another great recession?

The unavoidable answer: A new, broader vicious cycle in which a banking crisis undermines the economy and the sinking economy aggravates the banking crisis.

Can a Banking Shutdown Really Happen in Modern Times?

It already has happened, although on a smaller scale.

In January 1991, Governor Bruce Sundlun of America's smallest state—Rhode Island—declared a banking emergency and shut down all 45 state-chartered savings banks and credit unions in his state. Hundreds of thousands of savers were locked out. Thousands marched on the streets of Rhode Island's capital in protest. And that was *after* repeated assurances from the governor that all the savings banks were "safe and sound." Shortly thereafter, we saw a similar situation occur in Maryland.

And, as you saw in Chapter 3, the insurance industry had a similar problem in the 1990s: In response to massive failures, state insurance commissioners imposed a blanket moratorium on policy cancellations and policy loans, affecting close to six million people.

All of these shutdowns occurred largely *despite* government oversight and *despite* the virtual absence of derivatives among the institutions affected at that time. Therefore, it stands to reason that, in the twenty-first century, with more than half a *quadrillion* dollars in unregulated derivatives, we could see similar—or broader—shutdowns.

How Would a Banking Shutdown Affect Me?

In the past, we've seen some shutdowns that eventually helped resolve the crisis, and we've seen others that only made it worse. But no matter how it's resolved, if the banks have made big blunders and suffered large losses, it's individual investors and savers who are typically asked to make the biggest sacrifices and pay the biggest price. No one else has the money.

What might happen in the wake of a twenty-first century meltdown? Based on other banking holidays and financial moratoriums in modern history, it's safe to conclude that it would cause severe hardship for countless savers around the world.

The first and most obvious hardship is that you could be denied immediate access to some or all of your money. What about government guarantees like FDIC insurance in the United States? In an ultimate crisis scenario, some proportion of those guarantees would have to be suspended so as to give banking regulators time to sort out the mess.

"Your bank is not truly bankrupt," banking officials declare. "It's merely illiquid."

"Your money is still safely guaranteed," they insist. "You just can't have it right now."

The second and more long-lasting hardship is the possibility that, by the time you do regain access to your money, you would suffer losses. In theory, there are two possible scenarios:

1. Scenario A: The government establishes a banking reform program that directly penalizes savers. You're given two choices, neither of which would make you happy:

   1. *Opt in* by leaving some or all of your funds on deposit at your bank for an extended period of time, earning below-market interest rates. Your bank is then allowed to use the extra interest to recoup its losses and build its capital over time—income that should have been yours.

      Problem: You take the chance that the government's program may not work on the first attempt and that it will be replaced by another, even tougher program in the future. No matter what, you suffer a continuing loss of income and restricted access to your cash.

   2. *Opt out* of the program and withdraw your funds immediately, accepting a loss that approximately corresponds to the actual losses in the bank's investment and loan portfolio. Insured depositors suffer less severely than uninsured depositors. And those in strong institutions come out whole or almost whole, while those in weaker banks suffer the larger losses.

      Problem: Unless your bank has been cautious and well capitalized, you suffer an immediate loss of principal. Plus, to discourage savers from opting out, the government may structure the program so that everyone demanding immediate reimbursement pays an *additional* penalty.

   This is essentially how the authorities handled the large insurance failures of the early 1990s!

2. Scenario B is associated with an inflationary environment: The government presumably saves the banks and makes taxpayers foot the bill. But with tax revenues lacking, it also must print more paper money and gut the value of your dollars. Officials *say* they're giving you "all your money back," but, in reality, the money they give you is worth a lot less. You lose a large portion of your purchasing power. It's a palliative that resolves nothing. It merely postpones a more substantive resolution. Even if it's used, it does not end the crisis.

In either scenario, how can the government break its promise to millions of depositors? If the losses are too large and the nation's available resources are too small, they have no other choice. They must either distribute the losses, or cheapen the currency, or both.

How Can I Avoid These Huge Risks?

First and foremost, if you must do business with a bank, make sure it's financially solid. To check the safety of your bank—or to find a safe bank near you—follow the steps provided here:

HOW TO CHECK AND MONITOR THE SAFETY OF YOUR BANK

Many large U.S. banks have taken excessive risks with your money in recent years. And although your account is insured by the FDIC up to $250,000, if your bank fails, you could miss out on interest that you were promised, lose access to lines of credit, and suffer the inconvenience of waiting in line for your funds. Therefore, we recommend you take these steps to make sure your bank is safe now and remains so in the future.

Step 1. First, become familiar with the meaning of the Weiss Financial Strength ratings:

A = excellent

B = good

C = fair

D = weak

E = very weak

+ = the upper third of each grade range

− = the lower third of each grade range

Step 2. Double check the rating of your bank or banks by using our free Weiss Watchdog service at www.weisswatchdog .com. Simply:

- Provide your name and e-mail address for alerts when the ratings change

- Enter the name of your institution

- Make sure it's the right one by verifying its head-quarters state

- Instantly get its rating

Step 3. With the rating in hand, follow these guidelines:

- If your bank is rated B– or higher, it implies your bank's relative safety is good or better and no further action is needed.

- If your bank is rated C–, C, or C+, it's a yellow flag, and this is the type of situation that can make the free Weiss Watchdog monitoring service especially important (see Step 4).

- If your bank is rated D+ or lower, it's a red flag. Seriously consider moving your money elsewhere, while weighing the cost of any interest penalties. For uninsured deposits, the interest penalty is a small price to pay for safety. For insured deposits, it will depend on how much you value your peace of mind.

- If your bank is rated E+ or lower, the likelihood of failure is high. So we recommend even prompter action to seek stronger institutions.

Step 4. Whenever the rating on your institution changes, the Weiss Watchdog will send you an e-mail alert. If it's an upgrade, naturally, no further action is needed. But if your

(Continued)

bank's rating is downgraded, it may indicate the need for further action on your part. A downgrade to a D+ or lower is a bad sign. A downgrade to an E+ or lower is worse. The e-mail will give you further instructions.

Step 5. If you're shopping for a bank, start with our list of the largest banks with a B+ rating or better, or consider the next step. If you want to check the rating of a bank near you, follow the preceding Steps 1 through 3.

Step 6. If you cannot find a safe bank near you, or you'd prefer the additional flexibility and convenience they offer, consider using one of the Treasury-only money funds cited in Chapter 10.

Whether we have a broader banking crisis or not, it always pays to do business with the healthiest institutions that will suffer the least disruption or losses.

Second, seriously consider moving a large portion of your savings out of banks entirely, switching them to the safest and most liquid place for your money in the modern world: short-term government securities, the subject of Chapter 10.

But first I have some equally urgent tasks we need to deal with—to straighten out the mess that many insurance companies are making with the financial future of millions of Americans, possibly including yours.

CHAPTER 7

HOW TO FIND SAFE INSURANCE COMPANIES

In the new millennium, while many of the nation's largest banks plunged headlong into the mortgage boom, got smashed in the housing bust, and are still knee deep in risky derivatives, most of the nation's largest insurers watched from the sidelines.

Have some insurance companies made imprudent decisions that could put your money at risk? Our data say "absolutely," and I'll name the ones we believe to be the prime suspects in a moment.

But when viewed alongside the wild escapades of the world's largest banks and brokerage firms, the adventures of most big insurance companies are tame by comparison.

This is good news. It means that there's at least *one* financial industry in the United States that has the potential to weather a major storm without mayhem and moratoriums. It also means that, when the economy is ready for a true recovery, there should be at least one major group of companies with the capital and cash available to buy up some cheap assets.

This alone, however, does not guarantee your insurer is safe. As you saw in Chapter 3, some major insurance companies have also committed their share of financial sins in the past—investing heavily in junk bonds and speculative real estate, skating on the thin ice of slim capital, making more promises than they could possibly fulfill, and ultimately going bankrupt. And unfortunately, if too many companies are complacent, that could happen again.

The outstanding recent example: American International Group, the largest insurance company failure of all time. In this instance, the failure wasn't just a threat to its customers or investors, it was a threat to the financial system of the entire world. And this time, the cavalry coming to the rescue was not exclusively insurance regulators—that would hardly have been enough. Also galloping to the scene were the Federal Reserve and the U.S. Treasury Department, wielding the full financial firepower of the entire U.S. government.

Plus, there are other examples of insurance companies that have taken risks beyond their means.

The Six Steps to Finding the Strongest Companies

To find safe insurance, you need to avoid the weakest companies and find the strongest. (See Tables 7.1 and 7.2). And I feel this is so important in today's turbulent times, I am dedicating most of this chapter to the specific steps I recommend . . .

Step 1. Fundamental principles. Take a minute with me right now to learn the two fundamental principles for evaluating the safety of an insurance company. They are actually based on two simple questions you should ask your insurer:

- Your first question: "What risks are you taking with my money?"
- Your second question: "How deep are your pockets?"
    In other words, "How much of your own net worth (capital) do you have available to cover me for any losses you might take with my money?"

Table 7.1 Weakest Large Life and Annuity Insurers (with assets of $100 million or more)

Company	Domicile State	Weiss Financial Strength Rating	Total Assets ($Mil)
Ability Ins. Co.	NE	D	196.7
Bankers Conseco Life Ins. Co.	NY	D	285.1
Conseco Life Ins. Co.	IN	D	4,354.0
Conseco Life Ins. Co. of Texas	TX	D	752.4
Jefferson National Life Ins. Co.	TX	D	1,576.5
North Carolina Mutual Life Ins. Co.	NC	D	150.7
North Coast Life Ins. Co.	WA	D	128.0
Security National Life Ins. Co.	UT	D	379.6
Wilton Reassurance Co.	MN	D	1,351.3
Wilton Reassurance Life Co. of New York	NY	D	1,169.7

A = Excellent; B = Good; C = Fair; D = Weak; E = Very Weak.
Weiss Ratings based on second quarter 2010 data.

In sum, how much *risk* and how much *capital?* The more risk the company takes, the more capital they should have to back it up. And in essence, these are the same kinds of questions we ask when we determine our Weiss Ratings of financial institutions.

When we first developed our ratings many years ago, we called it *risk-adjusted capital.* Later, the regulators developed a similar model, calling it *risk-based capital.*

The trouble is that getting the answers from financial institutions isn't easy, especially in the insurance industry. You'd have to drive to your state capital, go to the state insurance department, plead with the commissioner's staff, and then, if you're lucky, you'd get a chance to look over the official financial filings of your insurance company—up to 1,000 pages of schedules and tables that even a CPA would have trouble figuring out. Instead, move on to the next step . . .

Table 7.2   Strongest Large Life and Annuity Insurers (with assets of $10 billion or more)

Company	Domicile State	Weiss Financial Strength Rating	Total Assets ($Mil)
Allstate Life Ins. Co.	IL	B+	58,806.8
American Family Life Asr. Co. of Columbus	NE	B+	80,985.6
American United Life Ins. Co.	IN	B+	14,905.8
Fidelity Investments Life Ins. Co.	UT	A−	14,228.7
Guardian Life Ins. Co. of America	NY	A	32,034.7
John Hancock Life Ins. Co. of New York	NY	A−	16,285.6
Massachusetts Mutual Life Ins. Co.	MA	A	122,461.5
Midland National Life Ins. Co.	IA	B+	27,633.8
New York Life Ins. Co.	NY	A−	118,743.7
New York Life Ins. & Annuity Corp.	DE	A−	91,967.7
Northwestern Mutual Life Ins. Co.	WI	A−	172,521.0
Pacific Life Ins. Co.	NE	A−	93,015.3
Penn Mutual Life Ins. Co.	PA	A−	11,328.1
Principal Life Ins. Co.	IA	B+	115,501.8
Southern Farm Bureau Life Ins. Co.	MS	A	10,785.3
Standard Ins. Co.	OR	B+	14,448.9
State Farm Life Ins. Co.	IL	A+	48,981.7
Symetra Life Ins. Co.	WA	B+	21,933.6
Teachers Ins & Annuity Assn. of America	NY	A+	206,720.5
United of Omaha Life Ins. Co.	NE	B+	14,242.4
USA A Life Ins. Co.	TX	A	15,780.9

A = Excellent; B = Good; C = Fair; D = Weak; E = Very Weak.
Weiss Ratings based on second quarter 2010 data.

Step 2. The Weiss Rating. Get the company's Weiss Rating, which takes into account the risks in their investment portfolio and operations, the capital and reserves they maintain, their earnings, and hundreds of other factors. Simply log on to www.weisswatchdog .com, and enter the name of your insurer. Or you can go to your public library and ask for the Weiss Ratings *Guide to Life and Annuity Insurers.*

The Weiss rating scale for insurers is the same as the scale for banks:

A = excellent
B = good
C = fair
D = weak
E = very weak
F = failed

And, as with banks, our recommendation is that you seek to do business strictly with companies meriting a grade of B+ or better.

Fortunately, there are many to choose from. The largest among them, based on the most current data, are listed in Table 7.2. Moreover, depending on what *kind* of insurance you need, you can choose from an even larger number of providers. (More on this aspect in a moment.)

Step 3. Be ready for a rating change. Simply enter the name of your insurer at www.WeissWatchdog.com and, as soon as the rating changes, the Weiss Watchdog will send you an e-mail alert with the downgrade or upgrade, an explanation of what it means, and instructions on what to do about it.

Step 4. Already have a policy? Then the parameters are similar to those we discussed earlier regarding banks:

If your company has a Weiss Financial Safety Rating of B+ or higher, that's ideal. And if its rating is B or B−, it's also acceptable for policies that you already own.

If its rating is C+, C, or C−, it's a *yellow flag.* Don't panic. But watch it carefully. If it doesn't cost you anything to switch to a stronger company, do so now. If there's a heavy penalty, which will diminish over time, be sure to monitor it carefully.

If your company's Weiss Financial Strength Rating is a D+ or lower, it's a *red flag.* When the U.S. Government Accountability

Office (GAO) conducted its study of our rating scale, it said our D ratings represented a warning to consumers of financial vulnerability, and we agree.[1]

You still have to weigh the cost and inconvenience of switching (plus whether you can get an equivalent policy with another company), but all things considered, when the company is rated D+ or lower, we feel the scale is tipping in the direction of *getting out*. (Table 7.1 includes a complete list of the life and annuity insurers in this category.)

Again, the type of insurance you buy can also be a factor that reduces or increases your risk, a topic I'll get to in just a moment.

Step 5. Other ratings. If your agent tries to promote this or that company based on their ratings by A.M. Best, S&P, Moody's, or Fitch, remember the inherent conflicts of interest and bias built into those ratings that we cited in Chapter 3. But, as long as you do keep those issues in mind, it can *still* be useful to refer to their information.

How do you sort out the alphabet soup of ratings from different ratings agencies? Fortunately, the GAO has already done that work for you, organizing each agency's scales in a table for easy comparison. As you can see in Table 7.3, the GAO first aligned its scale with the Weiss Ratings scale of A through F. Then, it sought to determine the equivalent scales of the other rating agencies.

A few noteworthy points to be aware of:

You may think A.M. Best's top rating is A+. It was, but it's not anymore. Now it's A++. That is another telltale symptom of grade inflation.[2]

Companies that do not merit a top rating from Best often advertise their A+ rating from Standard and Poor's. As you can see, however, the S&P A+ rating is actually fifth from the top of the S&P scale, as it is for Fitch. That A+ may look good in insurance company ads, but it doesn't look nearly as good when you see it in the proper context.

The B rating from Weiss truly is a good rating. Even our C rating is still in the *secure* range. We don't recommend you buy insurance from C companies. But as I mentioned earlier, if you're *already* with a C company, it's not cause for panic.

Table 7.3   Confused about What Insurance Ratings *Really* Mean? Refer to This Scale from the Government Accountability Office (GAO)

Ratings	Bands	Weiss[a]	Best[b]	S&P[c]	Moody's	D&P/Fitch[d]
Secure	1	A+, A, A−	A++, A+	AAA	Aaa	AAA
	2	B+, B, B−	A, A−	AA+, AA AA−	Aa1, Aa2, Aa3	AA+, AA, AA−
	3	C+, C, C−	B++, B+	A+, A, A−, BBB+, BBB, BBB−	A1, A2, A3, Baa1, Baa2, Baa3	A+, A, A−, BBB+, BBB, BBB−
Vulnerable	4	D+, D, D−	B, B−, C++, C+, C, C−	BB+, BB, BB−, B+, B, B−	Ba1, Ba2, Ba3, B1, B2, B3	BB+, BB, BB−, B+, B, B−
	5	E+, E, E−, F	D, E, F	CCC, (CC, C), (D), R	Caa, Ca, C	CCC−, CCC, CCC−, DD

If you're confused by insurance company ratings, you're not alone. So was Congress and the U.S. Government Accountability Office (GAO)! They spent many months comparing the Weiss ratings with those of other rating agencies—A. M. Best (Best), Standard & Poor's (S&P), Moody's Investor Service (Moody's), and Duff & Phelps (D&P), now Fitch. The GAO established a rating scale of five bands, which correspond to the five major ratings in the Weiss scale—A, B, C, D, E, and F (failed). Then, they placed the ratings of the other agencies into those bands.

If you are using the Weiss ratings, try your best to initiate new business strictly with companies rated B+ or better. If you are already doing business with an insurer, monitor regularly the safety of the companies with a C−, C, or C+ rating and seriously consider leaving the company if it is rated D+ or lower (taking into consideration any penalties plus the availability of alternative coverage).

If you are using the ratings of other ratings agencies, bear in mind that conflict of interest in the rating process compromises the objectivity of the ratings.

[a] Weiss and Best use additional symbols to indicate that they recognize an insurer's existence but do not provide a rating. These symbols are included in this table.

[b] Best added the A++, B++, and C++ ratings in 1992. In 1994, Best classified its ratings into *secure* and *vulnerable* categories, changed the definition of its B and B− ratings from *good* to *adequate*, and assigned these ratings to the vulnerable category.

[c] S & P discontinued CCC + and − signs, CC, C, and D ratings, and added the R rating in 1992.

[d] Duff & Phelps Credit Rating Co. merged with Fitch IBCA in 2000, and minor changes were made to the rating scale at that time. These changes were not reflected in the GAO's 1994 study, but *are* reflected in the above chart.

Source: U.S. General Accountability Office (GAO), with the updates described above.

Moody's, S&P, Best, and Fitch all have a full scale of low grades, but *they rarely issue those ratings.* At some of the agencies, there are actually *no* companies receiving the lower grades.

When you are evaluating insurance companies based on ratings from different rating agencies, be sure you have Table 7.3 by your side to give you a clearer picture of what the ratings mean.

Step 6. Your shopping list! Using these ratings, work with your agent to put together a final list of companies you're willing to do business with. But remember: *A high rating for the company doesn't guarantee a good deal on its insurance products.* That will depend on the benefits and costs each policy provides.

CHAPTER 8

HOW TO SHOP FOR THE BEST LIFE INSURANCE

When you buy a policy to protect yourself against a fire, it's called fire insurance. When it's for an accident, it's accident insurance. So when you want to protect your family from the consequences of your death, it should be called "death insurance," right?

Perhaps. But long ago, insurance salespeople discovered that no one wanted to talk about their death—let alone buy insurance for it. So taking a chapter out of George Orwell's *1984*, they called it "life insurance" instead.

It didn't seem to help much, though. Life insurance was still a very hard sell, and agents who pushed it too hard got a bad reputation for bringing up unpleasant subjects. "Want a row of seats all to yourself on your next flight to Chicago?" went a popular joke. "Then just tell your fellow passengers that you sell life insurance."

Prudential, the Rock-of-Gibraltar largest insurance company in the world, came up with another very "creative" solution. They figured out a way to disguise the life insurance as an annuity, developed a big sales force trained to obfuscate the real nature of the product, and sold it to millions of investors from 1982 through

1995. (Nearly all annuity policies sold by insurance companies do have a life insurance component. But that's a far cry from being an actual life insurance policy.)

It took many years of litigation before the regulators caught up with them. After much heated debate and negotiation, the company belatedly agreed to pay $2.7 billion in restitution to more than one million maligned customers, many times more than the largest previous settlement in insurance history. The violation? Prudential had sold insurance as a "retirement plan," failing to disclose the risks and using policy illustrations, which projected fabulous dividend accumulations as foregone conclusions. So did agents at New York Life and Allstate. Meanwhile, Equitable Life Assurance Society was fined $2 million for selling more than $100 million of improper life insurance policies.

The Prudential, Metropolitan, Allstate, and Equitable messes were finally cleaned up. However, serious problems remained—especially in the sale of deferred annuities to seniors.

Allianz Life Insurance Company of North America, for example, sold annuities to folks over 80, told them they could be surrendered, but then made sure they could *not* be surrendered without penalty for as long as 15 years. Plus, Allianz promised an immediate bonus that, in reality, didn't go into effect for at least five years after the annuity was purchased. Imagine yourself, a parent or a grandparent at 95 years of age, stuck with an annuity that's no good until age 100 and not surrenderable until age 110!

And if these are the kinds of shenanigans large, established companies get away with, what about fly-by-nights?

Fortunately, companies with stellar finances to begin with typically do not resort to those kinds of tactics. So to avoid the scams, the first (although not foolproof) approach is to do what I cited a moment ago—stick with the insurers meriting our highest financial strength ratings.

Unfortunately, consumers are often kept in the dark about everything that counts the most. The junk bond cover-up, the Orwellian newspeak of life insurance, the giant Prudential scheme, and the Allianz deception are just a few examples of the secrecy that still surrounds the insurance industry.

Result: It's hard to find out how much a product really costs. It's almost impossible to figure out how much you're paying in commissions. It's hard to know what the true yield will be. And unless it's term insurance, it's very cumbersome to compare the products of competing insurers side by side.

People in the insurance industry don't pay much attention to this issue because, they say, "It's always been that way." But anyone who comes to insurance from the investment industry is appalled. "Can't you tell me what your one-year yield is? Can't you tell me what your expense ratio is? Can't I compare your policy with a hundred other policies?"

The answers, respectively, are no, no, and no. Typically, you can't do anything even close. How does the insurance industry get away with this secrecy? By always maintaining that thin veneer of insurance on their investment products. They have to underwrite the policy (that is, decide whether you're worthy of their insurance coverage). So their message, in essence, boils down to: "You can shop around all you want. But first, *we* have to decide whether *we* will accept *you*."

If you're shopping for an ETF or mutual fund, you will get a prospectus that discloses all the risks. But if you're shopping for a cash-value life insurance policy, you get a *policy illustration* that often promises much but discloses little.

What about the actual insurance contract itself (that is, the actual product you're buying)? You often don't get to see that until *after* the underwriting process is complete. You'd have to go through this same process with several companies before you could make a comparison. Shopping around can become so impractical as to be virtually impossible.

Years ago, I proposed a solution to Congress: More disclosure to consumers.[1] Rather than place the entire burden of monitoring, baby-sitting, and punishing the industry on the states or the federal government, why not give consumers all the information they need to make their own, informed decisions? That way, they could vote with their dollars, naturally punishing the bad companies and rewarding the good ones.

Indeed, several of the largest insurance company failures in the 1990s could have easily been prevented if that kind of full disclosure to customers had been in place. For example, there would have been nothing wrong with Executive Life or First Capital selling high-yield annuities, provided they made it very clear up front—directly to the buyer at the point of sale—that their annuities were also very high *risk*. There may have been a small minority of investors willing to take that risk to get the higher yields. But instead of growing into giant junk bond insurers, these companies would have remained small, niche businesses.

The insurance industry rarely provides that kind of disclosure. So here's what to do . . .

Step 1: Decide whether you *really* need life insurance. If your agent or financial planner tells you that *everybody* needs some life insurance, tell him to take a hike. Some people need it. Some don't.

The purpose of life insurance is to replace the income of a deceased spouse, cover a mortgage, pay for a child's education, cover the costs of transferring an estate, or pay for living expenses during the early years following a death. Or it could be to provide an inheritance to a needy child or other relative that you were supporting. If you're not supporting anyone other than yourself, you don't need insurance to replace that support.

Let's suppose that you're a widow or widower with no children. You are in good health and have a comfortable lifestyle. What do you need life insurance for? You probably don't.

Or suppose you do have heirs. Do you need life insurance to help offset the costs they will have to pay in estate taxes? Maybe. But if your estate is under the large exemption allowed by current law, it's not subject to estate taxes. The most your children may need is some money to cover some basic expenses.

Moreover, the money you might have wasted on life insurance premiums could be much better spent on your own health or health insurance, so you can live a longer, more enjoyable life. Besides, why not spend some of it on your children's or grandchildren's education so they can be even more self-sufficient when you're gone?

The bottom line is that if you are not financially responsible for someone and you are not going to have a large federal estate tax bill, the agent who gives you a big pitch for life insurance is wasting your time.

However, if you *are* responsible for your heirs' well-being, or if they *do* need the money for their education, their mortgage, or for any other large expenses, then some life insurance may make sense—provided you can afford the premium.

Step 2: Make sure it's affordable. Your desire to provide for your children and grandchildren with some extra money is a kind and generous gesture. But remember: It may not be cheap. And it's certainly not free. Your premium money has to come from somewhere. If you have to sacrifice your own health care or adjust your lifestyle just to pay your premium, it's not affordable and may not be for you.

"But suppose," you ask, "even though I don't really need insurance, I *can* afford it. And suppose I really *want* to do something special for my children or grandchildren. Then what do I do?" Then consider giving them the money while you're still alive and able to appreciate their gratitude. Or contribute directly to their IRAs, other retirement accounts, or education funds.

For example, you could invest in one of the Section 529 education plans. You can open an account in any state, which can be used for tuition at any age, also in any state, and in any educational institution—not just college. Furthermore, an individual can have more than one Section 529 account. So if you want to set one up for a grandchild, you can do it separately from any investment or savings plans that the child's parents might have.

Step 3: Ready to buy life insurance? Okay. Then you'd better get started learning all the jargon. Do you know what a paid-up addition is? How about a mortality charge? Waiver-of-premium rider? If you don't, you're in good company. Most consumers who try to learn about life insurance are overwhelmed by the jargon. As a result, many simply bow to agents' sales presentations without knowing what they're buying or how much it costs.

Typically, once agents have their foot in the door, they begin speaking in a language that may as well be Egyptian hieroglyphics. And because most people are embarrassed by their ignorance, they do not ask questions. Actually, though, the fundamentals of life insurance are not that complicated.

You are the *insured*.

You buy the policy by paying *premiums* that entitle you to a specific *death benefit*.

The part of your premium that goes to the life insurance protection is known as the *mortality charge*. The rest may go into savings.

When you die, the *proceeds* of the policy (the death benefit) go to whomever you have chosen as the *beneficiary*.

Those proceeds can often be paid out as a *lump sum* or an *annuity* (an annual stream of income) and they are tax free to the beneficiary.

Step 4: Decide whether you want to just buy insurance, or buy insurance and an investment at the same time. If you've read this far, you can probably guess which one I recommend: With rare exceptions, you should stick with buying insurance from insurance companies and investments (ETFs or mutual funds) from investment companies

To buy pure insurance, stick with *term* life insurance, and avoid *permanent* or *cash-value* life insurance. Also, some term policies are guaranteed renewable, and give you some of the advantages of permanent insurance without the investment aspect.

As you've seen, insurance companies are usually not that good at handling your money. And even if they were, they just don't disclose the facts you need to be a prudent, informed investor. Another plus is that term insurance is less expensive than permanent insurance.

Term insurance can give you the death benefits you need. And if you want to save more money, you can simply take the difference between its premium and the premium of a permanent policy, and invest it elsewhere (following my guidelines in earlier chapters). Even if you have exhausted your tax-deferred retirement account options, you can always purchase a variable annuity.

One more advantage: With term insurance, you don't have to be quite as squeamish about the company's financial strength rating. Your savings are not at risk. So you can be a bit more forgiving if the company's rating is a bit lower: Shop for term insurance among companies rated B– or better.

Step 5: Figure out how much life insurance you need. Remember, the whole purpose is to help your heirs cover critical expenses after you're gone. So if you—or they—already have resources available to partially fund those needs, you need coverage strictly to fill any gaps, and perhaps give them a bit of an extra cushion.

Ask yourself what expenses you are trying to cover. Is it to pay off a mortgage? If so, it's fairly easy to estimate how much you'll need.

If it's to provide your spouse with enough money to maintain his or her current lifestyle, that's a bit more involved. Take a look at your current ages and life expectancies. Then consider your health, and make any adjustments that feel right for you. It's going to be a rough estimate. But that's the best you can do.

If you need some help, check out Weiss Ratings' free *Life Insurance Needs Worksheet* at www.weissratings.com/financial-planning. It helps you think through all of the expenses you might need to cover with the proceeds of a life insurance policy.

Step 6: Decide which type of term insurance you want. Here are your options:

- *Annual renewable term life insurance.* You buy it one year at a time, and your annual premium is recalculated each year based on your current age and life expectancy. Naturally, as you grow older, the premium will go up each year.
- *Level premium term life.* The idea is that you lock in your premium rate for a longer time period: 5, 10, 20, or even 30 years. That rate is established just once at the beginning of the policy, based on the average annual cost for the death benefit over that time. And it's the same during the entire term, regardless of your health. Or so they say. The reality is that some companies do not guarantee the premium for a 20- or 30-year term. The guarantee is often for only five years but you may not find out about that detail unless you read the fine print. Ask questions, read the entire contract, make sure you understand everything, protect yourself. An easy-to-understand explanation of life insurance can be found in the *Weiss Ratings' Consumer Guide to Term Life Insurance* (call 1-877-934-7778 for more information).

Step 7: Already in a permanent life policy? Then learn about what they're doing for you—or to you. There are two main types of permanent insurance: (1) *whole life* and (2) *universal life,* plus several variations of both. The one thing they all have in common is that they all have a death benefit and some kind of investment vehicle that provides for tax-deferred growth of your money.

The difference between term and permanent insurance is that permanent insurance has the added component of *cash value* (also known as *surrender value*). A percentage of each of your payments goes into the savings account that you own, and it gradually grows until it equals the death benefit at age 100. This is known as the *maturity* of the contract (or *endowment* of the policy).

If you would like to tap into your policy before it matures, you can take out a *policy loan*. That may sound great. But it's really your money, and they still charge you interest for it!

If you would like to terminate the policy before maturity, you will get the cash value (which is *not* the same as the death benefit). But you may also get slapped with a big *surrender charge*.

Beware of surrender details! Remember that I discussed how difficult it is to figure out how much agents make in commissions. One reason is that, on many life insurance policies, it's the equivalent to 100 percent (or more!) of the first-year premium. The company has to pay that money to the agent, and they get that money out of *your* pocket. Therefore, if you surrender your policy within the first year—or even beyond—your cash value could be *zero* because all of your first premium payment went to commission or an up-front revenue for the company. Some companies may pay the commission out over the first couple of years, and you can accumulate a bit more cash value. But many don't.

Step 8. Looking to buy a permanent life policy? Then consider the alternative types . . .

Type 1. Whole life insurance is issued to provide coverage for your entire life, with part of the annual premium you pay going into a reserve in which you own an interest. This is the *cash value* of your policy, invested by the company along with all of its other investments.

But I cannot say it often enough: With rare exceptions, the purchase of whole-life insurance is not recommended. The fact is that you have no control over the investments within the policy. They are not subject to the regulations of the SEC. Furthermore, if the insurance company becomes insolvent, your investments can go down with it.

Type 2. Universal life insurance provides you with flexibility to decide how much your premium payments will be and how frequently you will make them. And you can even increase or decrease your death benefit. In other words, as your financial situation and your insurance needs change, your policy can change to accommodate.

Here's how it works: Your premium is split out into a mortality charge (that is, the cost for the life insurance protection), expenses (including commissions and administrative fees), and a savings element (the portion that goes toward your accumulating cash value).

As you pay your premium and accumulate your cash value, interest is credited to that cash value. As long as there is enough in your cash account to pay for your monthly expenses, you don't have to put any more money into it.

But, let's step back for a moment to a place where many people make a bad decision. Interest is credited to your cash value after your mortality charge and expenses are deducted. That interest rate could be one of two types:

(1) *Current interest,* which is a rate that is declared by the company and dependent on the company's performance with the current market conditions.

(2) A *guaranteed minimum,* specified in your contract.

This is important because many people will purchase a policy based on those policy illustrations that make assumptions about how much their cash value will increase under *ideal market conditions.* That last detail can often be omitted when an insurance agent is trying to sell a policy. Therefore, many people make their purchase decision based on erroneous assumptions that may be unlikely to pan out. They buy a policy because they are told that it will probably increase to a certain dollar amount, when in reality that kind of increase may simply be unlikely to happen.

Type 3. Variable Universal Life Insurance is a variation on universal life with one addition: It lets you decide not only how much money you're going to invest, but where your money is going to be invested. As with a variable annuity, your money is kept in separate accounts, segregated from the insurance company's assets.

That's a plus. And, as with a variable annuity, you assume the investment risk. If you choose great investments, you win. If you make bad choices, you lose. One problem, however, is that the commission and other expenses for these policies can be a big drag on your portfolio.

Now that you understand the different types of life insurance, let's move on to the next steps.

Step 9: Take full advantage of your *free-look period*. This is a 30-day window during which you can review the policy and send it back for a refund. And you *are* insured during this period.

Step 10: Review your policy periodically. Unfortunately, many people buy a policy, put it in a drawer, and never look at it again. It's as if buying it was enough, and now they're covered no matter what. But any policy of a couple of years or more should be periodically monitored for its current relevance and value. Indeed, there are several events that should automatically trigger a review policy and perhaps a change:

- If your health has changed significantly.
- If your spouse or other beneficiary has passed away or changed status in some other way.
- If the insurance company's financial situation has changed enough to warrant a policy change.
- If you have taken any loans from your policy. You could be in danger of your coverage lapsing and owing tax on your loan if you don't replace the money.

Step 11: Get unbiased, conflict-of-interest-free advice. One of the most underhanded aspects of the life insurance industry is that, in the third millennium, you are not likely to encounter any individuals who introduce themselves as life insurance salespeople. Instead, you will encounter *pension consultants, financial advisers,* and *financial planners*. Even stockbrokers and bank tellers are selling life insurance when they can.

At one investment seminar, the speaker at a workshop passed out literature that declared, in bold letters, "I won't sell you insurance." However, several customers who got his "free consultation" reported that he tried to sell them some very expensive life policies.

Salespeople everywhere have been actively creating new titles for themselves, finding new ways to get in front of prospective buyers. Regardless of their shifting titles, however, the substance of what they do has not changed: The life insurance agent, by any name, is someone who *works on behalf of the insurance company*. He or she solicits the business of consumers like you, using a variety of tactics to get a foot in your door.

Now, you might think that a possible strategy is to just ask the person who has approached you if he is a life insurance agent, and if the answer is "yes," you will simply say, "No, thank you." But it's not that easy. In fact, he might even say something like, "I'm no agent, I'm a *broker*; I work for *you*." The truth is that brokers—and all other people who sell life insurance products for commission—are working for *themselves*.

Insurance brokers may indeed research most of your possible options and gather the material that you will need to make your decision. But how do you know that they haven't limited the search to the companies that pay them the highest commission?

Then there's the *financial planner* who wants to analyze your financial situation, and create a personalized, comprehensive financial plan (or estate plan) for you. When you meet, however, you discover—if you're paying close attention—that beneath all the talk of saving on taxes and growing your money, your new financial plan really revolves around an insurance policy that you may not need.

Always ask: "Who do you work for?" "In what capacity?" You might even ask, "Who owns the company you work for?" And although you might get some kind of explanation that hints about compensation, always ask: "Will you earn a commission from the sale of this product?"

Amid all of the specialists trained to sell you insurance products, there *are* ethical people who are waiting to serve you right now. You just have to find them. Your best weapon is your own education about what you are up against plus a healthy level of skepticism about the sales process.

There are agents who know exactly what they are doing when they sell you a policy that is inappropriate or unnecessarily expensive and gives them the highest commission. There are also agents who know exactly what the policies say and mean, and they are on a mission to find you the best deal and even educate you.

But somewhere in the middle (and I'm afraid this accounts for the vast majority of agents), there are also well-meaning people who were sold a bill of goods while they were being trained in insurance products. They tell you what you want to know (*according to what they have been told*), and they have no intention of cheating you! But you get cheated anyway because your well-meaning agent is in the same position you are in: He believed what the experts said.

What are you supposed to do? Is there a foolproof way to differentiate between the sharks and the ethical agents? Unfortunately, no. But you can use a fee-only insurance adviser. Many certified financial planners (CFPs) work strictly on a fee basis. The money they charge for their advice will be small in comparison to the amount they can save you. Make sure you look for a *certified* financial planner, as anyone can call herself a financial planner. And CFP or not, be sure to always ask if the person will get any commission from the sale of insurance products.

If not, look to an online quote service for help (for example, www.quotesmith.com or 800-556-9393, www.quickquote.com, www.insure.com, or www.term4sale.com). Just beware that free quote services earn their money from insurance company ads or referrals. It's okay to use these web sites as long as you understand that they will only show the rates from companies that have contracted with them or agreed to be on their site.

CHAPTER 9

HOW TO FIND THE BEST ANNUITIES

Annuities are invariably the investment most commonly recommended to folks over 50. However, many annuities lock up your funds and commit you to a single investment program—not always a good idea when things are changing so quickly. In these uncertain times, I believe the key to your success will be *flexibility*. Our financial markets are so volatile and fragile, it's almost impossible to imagine a world without big surprises that could upset our best-laid investment plans.

Take inflation and interest rates, for example. Almost every tax advantaged financial product you buy today makes assumptions about these two key factors, usually assuming they'll remain pretty much where they are now for the life of the plan.

But the reality is that no one knows what inflation and interest rates will be 10 or 20 years from now. We could have a return to double-digit inflation, or we could even have chronic *deflation*. Some interest rates could decline even further or they could spike higher than anyone dreams possible. In either scenario, the dangers—and opportunities—could be enormous.

In this environment, you must keep a substantial portion of your money *liquid*; you must avoid, as much as possible, precisely the investments or programs that salespeople like to promote the most—the ones that lock you in. Try to:

■ Steer clear of annuities and insurance policies that involve large start-up commissions or large surrender charges (cancellation fees).

■ Avoid esoteric investments that are easy to buy, but hard to sell (for example, limited partnerships, municipal bonds that rarely trade, penny stocks with low trading volume, *special* opportunities in start-ups or private investments in business deals).

■ Stick primarily with investments that are traded in large volume in open markets–that you can sell at any time, with no penalty.

Don't get me wrong. There *is* a place for a long-term plan that helps you build your wealth without the continuing drag and drain of taxes. Your money grows more quickly. You reach your goals sooner. You retire with more.

But tax deferral does not come without a cost. Nearly all tax-deferred investments require that you sacrifice liquidity. The IRS will hit you hard with penalties for early withdrawal of your funds before age 59½, and the insurance company charges additional penalties.

To begin with, don't put *all* your savings into tax-deferred investments. Use these vehicles only for a modest portion of your overall nest egg. This way, the bulk of your funds will stay completely liquid and under your direct and immediate control.

Also make sure that the money you do set aside for tax-deferred programs is money that you're reasonably sure will *not* be needed for living expenses and other needs.

Next, follow along with me as I help you ask–and answer–six key questions about annuities.

Question 1: What Is an Annuity, Anyhow?

Insurers use statistics to make the odds. Then, they use those odds to determine how much you have to pay in premiums and what the payouts will be. You always bet against the house (the insurance company). No matter which side you want to be on–life or death–the house will take the other side.

Life insurance is actually a way for you to bet on death.

When you buy life insurance, the insurance company is betting–and hoping–that you will live longer. The longer you live, the longer they can put off paying the death benefits to your heirs, and the more they can earn on your money in the meantime.

Annuities are a vehicle for you to bet on your life–the reverse of life insurance. The insurance company is betting, in effect, that you will die *sooner* than average. If so, *they* win the bet and make more. If you fool them and live longer, *you* win the bet and make more.

Why is an annuity a kind of insurance? Because it's *your protection against the risk that you might outlive your income*. What confuses most people is that there are two entirely different kinds of annuities you can buy, and one of them isn't really an annuity at all.

Immediate Annuities versus Deferred Annuities

If you are near or at retirement age, you can buy an annuity immediately. So it's called an *immediate annuity*. This is the true annuity and functions exactly as described earlier. You pay a lump-sum premium *now* and start getting your monthly income checks right away.

The insurance company is, in effect, saying to you: "Give us your principal and we will give you a monthly check for as long as you live. If you live longer than average, you will receive more checks than those who don't live as long. If you die sooner, we pocket the difference."

If you are *not* yet ready to retire, but you want to start saving for that time, you don't need to put up all your money right away. You buy a *deferred annuity*. This is not insurance. It's not even a true annuity. Rather, it's an *investment savings plan* in which you accumulate funds on a tax-free basis toward the *future* purchase of an immediate annuity.

Similarly, the insurance company that's selling you a deferred annuity isn't really acting as an insurance company. It's acting as an investment company that's competing with mutual funds for your investment dollars.

Deferred annuities are not insurance. They're investments. The proof is that they come with the option to either convert to an immediate annuity or to take the proceeds in a lump-sum settlement. If you take the lump-sum settlement, it's purely an investment from the first to the last day. You buy. Then you sell. End of story.

Indeed, many people who buy deferred annuities never intend to convert them into an immediate annuity. They use the deferred annuity as an investment vehicle and for its tax advantages. Then they simply take out the cash when they retire. Nothing wrong with that. Just make sure you recognize it for what it really is—an investment like any other.

Variable Annuities versus Fixed Annuities

When you buy a deferred annuity with an insurance company, you can either retain control over where your money is invested, or you can leave those decisions entirely up to the insurance company.

Variable annuities give you the control. You choose from a range of options (for example, a mutual fund investing in stocks, a bond fund, or a money market fund), and you assume the investment risk. If the market value of your investments goes up, you reap the benefits. If it goes down, you suffer the losses.

You are, in effect, investing in mutual funds affiliated with the insurance company—and with the additional advantage of tax deferral.

As with mutual funds, your investment is kept in separate accounts that are segregated from the insurance company's general pool of assets. When you're ready to get your lump-sum distribution, you get your fair share of what's in those accounts, depending on the performance of the funds.

With *"fixed"* annuities, you let the insurance company make all the investment choices, and they assume a part (but not all) of the investment risk. Your money goes into a general pool. No matter what happens, the company guarantees you a certain bare-bones minimum result.

Two warnings: I put the word *fixed* in quotes for a reason. It's not really fixed. Also, there's a big difference in the *safety* of variable versus fixed annuities. More on both of these in a moment.

Question 2: Do I Really Need an Annuity?

No matter how attractive it might sound, and no matter what the salesperson may tell you, *buying an annuity is not a foregone conclusion.* Remember, when you invest in a deferred annuity, you are giving up some liquidity. When the time comes to buy the real thing, an immediate annuity, you are completely giving up your principal to the insurance company. It's irreversible and final.

There is another option: Instead of buying an annuity, you can direct your own retirement investments. To help you make this critical decision, let's take a closer look at how an annuity works and how it compares with other investments.

Let's say you put $100,000 in a deferred fixed annuity at age 50. And let's assume there are no front-end charges or maintenance fees. Furthermore, let's assume the original crediting rate (yield) is 5 percent guaranteed for one year.

On the first anniversary of your policy, your account value will have grown to $105,000. So far, the account pays interest just like a certificate of deposit (CD), with the sole difference that you do not have to pay income tax on the $5,000 worth of interest income.

The problem is that the one-year guarantee period on your crediting rate has now expired. So the insurer will reassess your rate. If interest rates are rising and their investments are performing well, they will probably raise your rate. But the company also has the option to lower your rates for the coming year if they feel a need to do so.

Sure, it is in the interest of the company to keep rates competitive, but if interest rates on competing investments are going down, theirs will probably go down, too. They can't drop your rate below their minimum guaranteed rate, but that's usually set pretty darn low. Then, each year thereafter, the company reassesses their investment performance and declares a rate for the coming year.

That's why the term *fixed annuity* is deceptive. I can't even count the number of people who have told me they didn't read the fine print and were shocked when their rate went down. They'd never let a mutual fund get away with a product name like that. The truth is that the rate is fixed for only one year at a time.

The growth in your account value will depend on the rate declared each year. For the purpose of illustration, let's say the rate is

5 percent in year two, and 6 percent in year three. Your $100,000 annuity would be worth $110,250 at the end of the second year and $116,865 after three years.

Now, let's say you need to withdraw some money. Under the terms of your contract, you are allowed to withdraw 10 percent with no surrender charges. That would be $11,686. If you need $20,000, you'd have to pay a surrender charge on the remaining $8,314.

Surrender charges often start at 7 percent for the first year and decline by 1 percent each year (that is, 6 percent in the second year, 5 percent in the third year, and so on), until you get down to zero charges in your eighth year and beyond.

So, if you are making a withdrawal during the fourth contract year, the charge would be 4 percent of $8,314, or $332. Your account balance now stands at $96,533.

You would also have to pay regular income taxes on the interest income portion of the funds that are being withdrawn plus a 10 percent tax penalty if you're under 59½. This is generally not as bad as it sounds since you still have had the advantage of deferring the income taxes for the first three years.

This is the most common example. And it's simple. But there are many policy features that can vary substantially from company to company and policy to policy that you should know about—surrender fees, other fees, and bailout rates.

Surrender fees. Although surrender fees commonly start at 7 percent and are scaled down to zero percent after seven years, some companies charge more—9, 10, sometimes even 15 percent!

Even if you are fairly sure you will not need access to your money soon, don't even think about getting stuck in policies with such huge fees. Unexpected things do happen.

Bailout rates. While they are not as popular as they were several years ago, certain contracts offer a bailout provision in their annuity contracts. This provision allows you to withdraw all of your funds without penalty if your interest rate drops below a set figure. This is typically a rate that is just above the guaranteed minimum.

The bailout option will be especially useful if the rate decline is due to specific problems in the company's investments. However, if the rate drop is due to generally declining interest rates, you may not be able to find a comparable investment with a better return elsewhere.

Front-end load and other fees. Few policies now on the market carry either front-end loading fees (fees subtracted from your cash value when you first purchase the policy) or yearly maintenance fees. However, policies with between 1 and 3 percent in front-end loads and with yearly fees of $25 to $100 do exist. Avoid them.

Settlement options. Most policies provide at least two ways to use the proceeds of your deferred annuity when it matures. You can choose between two options:

1. *Lump-sum withdrawal.* You take out all of your accumulated cash values when the contract matures or at retirement.
2. *Annuitization.* You convert it into an income annuity, putting you in the same situation as someone who is buying an immediate annuity. This will typically pay out the funds to you monthly for the rest of your life. The actual amount of the monthly check will depend on the investment climate at the time of annuitization. As a result, most policy illustrations will show both a guaranteed payout (the minimum the company will offer) and a current rate payout (the amount it would be if the current interest rate were in effect at the time of annuitization).

Question 3: To Annuitize or Not to Annuitize?

The term of your deferred annuity is up, and you face a decision: Do I take all my money in a lump sum? Or do I annuitize (that is, use the money to buy an immediate annuity)? Even if you don't have a deferred annuity, and you're at or near retirement age, your question is similar: Do I buy an immediate annuity, or not?

Whatever you decide, don't be overly influenced by insurance agents, stockbrokers, or financial planners who sell annuities. Two warnings include:

■ A lot more depends on *your* individual circumstances than the salesperson may indicate. For example, if you feel you're healthier than the average person, or you come from a family of people who usually enjoy long life, annuities have an additional advantage to you, beyond the standard advantages. Otherwise, the annuity may have additional *dis*advantages for you.

■ Many salespeople will push the annuity that will give them the largest commission, not necessarily the one that's best for you.

Aside from a short grace period (which may vary from 10 to 30 days, depending on each state's laws), once you've bought an immediate annuity, that's it. You're in for life.

If you can accept this disadvantage, the advantages are still worth considering:

Advantage 1: Loved ones can be provided for. You can purchase an annuity called a *joint and survivor annuity.* In that way, some or all of the annuity income will continue going to the survivor when the original annuitant dies. Also, with one of the most common contracts, called "10-year certain and life," monthly checks keep coming for a minimum of 10 years and for as long as you live thereafter. If you die before the 10-year period is up, the checks are sent to a designated beneficiary for the balance of the 10-year period.

Some companies may give you the option of buying a certain and life annuity that ranges between 5 and 20 years. The payout amounts differ from company to company, perhaps by as much as $60 a month on a $100,000 annuity. So compare monthly income payments carefully.

Advantage 2: Reduced income taxes. You may have to pay taxes on as little as one-third of your monthly check, depending on your contract and your age. If you're in a 28 percent tax bracket, for example, and your monthly annuity check is $400, you may only owe taxes on approximately $130. So all you'd owe Uncle Sam each month is about $36. (However, in some states you may have to pay premium taxes.)

Advantage 3: Favorable monthly cash flow compared with CDs. Assume a 70-year-old widow in the 28 percent tax bracket invests in a $50,000, 5-year CD yielding 5 percent. She makes about $2,500 per year in interest, leaving about $1,800 in after-tax income.

By contrast, if she bought a $50,000 immediate 10-year certain and life annuity, she could get a check for roughly $385 a month, or $4,620 a year. The key is that this includes both interest and principal. The interest portion is $143, which after taxes, gives her $103 per month, or $1,236 per year. Adding in the principal portion, the total money she receives comes to $345 a month or $4,140 a year. That's a cash flow of 8.3 percent even after taxes.

Keep in mind that, with the CD, the bank will return your principal when the CD matures. In contrast, with the annuity, the insurance company keeps your principal and guarantees monthly checks.

Advantage 4: Annuity income for a lifetime. With other investments that pay out principal as well as interest (for example, a Ginnie Mae bond), when you deplete your capital, the checks stop coming. With an immediate annuity, because of the insurance aspect, the payout of principal does not result in a cutoff of your monthly checks. You continue to receive the checks for the rest of your life.

The insurance company—which bases payouts on average life expectancies and the earnings on its investment portfolio—is, in effect, betting that the funds paid *in* will cover all the funds paid *out*. That's why it's so important to buy annuities from strong companies that can back up their promises with their own reserves if they miscalculate their earnings or their liabilities.

Question 4: Can You Give Me an Example of a Typical Immediate Annuity?

Let's assume the following:

You're 65 years old.
The immediate annuity costs $100,000.
The payout is $850 per month.

It has a provision called *10-year certain and life*. (This stipulates that payments are guaranteed for a minimum of 10 years and for as long as you live thereafter. In case of premature death, payments would go to your designated beneficiaries.)

Since the payout is $850 per month, your benefit amounts to $10,200 per year. After 10 years, you will have received a total of $102,000 and will have recouped your original $100,000 investment. In other words, the 10-year certain provision protects you against an outright loss of principal.

Now let's explore another route. Instead of putting your $100,000 nest egg in an annuity, suppose you put the money in a 10-year U.S. Treasury note.

If the average yield is, for example, 3.5 percent, or $3,500, during the first year, your interest will be *less* than the $10,200 paid out by the annuity. But unlike the annuity, *you have not given up your principal.* You still have your original $100,000. So to maintain your income, you can simply withdraw the difference (that is, $6,700) from your principal.

For the second year, your principal would be $93,300. Interest for the year would be $3,266, and you'll have to withdraw $6,934 to maintain your income level.

As your principal shrinks year after year, earnings will also diminish. To maintain your income level, you'll have to dig deeper into principal each year at an accelerating rate. *Eventually,* it will be reduced to nothing. For many people, however, losing their principal eventually is a lot better than giving it up immediately as with an immediate annuity.

Table 9.1 shows you what happens to your money. As you can see, your nest egg will be gone after 14 years. At age 79, you will either have to reduce your living standard or look for another income source. If you live beyond 79, you'd be better off with an annuity. If you don't live past 79, you'd be better off with a self-directed investment program.

(*Note:* For this illustration, I have assumed that when you cash out your annuity, it has been in force for at least 10 years and you are at least 59½ years of age. If these conditions are not met, your proceeds may be subject to a substantial excise tax. Review the matter with your tax adviser.)

Table 9.1 The Disadvantage of a Fixed-Rate Long-Term Bond Compared to a Fixed Annuity

Your Age	Principal at Beginning of Year	Interest	Withdraw Enough Principal to Equal	Principal at End of Year
65	100,000	5,000	10,200	94,800
66	94,800	4,740	10,200	89,340
67	89,340	4,467	10,200	83,607
68	83,607	4,180	10,200	77,587
69	77,587	3,879	10,200	71,267
70	71,267	3,563	10,200	64,630
71	64,630	3,232	10,200	57,662
72	57,662	2,883	10,200	50,345
73	50,345	2,517	10,200	42,662
74	42,662	2,133	10,200	34,595
75	34,595	1,730	10,200	26,125
76	26,125	1,306	10,200	17,231
77	17,231	862	10,200	7,892
78	7,892	395	8,287	0

This illustrates the one *disadvantage* of putting your money in a fixed rate bond instead of an annuity: As you draw down your principal to cover expenses, its ability to generate interest for you also diminishes over time. An annuity insures you against this problem. But don't forget the advantage of a bond: You retain control over the asset at all times. That means you can sell it in the open market, either at a profit or a loss, and pull out all the remaining cash. You cannot do that with an annuity.

Question 5: How Can I Make Sure My Insurance Company Doesn't Die before I Do?

One of the greatest potential tragedies of our times is that many investors may go through all the sacrifices of planning for retirement, only to find out that their insurance company has died before they do.

Consider this historical example: A few years ago, the phone rang at the home of Vincent Triglia in Jamestown, New York.

A friendly salesman at a local bank said that he had noticed Triglia's money sitting in CDs, and was calling to suggest another investment: tax-deferred annuities.

Mr. Triglia said he didn't want to put one penny at risk. The salesman said the annuities were 100 percent guaranteed, just like bank deposits—only better, because up to $500,000 per account was covered.

So as each CD matured, Mr. Triglia shifted all $350,000 of his savings into annuities issued by one insurance company, Executive Life of New York. At that time, the company carried a high rating from all the established rating agencies.

But later, when Mr. Triglia tried to withdraw $58,000 to build a home, he found that his money was frozen in a moratorium. After formally applying in April 1991 for the cash, he received a letter telling him that the New York State Insurance Department had just seized the company, following the collapse of its affiliate, Executive Life of California.

Mr. Triglia wasn't the only victim. As I explained in Chapter 3, nearly 2 million American households suffered a similar disaster.

Don't let this happen to you! Before you even consider a specific annuity, look at the longevity of the insurance company itself. What good is it to buy a product with high yield and great payout promise, if the company doesn't stick around to fulfill that promise? What good is it if you win that bet with your insurance company, living longer than they expect, but they don't pay up? There are two ways you can greatly reduce this risk:

1. *Always check the company's Weiss Financial Strength Rating at www .weisswatchdog.com.* If it's B+ or better, the chances of a failure are greatly minimized. Of course, this is no guarantee that some of the B companies won't eventually run into trouble. But the chances are small, and we are bound to downgrade them long before insolvency.
2. *You can use variable insurance products instead of fixed products.* In variable annuities (and also in variable life insurance policies), the funds you invest are kept in separate accounts, segregated from the insurance company's general pool of assets. If the company fails, there may be some inconveniences and annoyances. But unlike fixed annuities and whole-life or cash-value insurance, you will probably still be able to take your money out normally.

Question 6: I Know There Are Rip-Offs Out There. But How Do I Avoid Them?

When you buy a fixed annuity, you can accumulate a nice nest egg, tax-deferred. And when you retire, the insurance company promises to either give you a lump-sum check or send you a monthly check for as long as you live. But it won't work for you unless you avoid the most common rip-offs.

Rip-off 1: More risk than you bargained for. In the early 1990s, many investors in Executive Life of California, Mutual Benefit Life, and other large insurance companies that failed lost up to half their principal. That wasn't so long ago. And if it happened once, it can happen again.

The money you invest in fixed annuities is inseparable from the insurance company's general pool of funds. So if your insurer fails, you could meet a similar fate.

Rip-off 2: High surrender charges that lock you in. If you cancel during the first year, you will most likely be hit with a surrender charge between 5 and 10 percent of your principal. That's a big loss just for changing your mind.

Although the charge typically diminishes by one point each year, it still means that most annuities are far from liquid. To avoid or reduce these charges, do the following:

Make sure that you invest strictly funds that you definitely will not need in the short or medium term.

Stick with annuities with surrender charges of 7 percent or lower. No-surrender annuities do exist, but your financial adviser will usually not suggest them, because they pay him a lower commission.

Favor annuities that will allow you to take out a portion of your funds, typically 15 percent each year, with zero surrender charges.

Look for those annuities that will at least let you withdraw your money if you are hospitalized or confined to a nursing home for a certain period of time.

Rip-off 3: Front-end loads. Some companies advertise "no surrender charges." The implication is that you're free to cancel any time you want. The catch is that, to get in the door, they charge huge *front-end* loads, which you sacrifice immediately, whether you cancel later or not. I found one with a front-end fee as high as 15 percent!

Rip-off 4: Teaser rates. Some companies lure investors with high first-year rates. Then they lock the door with steep surrender penalties, which continue even after the rate drops sharply. Always ask: "What rate are your one-year-old policies paying right now?" But, remember, a rate that is too high may reflect higher risks.

Rip-off 5: Misleading policy illustrations. The illustrations may:

- Exaggerate the real returns you can expect by making optimistic assumptions about the future level of interest rates.
- Disguise the fact that mortality charges and expenses can change, potentially draining the account value severely.
- Fail to disclose whether their policies have performed as well as their policy illustrations.

Shop around! There are hundreds of different annuity products available. There are many companies with a Weiss Financial Strength Rating of B+ or better that can be found at www .weissratings.com/annuitylist. Or check and monitor the rating of your company at www.weisswatchdog.com.

Bear in mind, though, that the safest companies don't always offer the best deals. Before you buy from them, always weigh the costs and the benefits, using the questions and answers in this chapter as a guide.

And always remember: There are inherent disadvantages to locking your money up—something that frequently is required of you with life and annuity insurance. For the cash that you'll need for opportunities—or emergencies—you need to find the safest and most *liquid* place for your money.

CHAPTER 10

THE SAFEST AND MOST LIQUID PLACE FOR YOUR CASH

With bubbles, busts, recession, and depression, it's not enough just to avoid losing money and preserving your savings; that's just one side of true safety.

The other, equally important, side that most people miss is *liquidity*–immediate access to your money, allowing you to actually have it in your hands and use it whenever you want to–without waiting; without penalties; and without bottlenecks, shutdowns, or disasters of any kind standing in your way.

That's your paramount goal in bubbles, busts, recession, or depression: Both capital preservation *and* liquidity.

Just remember that in the real world, *absolute* perfection is not possible. However, the single investment in the world that's at the top of the true-safety charts is *short-term* government securities.

I'm not talking about Treasury bonds, which are long term (from 10 to 30 years' maturity). And I'm not talking about Treasury notes, which are medium term (up to 10 years). I am referring strictly to Treasury *bills* (less than one year) or money market funds that own exclusively short-term Treasury securities (usually averaging less than 30 days in maturity).

You can buy them directly from the U.S. Treasury Department. Or for added convenience and liquidity, you can get them through a Treasury-only money market fund.

In recent years, because of the Fed's policy of reducing short-term interest rates to practically zero, the yield on Treasury bills has been a mere fraction of a percent. But the paramount goal of this chapter is to help you secure the return *of* your money. For better returns *on* your money, refer to subsequent chapters.

We think this policy will change, and because of pressures beyond its control, the Fed will be forced to let interest rates rise back to normal levels. But even if interest rates stay low, Treasury bills give you the following advantages:

- *The Rolls Royce of government guarantees.* You get the best, most direct, and most reliable guarantee of the government, over and above any other guarantees or promises the government may have made in the past or will make in the future.
- *No limit.* You can invest $1,000 or $100 million, and you get the same full guarantee.
- *Exempt from local and state taxes.* There's no difference between bank deposits and Treasuries when it comes to paying federal income taxes. You have to pay on both. But there *is* a significant difference with respect to *local and state* income taxes. Your income from Treasuries and Treasury-only money funds is exempt. Your income from banks is not.

Four Additional Advantages of Treasury-Only Money Market Funds

When you buy short-term Treasuries through a Treasury-only money market fund, beyond the three advantages cited earlier, you also benefit from the following four *additional* advantages:

1. *Low fees.* When a bank quotes you yields, it always quotes the yields *before* deducting all service fees. Because of these fees, it's

almost impossible for most bank customers to collect anything near the advertised yield. In contrast, with a Treasury-only money fund, when the fund quotes you its yield, it is invariably *after* deducting its fees and expenses.

2. *One account for both checking and savings.* At banks, most customers divide their money between checking accounts or savings accounts, where they give up interest; and certificates of deposit (CDs), which lock them in and force them to give up liquidity. In contrast, a Treasury-only money fund lets you keep nearly all of your cash assets in one single account. You get maximum liquidity and yield on your entire balance, and you don't have to shuttle back and forth between checking, passbook savings, money market accounts, CDs, and other complex combinations. You can have one large account that meets nearly all your cash needs.

3. *Truly free checking.* Nearly all banks charge you, one way or another, for checking privileges: a fee for each check you issue, a flat monthly service fee, or a combination of both. Banks say they're giving you "free checking," but require large minimum balances, paying little or no interest. In contrast, most Treasury-only money funds do not charge you any extra fee for check-writing privileges. You can write as many checks as you want, as often as you want. This is not true for all money funds. Some levy certain charges for special services, but they're almost always lower than the charges at banks.

4. *Immediate liquidity.* With bank CDs, there is invariably a penalty for early cancellation. With Treasury-only money market funds, there is no such thing. You can have your funds wired to your local bank overnight. Or you can write checks against it, much as you'd write checks against any bank checking account.

For investors who want to prioritize safety, there is only one disadvantage beyond the low yields: The danger of a decline in the purchasing power of your dollars. However, that's a separate issue I address later in this chapter and in Chapter 17. In the meantime, I realize you probably have several questions. So let me do my best to answer them right here.

Why Are Treasury Bills Safer than Bank CDs?

You might ask: *The FDIC is also backed by the U.S. government, so if I have money in an FDIC-guaranteed account at my bank, what's the difference? Why should I accept a lower yield on a government-guaranteed three-month Treasury bill when I can get a higher yield on a government-guaranteed three-month CD?*

Without realizing it, you've answered your own question. If the yield is higher on the bank CDs, that can mean only one thing—that, according to the collective wisdom of millions of investors and thousands of institutions in the market, the *risk* is also higher. Otherwise, why would the bank have to pay more to attract your money? Likewise, why would the U.S. Treasury be able to get away with paying so much less and still have interested buyers for its securities?

It's because the risk is higher for CDs but lower for Treasury securities. It's because even within the realm of government guarantees, there is a clear pecking order of priorities.

- The government's first-priority guarantee: maturing securities that were issued by the U.S. Treasury Department itself.
- The second-priority guarantee: maturing securities that were issued by other U.S. government agencies, such as the Government National Mortgage Association (Ginnie Mae).
- A third priority: the Treasury's backing of the FDIC.

This is not to say the Treasury is not standing behind the FDIC at this time. Rather, my point is that, in the event of a serious financial strain on the U.S. government, FDIC-guaranteed bank deposits will *not* be the first in line. FDIC officials may seek to deny this, and Treasury officials may seek to pooh-pooh the distinction. However, the differential in yields between CDs and T-bills tells the true story, accurately reflecting a very tangible difference.

Let's say I have a Treasury bill or a Treasury-only money fund. And let's say you have a CD in a weak bank. What do you have in terms of a guarantee? You have coverage up to $250,000, which in turn is backed indirectly by the Treasury. In contrast, I have a *direct* guarantee from the Treasury Department *without* any cap, and without any decision-making process that could hold things up.

Aren't You Ignoring the Government's Own Sinking Finances?

Isn't the U.S. government also having its own share of financial difficulties with huge budget deficits? If those difficulties could get a lot worse, why should I trust the government any more than I trust other investments? Why should I lend my money to Uncle Sam? Aren't you ignoring this?

No. The United States is the world's largest economy with the most active financial markets and the strongest military in the world. Despite Uncle Sam's financial difficulties, this has never been in doubt; and even in a financial crisis, that's unlikely to change.

More importantly, the U.S. government's borrowing power—its ability to continue tapping the open market for cash—is, by far, its most precious asset, more valuable than the White House and all public properties; even more valuable than the gold in Fort Knox. Those assets are like Uncle Sam's house, backyard, and pocket change. His borrowing power, in contrast, is like the *air he breathes to stay alive.*

Also remember this: The U.S. Treasury Department is directly responsible for funding the utmost, mission-critical operations of this country, including defense, homeland security, and emergency response. The Treasury will do whatever it takes to *continue* providing that funding, and that means making sure they *never* default on their maturing Treasury securities.

Even in the 1930s, when a record number of Americans were unemployed and when we had a head-spinning wave of bank failures, owners of Treasury bills never lost a penny. Even in the Civil War, Treasuries were safe. Investors financed 65 percent of the Union's war costs by buying Treasury securities. The war was far worse than those investors had anticipated, leaving over half of the economy in shambles, raising serious concerns among those investors. However, the U.S. government made the repayment of its maturing Treasuries the *number one* priority over all other wartime obligations. Investors got back every single penny, and more.

My main point: The crisis ahead will not be nearly as severe as the war that tore our nation apart. If Treasury securities were safe then, they should be safe today.

How Might I Cash in My Treasuries During a Banking Shutdown?

Suppose there's a bank holiday and I need to cash in my Treasury bills. Since the Treasury Department and the Treasury-only money market funds use banks for transfers, won't I be locked out of my money, too?

We actually have a real precedent for a similar situation. In Rhode Island in 1991, when the governor declared a statewide bank holiday, all the state-chartered savings banks were closed down. Every single citizen with money in one of those banks was locked out.

At the time, one of our *Safe Money Report* subscribers happened to have a checking account in one of the closed Rhode Island banks. Thankfully, he had almost all of his money at the Treasury Department in Treasury bills, so his money was safe. But he called and asked: "The Treasury is set to wire the money straight into my bank account, which is frozen. Will the money the Treasury wires me get frozen, too?"

In response, I told him to check his post office mailbox. Instead of wiring his funds, the Treasury had taken the extraordinary measure of cutting hard checks and mailing them out immediately. They wanted to make *absolutely* sure he got his money without any delay.

The moral of this story is that even in a worst-case banking scenario, the Treasury will do whatever is necessary to get your money to you. We can't forecast exactly how. But they will probably send you hard Treasury checks. And they'll probably designate special bank offices in every major city where you can cash them in. Ditto for Treasury-only money market funds.

Suppose the Government Devalues the Dollar?

Throughout history, many governments have defaulted on their debts in a more subtle way—by devaluing their currency. Why are you recommending Treasuries, which are denominated purely in dollars, if one of the consequences of this disaster could be a sharp decline in the dollar's value?

I cannot deny the risks. But the solution is not to abandon the safety and liquidity of short-term government securities. The solution is to separately set aside some money to buy hedges, such as gold and foreign currencies, against inflation and other unexpected events.

The big picture: In busts, recession, or depression, many other supposedly safe investments will be called into question—most stocks, of course, but also bank CDs, annuities, high-rated bonds in large companies, and even widely traded tax-exempt bonds issued by cities and states. It could be a financial war zone. But despite the wealth destruction everywhere, U.S. Treasury bills will stand head and shoulders *above* every other investment, returning 100 percent of your money plus at least *some* interest, with your money available whenever you need it.

How to Use Treasury Securities for Almost All Your Banking Needs

For most of your personal or business savings and checking, you don't need a bank, S&L, or credit union. All you need is a money market fund that invests exclusively in short-term U.S. Treasury bills or equivalent. The Treasuries the money fund buys enjoy the same U.S. government guarantee as Treasuries bought directly from the government. So insurance on the money fund itself is not an issue.

Whether you have a lot of money set aside or just small amounts, and whether you intend to use the funds actively or just let them stay put, I recommend these steps:

Step 1. Decide what type of account you want to open. For your personal checking account, it could be established as an individual, joint, custodian, or trust. You can also use your Treasury-only money fund to open a separate account for your individual retirement account (IRA) or other retirement accounts.

(Continued)

Step 2. Select a Treasury-only money market fund. I use American Century's Capital Preservation Fund, one of the first ever created. Or you can select any fund from the list provided on pages 156–158.

Step 3. Download the prospectus and application from the fund's web site. Or you can also ask the fund to send the materials to you by first-class mail.

Step 4. If you are not sure about what forms and documents you should submit to open an account, now is the time to ask. Different account types require different forms. So be sure to get all the information you need to decide whether you're opening (1) an individual or joint account, minor custodian account; (2) a trust or guardianship, (3) an IRA, Roth IRA, or other retirement account or rollover.

Step 5. With these documents, also provide the basic wiring instructions to the fund. If there is no space on the application, put the following information in a separate, signed letter: your bank's name, city and state, your bank's ABA number, your bank's wire transfer account number, your account number at the bank, and all registered names on the account. (The account title on your bank account should be the same as the title on your Treasury-only money fund account.)

Step 6. Don't forget to sign the application. Then make your first deposit check payable to the Treasury-only money fund and mail it with your new account materials. You should receive written confirmation of your deposit in the mail within a few days and a checkbook within a couple of weeks.

Step 7. To maximize your safety and liquidity, transfer the bulk of your cash funds to the Treasury-only money fund account. These can include any investment funds you wish to keep liquid and available for upcoming opportunities, as well as most of your regular spending money and most of your keep-safe savings.

Step 8. Keep only a minimal amount in your local bank for its ATM machine and small checks.

Step 9. Use a major credit card for as many of your purchases as possible. Then, to avoid any interest charges, pay off your credit card, in full, each month with one check written from your Treasury-only money fund.

Step 10. Write all of your checks that are above the fund's per-check minimum from the Treasury-only money fund account. These could include checks for paying your mortgage, rent, monthly credit card bills, utility bills, and any large purchases at establishments that give you a better price for non–credit card purchases.

Step 11. If you need a large amount of cash or want to buy traveler's checks, just call your Treasury-only money fund and give them instructions to transfer the money to your local bank. In most cases, if you call before 3 P.M. Eastern Time, you should have the funds in your account the next business day.

Step 12. At most funds, you may deposit your salary and any checks payable to you directly into your account. Just endorse the checks with your signature on the reverse side and include the words "for deposit to," followed by your account number at the fund. Then simply mail your deposit to the fund. (You may use the deposit slip and envelope that most funds provide you with your monthly statement.) You will receive monthly statements from the fund showing all your checking transactions, plus any other activity including deposits, dividend income credits, and so on. Canceled checks, however, are typically *not* returned to you automatically, unless you specifically ask for them.

(Continued)

That's it! With these steps, you will now have superior safety and liquidity overall. Moreover, except for the small amounts of money in your local banking account, you should not be negatively affected by a broader banking crisis.

Another alternative: If you feel you will not need your cash available to you at all times, you can also open an account directly with the U.S. Treasury Department, using your Social Security number, through the Treasury Direct program (www.TreasuryDirect.com). Just be sure to exclusively buy Treasury bills at this time—not Treasury notes or Treasury bonds. And if you are not familiar with the important differences among them, see the discussion at the start of this chapter.

MONEY MARKET FUNDS INVESTING IN SHORT-TERM U.S. TREASURY SECURITIES OR EQUIVALENT*

American Century Capital Preservation Fund
(800) 345-2021
www.americancentury.com
Symbol: CPFXX

Cavanal Hill US Treasury Fund
(800) 762-7085
www.cavanalhillfunds.com
Symbol: APGXX

BB&T US Treasury Money Market Fund/Trust Shares
(800) 228-1872
www.bbtfunds.com
Symbol: BBUXX

*Some of these funds may intermittently be closed to new money. Please contact your money market fund of choice before investing.

Citi US Treasury Reserves
800-625-4554
www.leggmason.com
Symbol: CISXX

Dreyfus 100% US Treasury Money Market Fund
(800) 645-6561
www.dreyfus.com
Symbol: DUSXX

Evergreen Treasury Money Market Fund, Class A
(800) 343-2898
http://www.evergreeninvestments.com
Symbol: ETAXX

Fidelity US Treasury Money Market Fund
(800) 343-3548
http://www.fidelity.com/
Symbol: FDLXX

First American US Treasury Money Market Fund
(800) 677-FUND
www.firstamericanfunds.com
Symbol: FOEXX

Gabelli US Treasury Money Market Fund
(800) 422-3554
www.gabelli.com
Symbol: GABXX

Huntington US Treasury Money Market Fund Trust
(800) 253-0412
www.huntingtonfunds.com
Symbol: HTTXX

JPMorgan 100% US Treasury Securities Money Market Fund
(800) 480-4111
www.jpmorganfunds.com
Symbol: HTSXX

(Continued)

RMK Select Treasury Money Market Fund
(800) 222-8866
http://www.morgankeegan.com
Symbol: FITXX

Schwab US Treasury Money Fund
(800) 435-4000
www.schwab.com
Symbol: SWUXX

T. Rowe Price US Treasury Money Fund
(800) 225-5132
www.troweprice.com
Symbol: PRTXX

US Treasury Money Fund of America
(800) 421-0180
www.americanfunds.com
Symbol: UTAXX

US Treasury Securities Cash Fund
(800) 873-8637
www.usfunds.com
Symbol: USTXX

Vanguard Admiral Treasury Money Market Fund
(800) 662-7447
www.vanguard.com
Symbol: VUSXX

CHAPTER 11

ALL-WEATHER INVESTMENTS FOR THE BEST AND THE WORST OF TIMES

If you have followed the instructions I've outlined so far, you are now ready for almost any crisis.

You have completed your primary mission: to cut your losses in real estate, sidestep the continuing dangers in stocks and bonds, escape a potential banking crisis, build a nice nest egg of cash, and put the cash away in the safest possible place. But just to make sure, let's run through this quick checklist:

☑ You've done the best you can to reduce debts, secure your job, and save money. If not, please see pages 15 and 17.

☑ You've taken steps to sell off vulnerable real estate that you don't live or work in and, provided it's consistent with your personal goals, perhaps your home as well. If not, you may have very valid reasons for holding the real estate. Just remember that no property is totally immune to busts, recession, or depression. If you'd like to reconsider, go back to page 72. And for an update on the latest news that may affect your property values, visit the blog of *Safe Money Report* editor, Mike Larson, at blogs .moneyandmarkets.com/interest-rate-roundup.

☑ You've greatly reduced your exposure to a stock market decline by cutting down the size and risk of your holdings in stocks and stock mutual funds, whether in your 401(k) or a regular brokerage account. If not, take advantage of any major stock market rally to do so, following the instructions on page 86.

☑ If you had long-term bonds, you've gotten rid of most of those as well, regardless of issuer or rating. If not, please review page 42.

☑ Your bank account and insurance policy are with strong firms. If not, review Chapter 7 and be sure to check the safety of your institutions at www.weisswatchdog.com.

If the bust, recession, or depression are accompanied by falling prices, a very possible scenario, you can survive even in the worst of times. You can sit with your cash and let the crisis play itself out, without investing, without buying a thing.

Later when the crisis exhausts itself and markets hit bottom, you should also be able to buy more of the things you've always wanted, including a better education for your children, a nicer home, more shares in your favorite companies. By doing *nothing*, even earning close to zero in interest, you will grow wealth.

But suppose the Fed's money printing causes inflation. And suppose you want to go *beyond* just growing your wealth passively? Suppose you want go on the offensive and multiply the money in your account starting right now. This chapter, plus others that follow, show you how.

First, let me help you deal with this dilemma: You have not yet been able to get rid of real estate property that's falling in value. You have stocks in a pension fund beyond your personal control; shares in your employer's company that you're not allowed to sell; or a vulnerable business for which there is no buyer. You see the real possibility of more declines and losses ahead. You do want to sell, but you cannot. You want to escape, but you feel trapped. What do you do?

The answer: Hedge!

Erect a shield around your vulnerable assets that can help protect you from the dangers. I'm not recommending you use a hedge fund for this purpose. Despite the name, many hedge funds are actually *speculator* funds that can increase your risk. Rather, what I'm talking about is your own, personal hedging strategy.

How is that possible? In the past, it was actually quite complicated. You had to sell the market short or you had to use futures. And in either case, you could expose yourself to unlimited risk. Today, thanks to the advent of a special kind of exchange-traded fund (ETF), you can go a long way toward protecting yourself against almost any crisis.[1]

First, let me tell you about the flexibility of ETFs in general. Then, I'll walk you through the steps for using the ETFs that are designed especially for declining markets.

The Advantages (and Pitfalls) of Exchange-Traded Funds

Like mutual funds, ETFs buy a broad portfolio of investments and help you spread your risk among a diverse range of securities. But, as the name implies, exchange-traded funds are different in that they are traded on major exchanges, giving you the following advantages:

- *Broad diversity of choices.* You can buy ETFs that are tied to a broad market average like the Dow Jones, the S&P 500, or the Nasdaq Composite. You can buy them on particular stock market sectors like consumer goods, energy, financials, various foreign stock markets, and many more. Plus, you can buy ETFs on a variety of other asset classes like bonds, commodities, and foreign currencies.
- *Low minimum investment.* Because ETFs are simply shares traded on the exchange, you can start with just a single share for $25 or less. So with a couple of thousand dollars you can buy a whole range of different ETFs across many different sectors or countries. Or you can try out an investment strategy *without* betting the farm on it.

- *No loads.* With ETFs, you also avoid the big loads (sales charges) that some mutual funds require. These loads not only cost you money, they also inhibit your ability to dump a loser or jump on a winner, meaning possible losses and lost opportunities that can cost you far more than the direct cost of the loads themselves. With ETFs, you do have to pay a broker commission. But if you use a discount or online broker, your commission costs can be slashed to the bone.

- *No special fees.* With ETFs, you sidestep some sneaky-but-legal expenses that mutual funds often charge investors. For example, mutual funds can charge you for their own marketing costs, under the rubric of 12b-1 fees. ETFs cannot. Plus, with ETFs, you also avoid some of the high management fees many mutual funds are known for. There are costs, but they are usually smaller. And since the money you save stays in your account, your money can compound at a faster pace.

- *Immediate transparency.* Mutual funds don't reveal where they've invested your money until the information is often outdated. ETFs tell you precisely what they own and how much every single day—all right on their web sites.

- *Up-to-the minute pricing.* Mutual funds are not priced until at the end of the trading day or, at best, twice a day. ETFs, in contrast, are priced continually through the trading day, so you always know what your shares are worth and you don't have to wait until the end of the day to sell them.

- *No switching restrictions.* Most mutual fund families discourage frequent switching. If you jump too soon too often, they may send you a notice and restrict your trading. In volatile markets, during which more frequent changes to your strategy may indeed be appropriate, this can be a burdensome restriction. With ETFs, aside from the commissions you pay, switching is not an issue. Moreover, since they are traded on the exchange much like stocks, you can use stop-loss orders to help protect your profits or cut your losses. Plus, you have a better chance to buy or sell at better prices by using limits—orders to your broker that specify the minimum or maximum price you'll accept.

- *The possibility of double and even triple leverage.* With certain ETFs, you can double or even triple your profit potential without borrowing money or opening a margin account with your broker. The ETF does the leveraging for you. With these ETFs, for every 10 percent move in the index, the ETF is designed to move 20 percent, and with some, even 30 percent.

■ *Overall advantage: Flexibility.* ETFs were *made* for flexibility, so you can buy and sell whenever you want as often as you want. No, I don't recommend trading in and out on a whim or too frequently. But in tough times with rapidly changing markets, ETFs give you the ability to avoid the buy-and-hold approaches that can burn a hole in your portfolio.

Of course, no investment vehicle is perfect. So you should also be aware of the possible pitfalls:

■ *Overtrading.* Sometimes, it's so easy to trade ETFs that investors wind up overdoing it, creating extra transaction costs and defeating the cost-efficiency advantage. But you have the ability to avoid this problem simply by buying and selling only when there's a good reason to do so.

■ *No ETF has a perfect model for tracking an index.* Although an ETF is *designed* to match a particular index, there could be differences in its performance and the performance of the index. Similarly, there's no such thing as a perfect double-leverage model. So, although double-leveraged ETFs are designed to move up (or down) at two times the pace of the index they track, they do not necessarily achieve that goal. There can be discrepancies, and those discrepancies can sometimes compound over time.

■ *Leverage is a double-edged sword.* Needless to say, leverage can work against you just as well as it works for you. Yes, it multiplies your profits when the market is moving in your favor, but it also multiplies your losses when the market is moving against you.

During a major stock market recovery, you can use the power of ETFs to go for substantial profits from the rise. But right now, my primary concern is to help you get the protection you may urgently need against bad times.

Protection against Stock Market Declines

Let's say a major market sector you're invested in falls 40 percent. But instead of losing 40 percent of your money, you bag a profit of 80 percent?

A fantasy? Not at all! There are now many ETFs designed to go *up* when the stock index they're tied to goes down. You don't sell short, use futures, or buy options. You just buy the ETFs like any stock. And with the profits you make in these special ETFs, you can offset some or all of the losses you might incur in vulnerable assets you may be holding. They're called *inverse ETFs*.

Let me make this point clear: Inverse ETFs are not merely designed to make money *despite* a market decline. They're designed to make money *because* of a market decline. The goal: The more the market falls, the more money you make.

Plus, they offer you the same advantages of standard ETFs that I discussed earlier. You can buy inverse ETFs on the overall market or individual sectors; the U.S. stock market or foreign stock markets; stocks or bonds; with leverage or without leverage. And you can buy them just like any other ETF–through your same broker, with the same low commissions and the same flexibility as ordinary ETFs. For example:

- If you have a lot of technology stocks, you could protect yourself with the ETF tied inversely to the Dow Jones U.S. Technology Index (symbol REW).
- If you have a lot of small caps, you could protect yourself with the ETF tied inversely to the S&P SmallCap 600 Index (SBB).
- If you have a broadly diversified domestic portfolio, you could use DOG or DXD, which move inversely to the Dow Jones Industrial Average. Or you could buy SH, SDS, or RSW, which move inversely to the S&P 500 Index.
- If you're exposed to emerging markets, you could use EUM or EEV, which are tied inversely to the MSCI Index and MSCI Emerging Markets Index, respectively.
- If you are exposed to long-term Treasury bonds and want to defend yourself against a decline in their market value, you could use PST or TBT, tied inversely to the daily performance of the 7- or 10-Year Treasury note and Treasury bond, respectively.

These are just a few examples. Many more are available. (See Table 11.1 on pages 170–172.)

Protection against Real Estate Declines

Consider this situation: Real estate continues to sink. Everyone you know who owns properties suffers major losses. But you double your money.

Again, this is not a pipe dream. It can be done with inverse ETFs tied to the real estate sector.

No, you cannot use ETFs to hedge directly against your properties. Unlike hedging against a stock or bond portfolio, there are no direct hedges you can buy for real estate. This means that, depending on the investments you select and how well you time their purchase or sale, there's a chance you could lose money in your real estate *and* lose money in your hedges. Despite this risk, however, it may still make sense for you, especially if you hedge in moderation.

One of the most convenient vehicles for hedging or profiting from real estate declines is an ETF that's tied inversely to the Dow Jones U.S. Real Estate Index.

Like many exchange-traded funds, this one focuses on a particular sector of the stock market–in this case, real estate–related companies such as real estate investment trusts (REITs).

And like other inverse ETFs, it is designed to go *up* in value when real estate stocks go *down* in value. Moreover, this ETF does so on a 2-for-1 basis. As an illustration, if the Dow Jones U.S. Real Estate Index goes down 10 percent, you stand to make 20 percent. If the index goes down 20 percent, you could make 40 percent, and so on. Its name: UltraShort Real Estate ProShares (symbol SRS).

An alternative is an inverse ETF tied to the Dow Jones U.S. Financials Index, which consists of bank and other financial stocks. Since the real estate sector is linked to the fate of banks, mortgage lenders, and other financial companies, this inverse ETF may be an approximate fit. It is also double leveraged, designed to rise 20 percent for every 10 percent decline. Its name: UltraShort Financials ProShares (SKF).

If you have the cash funds to spare, a more advanced approach is to diversify with multiple inverse ETFs. Although they may have no direct correlation to real estate, some of the same forces that can drive down home prices, such as a falling economy and scarce credit, can also hurt stocks. Overall, in a recession or depression, both should go down. If you are profiting from the decline in stocks generally, that can help offset the declining value of your real estate properties.

HOW TO BUILD YOUR PERSONAL HEDGE PROGRAM

Hedging is essential to protect you against risk in a declining market. But it is equally important to discontinue your hedge program when the market is ready to recover. If you hold your hedges indefinitely, they can work against you. See Chapter 14 for some telltale signs of a market bottom. Watch for my regular e-mail updates. And most important, make sure you sign up at www.weisswatchdog.com so that we can alert you whenever the rating of one of your banks, insurers, mutual funds, ETFs, or stocks changes. Here are the steps to follow:

Step 1. Determine how much money you want to set aside for portfolio protection. To help you think that through, let me first show you what the different possibilities are, and then I'll tell you which ones I prefer.

Possibility A. Let's say you have a $100,000 stock or mutual fund portfolio that is broadly diversified and approximately matches the performance of the S&P 500. And let's say you want to protect the entire amount using an inverse ETF that's single-leveraged—designed to go up 10 percent for every 10 percent decline in the S&P 500.

Problem: That could be very costly. For every dollar in your portfolio, you'd have to invest another dollar in the inverse ETF. And to do that, you'd have to come up with another $100,000 from some other source to throw into the game. If you were in Las Vegas, that would be tantamount to betting $100,000 on the red and then finding another $100,000 to bet on the black. You may think you can't lose. But the reality is, you can't win either; you're incurring costs or commissions; and, in the unlikely event of a double-zero scenario, you could wind up losing on both the red and the black.

Possibility B. Instead of full protection, why not settle for half protection? In other words, for every $1 of current value in your portfolio, you'd put up only 50 cents of your money into the inverse ETFs. Assuming a stock portfolio worth $100,000, that would mean investing another $50,000.

Possibility C. Use an inverse ETF that gives you double leverage. Now, to protect half of your $100,000 portfolio, all you'd need to invest is $25,000. Assuming your portfolio falls 10 percent in value, here's what you'd have:

Hedging Only HALF Your Portfolio with Double Leverage		
	Your Stock Portfolio	Your Hedge Portfolio
Before 10% Market Decline	$100,000	$25,000
After 10% Market Decline	$ 90,000	$30,000
Loss/Gain	−$ 10,000	$ 5,000

End result: A $10,000 loss in your stock portfolio, a $5,000 gain in your hedge portfolio, and a $5,000 loss overall. That cuts your risk of loss in half. Not bad. But you ask: Can't we do better than that? The answer: Absolutely, as you'll see with the next steps.

Step 2. Rather than invest new money in the inverse ETFs, raise that money by liquidating one third of your stocks. Then, here's what you should wind up with:

SELLING ⅓ of Your Stocks: THEN Hedging with Double Leverage		
	Your Stock Portfolio	Your Hedge Portfolio
Before 10% Market Decline	$66,667	$33,333
After 10% Market Decline	$60,000	$40,000
Loss/Gain	−$ 6,667	$ 6,667

(Continued)

You'll have $66,667 left in your portfolio, and $33,333 available to invest in an inverse ETF with double leverage. If the market falls 10 percent, you'll have about a $6,667 loss in your portfolio and about a $6,667 gain in your inverse ETF.

End result: No loss (except for commissions and costs). This simple step brings you two advantages: First, you won't have to dig into your cash assets to fund your hedge strategy. And second, you'll get *close* to full protection for the balance of your portfolio.

This is my favorite approach. You could stop there and you'd have achieved your goal of risk protection. But if you want to apply some additional intelligence (with some additional risk), you could do even better by following some advanced steps.

Step 3. (advanced). Instead of liquidating one-third of your stocks across the board, strictly get rid of the ones that are in the *riskiest* sectors. In my regular e-mails that I send from www.MoneyandMarkets.com, I give you indications of which sectors I feel are the most vulnerable. But no one can know that with precision all the time. So let's assume we're only half right and we get the following results:

■ Overall market: down 10 percent

■ Weakest sectors: down 20 percent

■ Strongest sectors: down 5 percent

In this scenario, we're half right in the sense that the strongest sectors outperform. But we're also half wrong because, instead of rising as we expected, they still go down, although not as sharply. I think that's a reasonable expectation. But even in this situation, you wind up a winner:

SELECTIVELY Selling ⅓ of Your Stocks: Then Hedging with Double Leverage		
	Your Stock Portfolio	Your Hedge Portfolio
Before 10% Market Decline	$66,667	$33,333
After 10% Market Decline	$63,334	$40,000
Loss/Gain	−$ 3,333	$ 6,667

Since your portfolio is in the stronger (or less weak) sectors, your loss is reduced from 10 percent to 5 percent, or only $3,333. Meanwhile, you're still gaining 10 percent on your hedges, or $6,667. End result: Despite the market's overall decline of 10 percent, you actually come out ahead.

Step 4. (more advanced). Assume the same scenario as the previous example. And assume the same steps to liquidate the riskiest sectors while holding the strongest.

But, in addition, instead of strictly using an inverse ETF that matches the S&P 500, use inverse ETFs that are designed to make you money when specific sectors are going down, targeting those that we believe to be the weakest. Again, there's no guarantee that we're going to be right. But, assuming we're halfway right (as in Step 3), here's how it would turn out:

You'd still have a $3,333 loss in your stock portfolio. But, on the other side of your portfolio—the inverse ETFs—the bad sectors fall 20 percent. So your double-leveraged ETFs give you a gain of 40 percent, or $13,333 (minus commissions and costs, of course). Your net gain overall: $10,000. End result: You've just turned what could have been a $10,000 loss in your portfolio into a $10,000 gain instead. That's what I call turning lemons into lemonade.

Selective Sell ⅓ of Stocks and Selectively Hedge		
	Your Stock Portfolio	Your Hedge Portfolio
Before 10% Market Decline After 10% Market Decline	$66,667 $63,333	$33,333 $40,000
Loss/Gain	−$ 3,333	$13,333

Step 5. (for Treasury bond investors). If you have a heavy load of long-term bonds in your portfolio, a risk that you may face at various stages of a global financial crisis is the risk that interest rates will rise sharply, driving the market price of your bonds sharply lower. To hedge against this risk, consider using UltraShort Lehman 20+ Year Treasury ProShares (TBT), designed to rise 20 percent with each 10 percent decline

(Continued)

in the daily performance of the corresponding Treasury bond. (Although Lehman Brothers is bankrupt, that does not have any impact on this fund, which is based on an index Lehman created and which is run by an unrelated company.)

Your Next Steps

Fortunately, all of the ETFs you'll need for this program are now available for purchase. And to help you find the ones that best match your portfolio, I have compiled a complete and current listing for you in Table 11.1.

Table 11.1   Inverse ETFs Available for Your Protection in Down Markets

Index or Sector You Want to Hedge Against	Inverse ETF You Can Use	Leverage	Symbol
Dow Jones AIG Commodity Index	ProShares UltraShort DJ-AIG Commodity	Double	CMD
Dow Jones Industrial Average SM	Short Dow30	Single	DOG
Dow Jones Industrial Average SM	UltraShort Dow30	Double	DXD
Dow Jones U.S. Basic Materials SM Index	UltraShort Basic Materials	Double	SMN
Dow Jones U.S. Consumer Goods SM Index	UltraShort Consumer Goods	Double	SZK
Dow Jones U.S. Consumer Services SM Index	UltraShort Consumer Services	Double	SCC
Dow Jones U.S. Financials Index	Short Financials Proshares	Single	SEF
Dow Jones U.S. Financials SM Index	UltraShort Financials	Double	SKF
Dow Jones U.S. Health Care SM Index	UltraShort Health Care	Double	RXD
Dow Jones U.S. Industrials	UltraShort Industrials	Double	SIJ
Dow Jones U.S. Oil & Gas Index	UltraShort Oil & Gas Proshares	Single	DDG
Dow Jones U.S. Oil & Gas SM Index	UltraShort Oil & Gas	Double	DUG
Dow Jones U.S. Real Estate Index	UltraShort Real Estate	Double	SRS

Table 11.1 (Continued)

Index or Sector You Want to Hedge Against	Inverse ETF You Can Use	Leverage	Symbol
Dow Jones U.S. Select Telecommunications Index	UltraShort Telecommunications	Double	TLL
Dow Jones U.S. Semiconductors Index	UltraShort Semiconductors	Double	SSG
Dow Jones U.S. Technology SM Index	UltraShort Technology	Double	REW
Dow Jones U.S. Utilities SM Index	UltraShort Utilities	Double	SDP
FTSE/Xinhua China 25 Index	UltraShort FTSE/Xinhua China 25	Double	FXP
Lehman Brothers 20+ Year U.S. Treasury Index	UltraShort Lehman 20+ Year Treasury	Double	TBT
Lehman Brothers 7–10 Year U.S. Treasury Index	UltraShort Lehman 7–10 Year Treasury	Double	PST
MSCI EAFE Index	UltraShort MSCI EAFE	Double	EFU
MSCI EAFE Index	Short MSCI EAFE	Single	EFZ
MSCI Emerging Markets Index	UltraShort MSCI Emerging Markets	Double	EEV
MSCI Emerging Markets Index	Short MSCI Emerging Markets	Single	EUM
MSCI Japan Index	UltraShort MSCI Japan	Double	EWV
NASDAQ-100 Index	Short QQQ	Single	PSQ
NASDAQ-100 Index	UltraShort QQQ	Double	QID
Russell 1000 Energy Index	Direxionshares Energy Bear 3X Shares	Triple	ERY
Russell 1000 Financial Services Index	Direxionshares Financial Bear 3X Shares	Triple	FAZ
Russell 1000 Growth Index	UltraShort Russell1000 Growth	Double	SFK
Russell 1000 Index	Direxionshares Large Cap Bear 3X Shares	Triple	BGZ
Russell 1000 Value Index	UltraShort Russell1000 Value	Double	SJF
Russell 2000 Growth Index	UltraShort Russell2000 Growth	Double	SKK

(Continued)

Table 11.1 (Continued)

Index or Sector You Want to Hedge Against	Inverse ETF You Can Use	Leverage	Symbol
Russell 2000 Index	Direxionshares Small Cap Bear 3X Shares	Triple	TZA
Russell 2000 Index	Rydex Inverse 2x Russell 2000 ETF	Double	RRZ
Russell 2000 Index	Short Russell2000	Single	RWM
Russell 2000 Index	UltraShort Russell2000	Double	TWM
Russell 2000 Value Index	UltraShort Russell2000 Value	Double	SJH
Russell MidCap Growth Index	UltraShort Russell MidCap Growth	Double	SDK
Russell MidCap Value Index	UltraShort Russell MidCap Value	Double	SJL
S&P 500 Energy Select Sector Index	Rydex Inverse 2x S&P Select Sector Energy ETF	Double	REC
S&P 500 Financial Select Sector Index	Rydex Inverse 2x S&P Select Sector Financial ETF	Double	RFN
S&P 500 Health Care Select Sector Index	Rydex Inverse 2x S&P Select Sector Health Care ETF	Double	RHO
S&P 500 Index	Rydex Inverse 2x S&P 500 ETF	Double	RSW
S&P 500 Index	UltraShort S&P500	Double	SDS
S&P 500 Index	Short S&P500	Single	SH
S&P MidCap 400 Index	Short MidCap400	Single	MYY
S&P MidCap 400 Index	UltraShort MidCap400	Double	MZZ
S&P MidCap 400 Index	Rydex Inverse 2x S&P MidCap 400 ETF	Double	RMS
S&P SmallCap 600 Index	UltraShort SmallCap600	Double	SDD
S&P SmallCap 600 Index	Short SmallCap600	Single	SBB
S&P Technology Select Sector Index	Rydex Inverse 2x S&P Select Sector Technology ETF	Double	RTW

Step 6. Refer to the Table 11.1. The indexes are listed in alphabetical order. So find the indexes or sectors that you would like to hedge against, based on the instructions I gave earlier. Then, in the next column, find the names of the inverse ETFs that match those indexes.

Step 7. In the Leverage column, please note that most are double-leveraged inverse ETFs, which is what we recommend for this strategy. But some single-leveraged inverse ETFs are also available. We also list triple leverage ETFs. But as of this publication, these are very new and not yet recommended for this hedge strategy. (For our current views on ETFs, see our updated commentary at www .moneyandmarkets.com/hedge).

Most important, be sure to act swiftly—and deliberately—before you suffer further damage to your portfolio.

Hedging against Real Estate Declines: A Possible Scenario

You should not expect inverse ETFs to defray more than a portion of the potential losses in your real estate properties. As an illustration, consider this hypothetical scenario:

- Your real estate properties are valued at $1 million.

- To help defray a possible loss, you invest $200,000 in SRS, the inverse ETF that's designed to rise 20 percent for every 10 percent decline in real estate–related stocks.

- Your real estate falls 20 percent in value, implying a $200,000 loss.

- But real estate stocks, which are more volatile, fall 30 percent. And since your inverse ETF is designed to go up 20 percent for each 10 percent decline in the real estate stocks, you have a profit of 60 percent, or $120,000.

- You have reduced your total loss from $200,000 to $80,000.

12

HOW TO PROFIT DIRECTLY FROM A MARKET DECLINE

Most people don't think about profiting directly from a market decline. They don't understand the concept, and they don't know how. That's a shame, because one of the key things you need to help get you through tough times is money. And in bad times, to acquire that money, sometimes the best defense is to go on the offense.

Others don't consider this opportunity because they think there's something sinister about making good money in bad times. The fact is that the more people who can build wealth, the better it will be for everyone.

In the 1930s, only a very small handful of investors turned the tables on Wall Street and actually transformed the three-year market decline into a profit opportunity. Bernard Baruch, an adviser to several American presidents, was one of them; Dad was another. Initially, the two men didn't know each other. Yet their approach to the market was similar. Here's how Dad described his experiences:

> I had gone to work on Wall Street as a typist at the age of 16. I knew very little about the stock market then. But I found it so exciting that I went back in 1929 as a customer's man (stock

broker). I traded some stocks for myself and a few clients. When the crash hit, I was as surprised as everyone else by the utter fury of the decline. But my portfolio was clean. Neither I nor any of my clients had one share of stock.

My good fortune was due to a combination of poverty and a healthy dose of skepticism. I saw the devastation in the farms. I saw how Florida real estate had gotten killed. I saw commodities falling. Yet, all around me, investors were going wild over stocks.

If people bought stocks with their own money, it might have been okay. But they were doing it on margin, with broker loans. These loans, which normally totaled around a half a billion or a billion dollars, surged to $8 billion in 1929. That was huge in those days! The entire gross national product was only a bit over $100 billion.

The rest of the world—and the rest of the country—was sinking. Why should Wall Street be any different? I couldn't understand the discrepancy. I wasn't about to risk my family's meager savings on something as uncertain as a surging stock market. Looking back, I can see that escaping the crash was a landmark event in my life. Had I been caught with some shares, no matter how few, I might have abandoned investments in disgust. Instead, I stuck around.

I met George Kato, a Japanese analyst who was in the United States for a few years and was in close touch with the most astute speculators of the day. Kato was like a big brother. He spent months teaching me his technical trading methods, about how to sell short, how much and when.

He showed me that selling short isn't difficult or complex. Instead of buying low and then selling high, you just reverse the transaction. You borrow the stock and sell it. Then, you wait for it to go down and buy it back at lower prices. The more it falls, the bigger your profits. This fascinated me. I wanted to learn more.

I soon discovered that some officials blamed short-sellers for the market declines. But that was pure hogwash! The stock market fell because the bubble was bursting. Moreover, short-sellers played a vital, constructive role in the market: Sooner or later, they would have to buy back the shares they borrowed, and that buying was the starter engine without which a market recovery would be very tough to get going.

Kato also introduced me to the trading strategies of other great traders—men like Jesse Livermore, who built up a fortune trading the market, and Bernard Baruch, who was also making money in the market's decline.

Baruch was a quintessential contrarian. He recommended watching the crowd and then doing exactly the opposite. If good news about the stock market shows up on the front page of the paper, sell. That was my approach as well.

I shared this new knowledge with my older brother, Al, who helped me throughout my career. We learned everything we could about selling short. So when the market rallied from November 1929 into early 1930, we were ready.

With this rally, almost everyone on Wall Street thought we were in a "new bull market." But I was skeptical. The volume just wasn't there. Deflation was spreading from commodities and real estate to other assets. The situation at the banks was getting worse by the day. The economy was sinking. The European markets had not recovered very much, and England was especially weak. When I saw nearly everyone turning bullish again, I just shook my head. I shorted every stock I could lay my hands on that had anything to do with England.

President Hoover tried to rally businessmen and failed to do so. Still, no one on Wall Street was paying much attention to the sinking business picture. They said the 1929 crash had been a "temporary lapse." They believed Hoover. I didn't. I borrowed $500 from my mother and started to go short the stock market—100 shares, 200, 300, building it up slowly at first.

To me, $500 was a lot of money. I grew up in a poor and tough immigrant neighborhood on the Upper East Side of Manhattan. I'd worked two jobs to help support my parents and family ever since I was a teenager. But I was confident because of my indicators.

The main indicator I watched was the Federal Reserve's figures on the broker loans of the large New York banks that issued their data weekly. I noticed that, instead of broker loans going up, as they normally would in a recovery, they were going down. This tipped me off that the banks were liquidating stocks. I figured the banks represented the smart money in those days, so I followed them. They didn't have any faith in stocks, so neither did I. As long as they sold, I sold. When they stopped selling, I stopped selling. The other brokers and analysts at the office laughed at me. They thought I was crazy to sell stocks short. But that only made me more confident.

My other benchmark was foreign currencies, especially the British pound. Britain was still the financial capital of the world. So when the pound fell, it had a direct impact. My brother and I charted the pound daily, and as soon as it broke a key low, we sold short more stocks that were closely tied to the pound's fate.

By the time the crash was nearing bottom, I had transformed my mother's $500 into six figures. She was overjoyed, and so was I.

But not every trade was a success. Each time the market surged, I lost money, and whenever my losses began to mount, I sweated bullets. When you use margin and borrowed money, like I did, the losses can pile up just as fast as the profits. At one point, just when I thought the market was going down still further, there was a terrific rally. I lost more than half my profits.

Fortunately, today, you can profit from a market decline *without* selling stocks short, and without risking a penny more than you invest. You can simply use the very same inverse exchange-traded funds (ETFs) I recommended for hedging purposes in the previous chapter.

You have the opportunity to earn greater fortunes in a bear market than most people made in the great tech boom of the 1990s or in the housing boom of the 2000s. You can make that money *before* each major decline, *during* the decline, and *after* the decline. You don't need a special brokerage account or even special expertise. In a moment, I'll show you how. But first, let me summarize what I have learned from Dad's experience:

From an early age, we are taught that *up* is good and *down* is bad. So most people don't like declines. But that kind of bias has no place in investing strategies. Especially in bubbles, busts, recession, or depression, serious investors must learn how to invest in both up *and* down markets.

Bernard Baruch's axiom to never follow the crowd is especially critical. If you follow the crowd, you could end up buying stocks when investors are the most enthusiastic (at the market's top) and selling when they are the most downtrodden (at the bottom). Don't fall into that trap. Even if Wall Street experts or your own friends deride your approach, do not let that stop you from making rational, prudent decisions.

You don't have to be an expert to make money in the market. In fact, sometimes, those who are new to the world of investing can see the big picture more clearly than veterans who have been cocooned on Wall Street.

Whenever the government makes a new announcement to bail out this or that company or to prop up this or that credit market or to announce a new economic stimulus package, you can typically expect bursts of optimism on Wall Street. But that's probably the worst time to buy and the best time to sell. If you see that kind of a rally in the market, consider using it as your window to get out, or to buy contrarian investments like inverse ETFs.

One last point: Do not expect profits all the time. In any kind of investing—in rising *or* falling markets—losses can and do happen.

Large Profit Potential with Inverse ETFs

With inverse ETFs, the potential for profit is quite extraordinary, even if the market is not moving dramatically. For example, between June 5 and July 15, 2008, as tech stocks fell, the inverse ETF that's tied to technology stocks enjoyed a gain of 30.9 percent, while the inverse ETF tied to the semiconductor index rose 37.2 percent. Those are large gains for such a short period of time.

Around the same time frame, stocks in the real estate sector fell even more sharply. Result: a gain of 46.1 percent in the corresponding inverse ETF between May 15 and July 15. And, because of the debt crisis, financial stocks took the biggest beating of all, driving up the inverse ETF in that sector by 106.7 percent in the same period.

As the markets became more volatile in September and October 2008, the potential gains in inverse ETFs were even larger. We saw a 61 percent gain in just 15 days as the technology sector fell between September 25 and October 10; an 89.1 percent gain in just 19 days as the real estate sector dropped between September 26 and October 15; an 89.6 percent gain in 19 days as the consumer services sector plunged between September 26 and October 15; and an 89.9 percent gain in 8 days as the financial sector slumped between October 1 and October 9.

Unfortunately, we can't go back in time to grab those profits. Nor is it possible to catch the tops and bottoms of each major move. But it's crucial to understand two things: First, unlike short-selling on margin, which exposed Dad to much higher risk, in each case I just cited, your risk in inverse ETFs is strictly limited to what you invest—not a penny more. And second, these kinds of gains can go a long way toward helping you through an economic crisis.

Just bear in mind that the market does not go down in a straight line; there are always going to be rallies, and sometimes they could be quite sudden. When that happens, the inverse ETFs *fall* in value. Like any other investment, the goal is to buy them low and sell them high. If you wind up doing the opposite, you will suffer losses.

If you cannot afford any losses, this strategy is not for you. But if you have risk capital and you can set aside a modest portion for an aggressive strategy in falling markets, follow these steps.

HOW TO GO FOR PROFITS IN A DOWN MARKET

Step 1. Review this chapter to make sure you understand the ins and outs of inverse ETFs.

Step 2. Recognize that you *can* lose money in inverse ETFs. So, for this strategy, allocate strictly the funds you can afford to risk.

Step 3. Apply essentially the same tried-and-tested discipline for investing in a bull market, but in reverse.

- In a bull market, astute traders seek to buy on dips and sell on rallies. When using inverse ETFs in a bear market, do the opposite: Buy the inverse ETFs on a stock market bounce; sell them after major stock market declines.

- In a bull market, astute traders wait for temporary bouts of bad news to help drive prices down and

(Continued)

give them a bargain-buying opportunity. They know that as long as there are solid signs that the economy will continue growing, the stock market can climb *a wall of worry*. When using inverse ETFs in a bear market, do precisely the opposite: Wait for good news to help drive prices up. Then, buy the inverse ETFs in anticipation of another decline. As long as it's clear that the economy will continue to contract, the stock market is likely to slide down *a slippery slope of hope*.

Step 4. Recognize that fundamental indicators that make sense in a bull market may not be appropriate for a bear market. For example,

- In normal times, the cheaper the stock in relation to its earnings, the more attractive it is. But in a depression, many companies have no earnings, rendering useless any measures of value based on earnings.

- Normally, the company's book value (assets minus liabilities) is another good measure. In a depression, however, as asset values fall and large debts are still outstanding, the book value is less than zero.

- How does one distinguish companies that are deep in the red from those that are *deeper* in the red? Not easily!

Step 5. Diversify among several stock market sectors while also using *inverse* ETFs that represent the most diverse basket of stocks. Examples of the most diversified ETFs include those with the symbols DOG or DXD, which move inversely to the Dow Jones Industrial Average; and SH, SDS, or RSW, which move inversely to the S&P 500 Index.

For more detailed instructions, visit www.MoneyandMarkets .com/Bear.

HOW TO *CONTINUE* MAKING MONEY EVEN WITH THE WORST DISASTERS

In the last chapter, I showed you how to make money by betting against the market.

Now, I want to show you how to escape the stock market entirely; shift to another investment world that's far removed from stocks; and make money regardless of bubbles or busts, inflation or deflation, prosperity or depression.

One of the few places that's possible: In the vast global market for world currencies.

The stock market may be crashing, and it would not interfere with your ability to make money in the currency market. The U.S. economy may be mired in depression and it would *still* not interfere with your ability to make money. No matter what happens in the global economy or the world's financial markets, there are always continuing profit opportunities in currencies.

I don't recommend currencies for all of your money or to all investors. But at a time when nearly all other investments are going down or yielding very little, it's a good alternative—to get away from the disasters and find a separate world of investment opportunity.

In the past, this market was beyond the reach of average investors. To invest in currencies, you had to be rich, take huge risks, or both. You typically had to open special accounts, watch the markets 24/7, and immerse yourself entirely in international finance.

Today, that's no longer the case. Thanks to new, revolutionary investment vehicles I tell you about in this chapter, you can invest in foreign currencies just as easily as you can buy traditional investments.

The advantages of currencies are many.

You Never Touch a Single Stock or Bond

You do not invest in shares of companies. Your investment does not hinge on factors like the ups and downs of a company's earnings, or the vagaries of a particular CEO. Nor do you own bonds, mortgages, or other debts that can go sour. So there's no issue with missed corporate earnings, company losses, bond defaults, or similar disasters that can drive most traditional investment vehicles into the gutter.

Just consider how many stocks have gotten killed because of poor earnings, and you'll understand how much of a relief this can be.

Even before the 2008 debt crisis, for example, United Healthcare Group missed earnings estimates by a meager 3.6 percent, and its stock promptly plunged by 32 percent. Washington Mutual missed its earnings estimates twice, and its stock plunged 70 percent. Hundreds of others met a similar fate. This is true in good times; it's even more so in bad times. In contrast, when you invest in currencies, those events rarely have an impact on your investment.

You Benefit from Unrivaled Liquidity

In bubbles, busts, recession, and depression, stock market turmoil is to be expected; and trading in many stocks—including some blue chips—can be subject to serious disruptions:

- The stocks may be hard to sell because of thin trading volume and few buyers.
- The exchange may stop all trading in the shares of companies in trouble or on the verge of a major announcement.
- Under extreme circumstances, the entire stock exchange can be shut down, potentially locking investors into serious losses.

Thanks to the high volume of trading with global participation by thousands of large institutions, these disruptions are extremely rare in currencies; the average trading volume in the global currency market is estimated at *$3 trillion dollars per day,* many times more than the volume traded on all the stock exchanges in the world combined.

Moreover, in stock markets, that trading volume is divided among thousands of individual stock issues, greatly reducing the volume of trading in each issue. And for small- or mid-cap stocks, the volume can be especially thin.

In the currency market, we see precisely the opposite: Approximately four-fifths of the trading volume is concentrated in just six major foreign currencies that trade against the U.S. dollar:

1. The euro
2. The British pound
3. The Swiss franc
4. The Japanese yen
5. The Canadian dollar
6. The Australian dollar

This means that there is vast liquidity in *each* major currency—a feature that's important to you for several reasons:

- The large volume of trading makes it extremely difficult for any individual or institution to manipulate the market.

- Prices are based on actual, *current* trading, making it very hard for a broker to give you a bad price.
- Most important, you will rarely get trapped in a position because of a lack of buyers—or get left out of a major move because of a lack of sellers.

With stocks, you typically can get into the investment easily enough. You put your order in, and, as long as you're willing to pay up for it, you can buy the shares. But later, to get *out* of the stock could be another story entirely.

The plight of investors in Bear Stearns shares in March of 2008 is a case in point. One day the closing price was $30. The next trading day, after the authorities made some emergency decisions behind the scenes, it was suddenly worth only $2, with more than 90 percent of investor money vanishing into thin air. This has never happened—and probably never *will* happen—in the major currencies.

Currencies Are an Entirely Separate Asset Class

Currencies give you an opportunity for diversification beyond traditional asset classes like real estate, stocks, and bonds. Plus, they give you the opportunity to *continue* making money during the most intense financial storms.

Example: Even following the 9/11 terrorist attacks, when the U.S. stock and bond markets were shut down for a full week, the currency market did *not* shut down, continuing to trade around the clock as usual.

There's Always at Least One Major Currency Going Up

Currencies always trade against each other in pairs: the dollar versus the euro, the euro versus the British pound, and so on. When one currency in the pair is going up, the other is going down, like a seesaw. Therefore, *by definition,* there must always be at least one currency that's rising in value.

For investors who feel more comfortable investing in something that's going up, the implication is that there's almost always a bull market in currencies. But you should feel equally comfortable investing in a currency that's going down, and the vehicles available make that possible.

Currencies Tend to Move in Long-Term, Sweeping Trends

Currencies are not normally affected by the vagaries of individual stocks or industries and are usually driven by far broader, economic factors like interest rates or economic growth. Since these factors generally do not shift in direction often or abruptly, currencies can stay in a single, long-term trend for many months and even years.

Naturally, as in any market, currencies don't go straight up or down; there will also be intermediate corrections or rallies. But as a rule, the trends in currencies tend to be more consistent and longer term, making it easier for investors to plan and profit.

Inflation versus Deflation in the Currency Market

As a rule, inflation is usually bad for the dollar and good for the dollar exchange rate of most foreign currencies. When the price of goods and services goes up, the value of each dollar in your pocket goes down. That's why, during the many years of U.S. economic expansion and inflation, the dollar's value usually declined, while the value of foreign currencies generally rose.

Conversely, deflation is typically good for the dollar and bad for the dollar exchange rate of most currencies. When the price of investments or goods and services falls, the value of each dollar rises.

Most people assume that if the U.S. economy is in trouble, the U.S. dollar must suffer as well. But that's not how it works. The currency market is a *relative* game; the dollar is always measured against other currencies.

So the relevant question is not "How well is the U.S. economy doing?" Rather, it's "How is the U.S. economy doing *compared* to the economy of the eurozone, the United Kingdom, Australia, or other major nations?"

In a global depression, the strongest currency will be associated with the country that can win the "least ugly" contest. No matter how ugly things get in the United States, if the situation is uglier abroad, the United States will win the contest and the U.S. dollar will tend to be stronger.

In 2008, for example:

■ Europe's banks had lent more than $2.7 trillion to high-risk emerging markets, such as Hungary, Ukraine, and Russia, all three of which risked collapse in the wake of a global depression.

■ Great Britain, Ireland, and Spain were mired in housing busts that were even more extreme than the housing bust in the United States.

■ Australia and Canada were highly dependent on commodities that had collapsed in value.

■ Brazil, Russia, India, and China were slammed by deflation, sinking global trade and vanishing credit.

Consequently, all their currencies fell against the dollar. The one outstanding exception: The Japanese yen, which was a major source of cheap funding and loans for international investors during the inflationary years. As those investors dumped their investments, they naturally had to pay back their Japanese yen loans, forcing them to buy yen and drive up its value.

But the dollar rose against the euro, the British pound, the Swiss franc, the Australian dollar, and the Canadian dollar. It surged against the Brazilian real, the Russian ruble, and nearly every other currency on the planet.

Typically, in a recession or depression, as long as commodity and consumer prices are falling, this trend is likely to repeat itself: A temporarily stronger dollar! But as long as the U.S. Federal Reserve continues to lead the world in printing paper money, the dollar is likely to *decline* in value.

The Most Convenient Vehicle: Currency ETFs

These are exchange-traded funds, offering the same advantages as the other ETFs described in previous chapters.

There are currency ETFs available to bet on the rise of each of the major foreign currencies—the euro, the British pound, the Swiss franc, the Japanese yen, the Canadian dollar and the Australian dollar. Plus, there are inverse currency ETFs available to bet on the *decline* of key currencies.

With these inverse currency ETFs, the more those currencies fall, the more money you can make. Plus, you can do it with two-for-one leverage. In the euro, for example, if the currency falls 10 percent, you stand to make 20 percent. Or, if the euro falls 20 percent, you can make 40 percent.

As with other ETFs, you can buy as little as one share of each, implying virtually no investment minimum. Or, with just $1,000, you could buy a whole range of different ETFs across several different currencies. Remember: You do have to pay a broker commission. But if you use a discount or online broker, your commission costs can be slashed to the bone.

Currency ETFs are readily available to anyone with a regular stock brokerage account. You buy and sell them just like a stock or any other ETF. You don't need any new accounts. They're extremely liquid. You just aim to buy them low and sell them high, like any other investment. (See page 188 for additional instructions.)

Bottom line: If your goal is to take no risk whatsoever and keep all your money 100 percent safe, then investing in currency ETFs would be a mistake. There is always risk of loss. But if you're looking for continuing investment opportunities even during a recession or depression, then not exploring this opportunity could be a mistake.

How to Invest in Foreign Currencies

Step 1. Recognize that, regardless of the instrument you use, foreign currencies are not low-risk investments. They are not for all investors and not for all of your money. Therefore, strictly allocate the funds you can afford to risk.

Step 2. To trade currencies, focus on currency ETFs, available through any stock brokerage account. These are issued by Rydex Funds, PowerShares, and others.

Step 3. During periods dominated by fear, risk, or deflation, such as witnessed in 2008, concentrate on betting on a rising dollar. Use primarily the PowerShares DB US Dollar Index Bullish Fund (UUP), and if you can take additional risk, also consider ProShares UltraShort Euro (EUO).

Step 4. During periods dominated by greed, confidence, or inflation, concentrate on betting on a falling dollar. Use primarily PowerShares DB US Dollar Index Bearish Fund (UDN), and also consider diversifying with ETFs such as CurrencyShares Japanese Yen Trust (FXY), CurrencyShares Swiss Franc Trust (FXF), and CurrencyShares Australian Dollar Trust (FXA).

Step 5. If you are a more aggressive investor seeking larger and quicker returns, look into World Currency Options traded on the Philadelphia Exchange (recently purchased by the Nasdaq). These options are securities structured like standard stock options and are available through any stock brokerage account that's approved for options trading.

Step 6. For more educational information on currency trading, visit www.moneyandmarkets.com/currencies.

CHAPTER 14

WHEN TO BUY THE BEST BARGAINS OF THE CENTURY

In the wake of a major bust, recession, or depression, the most important event will come when we finally hit rock bottom—your opportunity to build the kind of wealth that endures for generations.

Imagine buying a company like General Electric for what Thomas Edison's company cost soon after he invented the light bulb; or a stock like Microsoft for a few dollars per share; or the most solid, highest-paying dividend stock for as little as a third of its book value!

At the bottom of the next major decline, bargain opportunities like these will be so plentiful, your greatest challenge will be to refrain from buying too many too soon. But don't fret. It will not be a one-day event. So you won't have to rush out and do all your buying at once. Different stocks, sectors, markets, regions, and countries will hit bottom at different times, some earlier than the Dow, others not until weeks or months later.

One reason stocks will be so cheap is because the decline in corporate earnings is so deep; and most investors will see that clearly. What they will *not* see is that their own irrational fears and outright panic are part of the reason share prices fall so sharply, usually far *below* their true value.

That alone multiplies your opportunity: You can profit from a stock rebound that comes with the return of investor confidence, and you can profit *still more* with an actual recovery in earnings.

So even if you get nothing else out of this book, an enhanced ability to recognize the bottom, when it comes, could make the entire time you've spent with me well worth your while.

Remember: For those who see it coming—or just recognize it midstream—the biggest benefit of a recession or depression is falling prices. By simply waiting for the bottom, you can buy some of the world's most valuable assets for a pittance. That's precisely what my father did near the bottom of the great market decline of the 1930s, as he explains here:

In those days, I was working with my brother Al at the midtown branch of a small brokerage firm. The stock market had been battered to unheard-of lows, but the big spotlight was on banks. People were lining up for their money. Bank failures were spreading like crazy.

In an attempt to quell rumors of a bank holiday, Governor Lehman of New York pledged that he would never close the banks. In state after state, other officials made similar vows. Then, just a few months later, they turned around and did exactly what they said they would never do. One by one, they closed down the banks in their state. Confidence was shaken still further.

My brother and I decided to track the banking crisis more closely. We figured the money must be going somewhere. But where? Soon we discovered the obvious: If people are taking their money out of the banks, it must show up in the currency in circulation. That was one of the statistics tracked weekly by the Federal Reserve. And it was readily available for the asking.

Currency in circulation is the cash you carry in your pockets. But back then, most of it wasn't circulating at all. People were taking their money out of the banks and burying it in their back yards or stashing it under the mattress. It was dead money. Currency in circulation became our number one indicator of the banking crisis. Every Friday morning, we got the figures from the newspaper and plotted them on a graph.

In late 1932, it was climbing at a pretty steady clip. Then, in early 1933, the withdrawals accelerated, and the line on our chart began to rise more rapidly. We sensed that the banking crisis was approaching a climactic finish.

President-elect Roosevelt was to be inaugurated in a few weeks. He would have to do something dramatic to stop the cash hemorrhaging from the banks. As inauguration day approached, my brother and I began to speculate that Roosevelt might declare a national bank holiday. But we wanted more than guesswork—we needed solid data.

So on Thursday afternoon, March 2, 1933, two days before FDR was to be inaugurated, we decided not to wait for the next morning's paper to get the latest from the Fed. Instead, we hopped on the downtown express to the New York Fed's offices on Liberty Street to get the number in person, as soon as it was released.

The only people waiting in line at the Fed were a few messengers from some banks. No one else was interested in the currency in circulation. When we saw the number, we were shocked. It had surged far beyond anything we had imagined. That was Thursday night. Roosevelt's inauguration was going to be Saturday morning. We went home, plotted it on our chart, and boy, were we shocked! It was through the roof.

So we immediately set about to map out our buying strategy, checking the charts, double-checking the fundamentals, picking the stocks. Al said: "This is it! This is the end of the whole stock market decline! Roosevelt is going to have to do something about this. He's going to have to close the banks." I agreed.

Most people might think that a bank holiday—the crest of the worst financial crisis in modern history—would be the harbinger of a further stock market decline and a signal to run for the hills. We felt it was exactly the opposite. We believed that it was the government "capitulation"—the belated recognition by Washington that they had lost the battle against the banking crisis. Plus, it was also the first necessary step toward truly resolving it. We saw it as the climax of the deflation since 1929.

The new president would have no choice but to close the banks, inflate the economy and pump up the stock market. Besides, at these low prices, major blue chips had great value. We had no intention of running for the hills. Our sole purpose was to buy.

The next morning, we went straight to our firm's main offices downtown. We didn't stop at the midtown branch. We wanted to get our orders in to the man who talked directly to the floor traders. We bought everything we could lay our hands on. We bought GM, AT&T, GE, and Sears for pennies on the dollar. The tape barely moved, it was so dead. No more than 350,000 to 400,000 shares of stock were traded that day. That's less volume than what typically trades in just one large transaction in modern times. Some people thought it was the eye before the next storm. We didn't. We just kept right on buying.

The order clerk looked at us as if we were from another world. "How come you guys are buying?" he asked. "You're the only ones!"

We didn't tell him. It was none of his business. By the time the day was out, we had bought thousands of shares of stock for ourselves and for our clients, at bargain basement prices. As a matter of fact, they were just about the lowest they had fallen in the entire century.

The next day, Roosevelt was inaugurated. Immediately, he announced that he was closing not only the banks, but also the financial markets. All the stock exchanges were shut down. There was no trading. Everything was frozen. So if you owned stock, it was impossible to sell. If you didn't own stock, it was impossible to buy.

Investors wondered: "Is this the end?" . . . "Will the markets ever reopen again?" . . . "Is there going to be another crash?" Even at such low levels, people were afraid the market could fall a lot further.

But as we approached the end of the banking holiday, sentiment began to change. Confidence in the banking system recovered. Well-heeled investors made plans to start buying some stocks. When the stock market finally reopened, prices jumped up. There was a big gap between the closing prices before the holiday and the opening prices after the holiday. So it was too late to get in at the best prices. Lucky for us, we got in ahead of time. So we were in great shape. And because we had bought the stocks on margin, our profits were large. Too bad we didn't hold on for many more years. Instead we sold out for a short-term gain.

How to Recognize the Signs of a Bottom in the U.S. Economy and Financial Markets

Before we read too much into Dad's experience, one word of warning: Do not try to find an exact, point-by-point correlation between each of Dad's past experiences and what the future might bring. Instead, my task—and yours—is to step up from the level of specific detail to the higher plane of overarching principles, always careful to make sure we're not overlooking differences in the way things work today and the way they worked then. Here's what I recommend.

First, Look for the Debt Liquidation

In the boom and bust of the late 1920s and early 1930s, the debts to watch were bank loans to brokers and broker loans to investors. Dad tracked these carefully, and once they were mostly off the books, he began to look for a bottom in the market.

This time, the main debts to watch will be mortgages, mortgage-backed securities, and risky derivatives such as instruments called *credit default swaps*. When these are mostly cleaned out or well on their way to being rehabilitated, it may be a time to start looking for a bottom.

As the crisis progresses, I will alert you to the progress of the debt liquidation in my regular e-mails.

Warning: If the government attempts to guarantee an unrealistic, no-loss environment for investors, if they continue to merge weak banks with strong ones, or if they insist upon sweeping bad debts under the rug, it can only delay the needed liquidation. True debt liquidation can rarely occur without bankruptcies and a full accounting for actual losses.

Second, Look for a Major, Enduring Regime of Austerity by the Federal Government

This will be the critical juncture when Washington is forced to give up bailouts, stimulus, and money printing; the day they cut spending, reduce the budget deficit, and impose a regime of collective sacrifice with true, enduring *austerity*.

In Europe, this was the direction that some countries were forced to take in response to the sovereign debt crisis that struck in early 2010. And it's also the direction that the Tea Party movement was seeking as it won a series of victories in the U.S. midterm elections of November 2010.

However, mere talk—and even some initial steps—in the direction of austerity is not the same as an *enduring regime of austerity*. Moreover, politicians and their citizens rarely make the needed sacrifices that true austerity demands as long as they feel they still have other alternatives available. It is only when all of those alternatives are exhausted—and when austerity is clearly perceived by the majority of the population as the lesser of the evils—that we can begin to talk about the beginning of the end to the crisis.

Be on the alert for a sweeping policy change that essentially means the government is *getting out of the bailout business* and focusing its attention on saving its own good credit.

Government officials will probably not announce the change in precisely those words, of course, and there may be an attempt to sugarcoat the change to avoid alarming already-panicked citizens. (If you want to get my e-mail alert on this critical change, sign up at www.moneyandmarkets/alert.)

Third, Look for a Parallel Capitulation by Wall Street Stock Analysts and Bond Rating Agencies

At the peak of the 1990s boom, Wall Street analysts often looked for excuses to ignore tried-and-tested formulas of stock valuation. To justify touting companies that were grossly overvalued, they said the old formulas were no longer valid.

In the future, as we approach a true bottom of the market, they're likely to make the same mistake again, but in reverse. Many will have sold most or all their own stocks. They will be playing the market to profit from the decline or they'll be looking to drive prices lower so they can buy at even cheaper levels. Again, they will say that traditional valuation models are no longer valid—this time to justify panning the shares they used to tout. Stocks that seem undervalued, they'll argue, are really worthless.

At Wall Street's rating agencies, you may see a similar pattern. Instead of just piecemeal downgrades, watch for the day when the rating agencies revise their rating scales or models across the board, with the net effect of downgrading, in one fell swoop, the entire universe of companies or investments they cover.

Fourth, You Should See Similar Signs of Capitulation among People You Meet on a Daily Basis

- Real estate agents, who forever were saying "buy, buy, buy," will warn you to avoid the purchase of houses, condos, and land like the plague.
- You will see a major change in people's perception of prices, especially in the real estate area. At one point, they will still be

saying, "Wow! Everything is so darn cheap, it couldn't possibly get any cheaper. This is *the* best time to buy." But one morning, they will wake up and exclaim: "You know what! We got it all wrong. Nothing is really cheap right now. It's the damn prices they *used* to charge that were so ridiculously expensive. This is obviously the *worst* time to buy."

- Nearly everywhere, you will note a switch from hear-no-evil optimism to apocalyptic pessimism. You'll see respected Wall Street analysts advising investors to avoid stocks like the plague. You'll see the establishment press ask if this is "the death of the American dream." You'll even hear your friends wondering out loud if the world is, indeed, coming to an end.

Don't be swayed! Yes, there are bound to be some events that appear to lend credence to the direst of prophecies. It may indeed *seem* like the end of the world in some ways. But *that's when it will be the time for you to fulfill the promise you made to me in the first pages of this book*—to look beyond the darkness and recognize that you're actually near the *end* of the tunnel.

Fifth, Be on the Lookout for a Watershed Event

No one can define in advance what the watershed event will be. In Dad's time, it was Roosevelt's declaration of a national banking holiday, literally bringing closure to the entire decline. In the future, it could be:

- A change at the helm of the Federal Reserve and a radical shift in monetary policy
- Major reforms in the structure of foreign currency markets
- In an extreme scenario, a temporary shutdown not only of the banking system but also of nonessential production

No matter what, to be a true watershed event, it must make no pretense of rescuing debtors or saving lenders. Any major attempt to do so would merely imply a perpetuation of the bailouts, no end to the needed debt liquidation process, more false bottoms and more false rallies.

And rest assured: I will stay in touch. By e-mail or video chats, I will be there to always remind you of the wealth of resources our country still has. I will show you how, despite the trillions in losses, there is no loss in our immense pool of knowledge and talent. And I will do my best to guide you to the best opportunities.

Do Everything You Can to *Not* Miss This Opportunity

When you reach a bottom in the markets, there will be no scarcity of bargain opportunities. The critical questions will be:

Do you have the cash to buy them? If you're counting on raising the cash *then*–through the sale of other assets or by borrowing the money–you could be very disappointed. There could be virtually no buyers for your assets at a price that would bring you meaningful value. Credit will be practically nonexistent. You must have the cash ahead of time.

BASIC PRINCIPLES FOR BUYING AT THE BOTTOM

Principle 1. The biggest payoff from a major market decline is having the cash to buy real estate, stocks, bonds, gold, and other assets when they've reached a bottom. That, in turn, requires the courage and stamina to take your money out of the market now, put it away, let it sit there, and then pull it out to deploy at the right time to buy true values.

Principle 2. After a historical decline, the best time to buy something is when virtually no one else wants it. Wait until people's emotions are so powerful they forget the original reasons they started selling in the first place. Wait until people are selling just for the sake of selling. Don't trust the public mood in the worst of times any more than you would in the best of times. When everything looks the blackest, it could be the time for a real recovery.

Principle 3. It's a mistake to fly by the seat of your pants. Use a benchmark–an indicator you can rely on. In the 1930s, currency in circulation and the British pound was Dad's most reliable index. In modern times, I recommend tracking a series of crisis indicators that you can find on our web site at www.MoneyandMarkets.com/Indicators.

Which investments should you buy first? Begin with the highest quality across the board. In stocks, that means you won't have to hunt among the small, high-risk companies selling for pennies. The best, most-established blue chips will be cheap enough. In bonds, there will be quite a few high-quality issues to choose from. And in real estate, you'll have your pick of the choice properties in the best locations.

Should you jump at the opportunity to buy everything you can lay your hands on? No. In the first phase of the recovery, you're better off starting slowly and investing prudently.

Since you're confident it's the big bottom, should you hold on no matter what? No. Although you have every reason to believe it's the bottom, suppose you're wrong. Set reasonable risk limits, such as 10 or 20 percent of your investment. Yes, in the early 1930s, my father and uncle happened to pick a time that was close to the exact bottom. But they didn't become aware of that until many years later. At the time, based on the information they had, selling out for a good, medium-term profit was *not* the wrong thing to do. They needed the money for other opportunities. And a few years later, the market did fall again.

Should you stick mostly with the stock market? Not at all. It's quite possible that other asset classes will be the better place to start. In the next chapter, for example, Dad shows you how, if he had only known what he learned later in his career, he probably could have enjoyed far better long-term success by following a steadier path to wealth.

BONDS: YOUR FIRST GREAT INCOME OPPORTUNITY

Crisis breeds opportunity, good comes out of bad, and past mistakes can lead to future break-throughs. This is particularly true in bubbles, busts, recession, and depression. And it may also be true about the most powerful tool at your disposal to boost your income–interest rates.

In recent years, one of the most frequently used–and abused– tools of the Federal Reserve has been to cut interest rates. They cut interest rates to fight the technology bust, the 9/11 aftermath, the housing bust, the mortgage meltdown, the credit crunch, and the debt crisis. They cut interest rates to help avert deflation, debt defaults, and other disasters. Fed Chairman Ben Bernanke even sought to push down interest rates in order to *create* inflation.

This is not just an erudite debate about monetary policy, mind you. Near-zero interest rates are an ongoing threat to every penny you've saved or want to save. At the same time, if their policies backfire and interest rates explode higher, they can be a power-ful force that will give you one of the greatest opportunities of the century to boost your income.

First, let's see what the government has done with interest rates, and the consequences. Then, I'll tell you about the opportunities.

The Interest-Rate Boomerang

In the early 2000s, starting January 3, 2001, the Federal Reserve lowered short-term interest rates 13 times, to 1 percent, and then sat on them at that level for 12 months. In the late 2000s, when the financial crisis struck the globe, the Fed did it again, lowering short-term rates nine times to virtually zero. Then, as we saw in Chapter 2, when it ran out of room to lower short-term interest rates, the Fed targeted long-term interest rates by running the printing presses and buying up bonds in massive quantities.

In essence, their goal was simple: to inject plenty of money into the economic body and to make that money cheap—to ease the pain, make folks happy, and, above all, keep the party going. "Easy money solves everything" seemed to be their mantra. Except for one thing, of course: All of the problems that arise from having *too much* easy money.

Just minor side effects? Far from it! Too much of the money drug flowing through the bloodstream of society can have far-reaching, insidious consequences: It drives people to shop till they drop and borrow till they're suffocating. It kills their natural instinct to save for a rainy day and leaves them stranded in any storm.

It does precisely the same thing to small businesses and large corporations, charities, churches and schools, city governments, state governments, and the federal government itself.

Too much easy money is known to affect child rearing, schooling, career building, retirement, and estate planning. It can corrupt government, politics, sports, marriage, and even sex. Money is not fundamentally evil in the least. But too much, too fast, in the wrong hands, without the corresponding effort, corrodes culture.

Ironically, the folks at the Fed are fully aware that whenever you artificially manipulate or fix prices—of anything—it causes distortions and serious side effects. When the U.S. government set a high, fixed price for corn or wheat, it led to mountains of grain that rotted in the silos. When Iron Curtain countries set a low, fixed price for bread, milk, or butter, it created queues of shoppers so long that line-waiting became a common profession.

Here's the key: The interest rate is the *price of money.* So by controlling interest rates, the Fed is committing the same cardinal economic sin it so frequently disparages: *money price controls.*

If the Fed had just controlled the price of *a few targeted items*–like beans and corn or milk and bread–society could have dealt with the resulting distortions in one way or another. But that's not what they've done. By controlling interest rates, they've manipulated the single element that has the most sweeping impact on everything we buy, make, do, think, and dream: Money! That's far worse than ordinary price controls.

If the Fed had just applied their controls in a manner that was approximately *in sync* with the actual supply and demand for money, it wouldn't have been nearly as bad. The money surpluses would have been less frequent. And society could have probably dealt with them one way or another. But that's also not what they've done. For the past quarter-century, since Fed Chairman Paul Volcker left his post at the Fed in 1987, the Fed has *almost always* erred on the side of pushing interest rates lower! More cheap money!

If the Fed had just applied their controls *temporarily,* the economic, social, and political distortions wouldn't have been as pervasive. But even that level of restraint was not respected. Instead, except for a few brief interludes, the Fed shoved interest rates down, kept them down, shoved them down again, and kept them down some more.

If the Fed had given society *a chance to absorb* the money drug, deal rationally with the mountain of debts, and unravel the horrendous mess they created, then, perhaps, history might someday forgive them. But that's not what they did. As soon as the Fed decision makers realized that all its rate cuts were *still* not enough, they began a new radical policy they called "quantitative easing," pumping in more easy money to buy up government bonds, mortgage bonds, and even corporate paper.

How did all of this affect you? It depends on who you were. If you were a big spender or speculator, it was like money growing on trees and manna from heaven. You found it in your mailbox, stuffed with unsolicited credit cards. You could shake it from your home with click-the-mouse equity loans. Or it just landed in your lap in the form of fat bonus checks.

But if you were a prudent investor, a hardworking saver or simply retired, it was pure hell. Banks charged you to make a deposit, charged you again to withdraw your money, and then charged you for their charges.

By the time you covered all the fees, subtracted inflation, and paid your income taxes, you weren't just getting a low yield on your savings. You were actually *paying* for the privilege of letting *them* use *your* money. Worse, for many, the only escape from this no-income trap was to jump from the frying pan into the fire—high-risk investments that could chop up your principal.

It's obvious that the Fed artificially suppressed and repressed the price of money, pushing it far below its natural level. It should be equally obvious that the ultimate outcome is for the price of money to jump back up.

We've seen the same pattern over and over again: Whenever the government artificially hammers *down* the price of something, that price must ultimately bounce back up to its normal level—or higher.

That's what happened after rationing in World War II, after price controls by Nixon in the late 1960s, and after steel price controls under President Kennedy. It's what happened in Brazil, the Soviet Union, and most recently, in Zimbabwe. Price controls work for a short while. But then, like a pressure cooker, once the lid is popped, prices explode higher.

The same is likely for the price of money—interest rates. Once the lid is off, they could explode higher. That will be the prime opportunity for you to boost your income like never before, locking in some of the best yields of your lifetime.

When? How? Before I give you my answers, I'll let Dad give you his:

> In the early 1930s, I had one of the greatest income opportunities in history. I could have gotten high, juicy, double-digit yields on the best bonds of the strongest companies in America. And I could have locked in those high returns for 20 or 30 years with virtually no inflation. The yields on guaranteed government bonds were not as high, of course. But even there, the income opportunity was unusual. With stocks, I felt it was too risky to hold on for too long. A buy-and-hold approach to bonds, however, would have been just fine. It would give me

a more comfortable, more durable opportunity. Unfortunately, I missed it entirely.

One reason was that I was too focused on finding the bottom in the stock market. Another reason was that I made the mistake of believing the textbook theory on interest rates.

That theory was based almost entirely on the economy and inflation. When we had more growth and inflation, interest rates were supposed to go up. When we had less growth and inflation, interest rates were supposed to go down.

Nobody looked at interest rates as separate and apart from growth or inflation, and neither did I. Boy, was I in for a big surprise! In fact, just as I began to watch rates more carefully, every single thing I had read about interest rates went by the wayside.

Before we continue with Dad's story, I want to make sure you're completely familiar with bond prices and bond yields—why they're like two sides of a seesaw.

Let's say I buy a $1,000 face-value bond issued by Ford Motors, paying a fixed 5 percent. It costs me $1,000. So I earn interest of $50 per year.

Second, let's say Ford loses money hand over fist and investors begin to fear that the company might go broke. They dump their Ford bonds and drive the price down sharply. *Result:* The market price of the bond I bought for $1,000 falls to $500.

Next, you buy a bond exactly like mine. The only difference: Instead of paying full price, you pay only half price—the $500.

Now here's the key: Ford is still paying 5 percent interest on the original $1,000 face value bond. So you get the same $50 annual interest I'm getting.

The big difference: You're getting my $50 interest on a $500 investment. So the return on your investment is 10 percent, twice as much yield as mine.

Bottom line: The price of the bond fell in half; the yield doubled. Remember this, because it's critical: When the bond price falls, the yield goes up. One is just the mirror image of the other. Now back to Dad:

Here's what happened: After the stock market crash of 1929, interest rates fell sharply, which was to be expected, because of deflation. But then, something absolutely astounding took place: Although we were still in a deflationary era, although the economy was still sinking, interest rates began to surge dramatically. The immediate reason: Bond markets collapsed.

However, in the early 1930s, when I saw interest rates surging, I didn't understand the cause. It didn't make sense because we had deflation. And with deflation, the textbooks said interest rates were supposed to go down.

So I asked myself: Was inflation coming back? Did I read the textbooks upside down? The answer to both questions was a flat "no." Yields were surging because bond prices were crashing just like stocks. And that's when I began to look at *interest rates as a powerful fundamental force in their own right, separate from the economy or inflation.*

The yields on low-grade corporate bonds were the first to surge as their prices plunged. It was like an aftershock from the stock market crash. This made sense because these were bad bonds and they traded almost like common stocks. They were issued by companies that were expected to default on their payments, and a lot of the companies did just that. So it was natural that their bonds should fall in value or even become worthless.

As always, the lower the prices, the higher the yields. And wow! Did those yields surge! They went to 15 percent, 20 percent, 30 percent, even 45 percent. But what good was it if you lost your principal?

Then high-grade corporate bonds also got hit hard. Investors feared that any company—regardless of rating—could go belly up, and they were right! At some companies, finances deteriorated so quickly that, by the time the analysts got around to downgrading them, they were already at the bankruptcy courts. As the price of these high-grade corporate bonds crashed, their yields surged. And amazingly, they surged *beyond* their 1929 highs. Someone was obviously selling the heck out of them. But who?

You'd think that at least government-guaranteed Treasury bonds would be spared from this selling panic. They weren't. Investors sold them aggressively, driving their prices to new lows, following in the path of corporate bonds. Yields surged.

Where was all the selling coming from? One source was the U.S. Treasury itself. In the sinking economy, the government's tax revenues plummeted. So they needed to borrow more to replace the missing revenues. And that meant they had to issue more Treasury bonds—more bond supplies, lower prices, and higher yields.

But that still wasn't enough to explain it. It still didn't tell us what drove interest rates up when every textbook in existence said they should be going down.

It wasn't until later that my brother Al and I figured it out. To understand what was going on, we had to forget about inflation, deflation, money supply, the Federal Reserve. And all the theories economists swore by. Instead, we looked at bonds like any other kind of investment—no different from stocks or commodities. When investors sold them, they went down in price. When investors bought them, they went up.

These investors didn't give a hoot about textbooks. All they cared about was the fact that they needed cash. The banks needed cash to meet huge demands by savers withdrawing their money. Businesses needed cash to pay bills. Insurance companies needed cash to pay claims. So the execs went to their financial VPs to dig up something they could sell off for cash.

"What's this stuff?" they asked.

"They're bonds, sir," came the answer. "They're solid investments—not like stocks."

"Can you sell 'em?"

"Sure we can. But bonds are good for bad times. You shouldn't be selling them now because . . ."

"I don't give a damn if they're good, bad, or in between. Sell 'em! Raise cash!"

Thus, tremendous amounts of bonds were dumped on the market. High-grade bonds. Low-grade bonds. Muni bonds. Treasury bonds. It didn't matter what color or denomination. Everywhere, individuals, financial institutions, and businesses were getting rid of their bonds.

If they were low grade or on the verge of default, they got no more than pennies on the dollar. And even with higher-grade bonds, many investors were simply throwing the baby out with the bath water, driving prices to new lows.

I asked some of my business clients why they wanted to sell bonds. They saw some commodity prices rally temporarily and talked about "telltale signs of inflation returning," or the danger of *reflation,* as they called it. But later, I realized that their fear of inflation, although not irrational, was mostly an excuse. The main reason they sold the bonds was that they needed the cash.

Looking back, I wish I could have had the foresight to convert my winnings from the stock market crash into the highest-grade bonds. On top of the high yields, the purchasing power of the dollar improved. And throughout the entire depression, bonds outperformed virtually every other investment in the world, with far less risk.

But by the time we had figured it out, the opportunity was gone. As the depression progressed, rates fell back down again, and only those who had locked them in during that unusual period were able to enjoy the higher incomes.

What lessons can we learn for the twenty-first century? (See Figure 15.1.) Consider the similarities between interest rates today and those of the early 1930s:

- *Short-term interest rates.* As in the 1930s, when the economy starts sinking, most interest rates initially go down. And when the decline is accompanied by deflation, they fall even further.
- *Low-grade corporate bonds.* As in the 1930s, when the country is in the midst of a debt crisis, investors shun low-grade corporate bonds, their prices call, and their yields move higher. They are bonds issued by companies on the verge of default and bankruptcy. So naturally, to attract investors, they have to pay much higher interest.
- *Investment-grade corporate bonds.* Also as in the 1930s, a major debt crisis drives the price on higher-grade bonds (triple-B or better) lower and their yields up, although not as high as the yield on low-grade bonds.

Now, this brings us to pay dirt for your first, most powerful income booster for the depression and beyond.

The Great Buying Opportunity in Highest Quality Long-Term Bonds

As we go to press with this book, it is much too soon to buy long-term bonds. Their prices are far too high; their yields, too low. They're still being artificially supported by the Federal Reserve. If anything, the Fed has created a great bubble in bonds.

But much like the tech bubble and the housing bubble, this one cannot endure. It must end in a great bust, decimating the portfolios of most long-term bond investors. And it's *after* that bust that the true opportunity will come—to lock in a high yield *and,* if the government

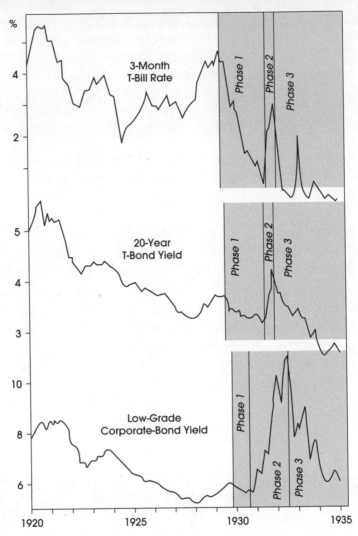

Figure 15.1   Mass Interest Rate Moves in the 1930s

In the 1930s, interest rates moved down, up, and then down again, in three distinct phases: In *Phase 1*, all interest rates declined because of deflation. In *Phase 2*, however, interest rates surged unexpectedly: The 3-month Treasury-bill rate jumped sixfold—from about a half percent to 3 percent; the yields on 20-year Treasury bonds surged beyond their precrash peak; and the average yield on low-grade corporate bonds exploded higher to 11 percent. Finally, in *Phase 3*, interest rates fell and mostly remained low for the balance of the decade. The best time to buy long-term bonds was at the end of Phase 2 or the beginning of Phase 3, when investors could lock in safe, high yields for many years, while, at the same time, enjoying stable or improving purchasing power for their dollars. Note: The time scales of the charts are not aligned.

Source: Federal Reserve.

can persist in regime of austerity, enjoy continuing improvements in the purchasing power of your money for years to come.

How much can you earn? Please bear in mind that you have to consider two key factors: the nominal interest that you collect *plus* the rate at which your money is becoming more (or less) valuable, due to falling (or rising) prices. The combination of these is the *real* yield you will be making. Here are just three possible scenarios:

1. *Good opportunity.* You lock in 8 percent on a 30-year Treasury bond. However, because of rising prices, the purchasing power of your dollar is eroded by an average of 3 percent per year. Your real yield (after subtracting inflation) is 5 percent per year.
2. *Great opportunity.* You earn a steady 5 percent on a 30-year Treasury bond or highest-grade corporate bond. *Plus*, because of *falling* prices, the purchasing power of your dollar improves by an average of 3 percent per year. Your real yield (after adding the improving purchasing power): 8 percent per year.
3. *Best-case scenario for you.* Long-term yields on the highest quality bonds temporarily spike higher, to, say, 10 percent, due to a bond price collapse similar to that described by my father. You jump in, buy long-term bonds, and lock in that high yield for 30 years. Prices subsequently fall and your purchasing power grows by an average of 5 percent for several years. Your real yield during that period: 15 percent.

Why would long-term yields on highest quality bonds spike higher? At the time this chapter was written, few people were expecting it. Fewer still were planning for it. But it is quite possible for the following reasons:

■ *Massive borrowing by the U.S. Treasury.* The Treasury must finance its ambitious bailout programs, pay for its gigantic economic stimulus packages, cover the resulting federal deficit, and roll over old debts coming due. And even if the government imposes a new regime of austerity, the initial consequence could be a decline in the economy, reduced tax revenues, even larger budget deficits, and still more government borrowing.

The more the government issues bonds, the greater the supply and the more they tend to push the price of existing bonds down, driving up their yield. Or, put another way, the more money the government needs to borrow, the more it bids up the cost of the money—the interest rate.

■ *Massive selling by bond investors to raise cash.* American consumers need cash to make their mortgage payment, pay their car loan, and make ends meet. They withdraw it from their bank account, take out policy loans on their life insurance, or borrow it from their 401(k). *Result:* Banks, insurance companies, and mutual funds must sell the government bonds they hold in their portfolios to raise the cash. Meanwhile, China and Japan, the biggest foreign holders of U.S. government securities, also reduce their holdings to avoid losses.

In this scenario, it doesn't matter if U.S. government bonds are the best investment in the world and the best place for safety. To raise cash, investors all over the world have to sell anyhow. Most would prefer to sell their other holdings, such as common shares and corporate bonds. But that escape hatch is shut because the prices are so bad, there are so few buyers, or both. So they sell the good stuff—their best long-term bonds.

■ *Warning signs of inflation.* There are inevitably intermediate periods of rising prices, and the return of inflation drives interest rates back up.

Moreover, U.S. and foreign investors have all kinds of fears, real or imagined—not only the ghosts of past inflation returning to haunt them, but also the monstrous budget deficits that loom larger with each new announcement of another government bailout.

The biggest fear of all is that, in its battle to rescue others, rather than lifting them up, the U.S. government's credit and credibility will be dragged down. Rather than bestowing its own highest-of-high credit rating onto all those it blesses, its credit is soiled by the dirt-low ratings of all those it tries to save.

For reasons I explain later, I continue to hope that those ultimate fears, although not unfounded, are unlikely to come to fruition. Despite everything, I do not believe the U.S. government will go bankrupt, shut down, or cease to exist.

Yet, whether justified or not, the fears are real in one sense: They are the emotions that drive behavior. Orderly selling becomes panicky dumping. Bond prices collapse. Interest rates surge dramatically higher.

And therein lies your big opportunity: to buy the highest quality corporate bonds or even government-guaranteed bonds at bargain-basement prices, to lock in high yields for 30 years to come, and to do it all in an era when the purchasing power of your money is likely to be stable or even grow! But that will be just the first of the income-boosting opportunities ahead.

HOW TO MAXIMIZE YOUR YIELD WITH SAFETY

Step 1. Put your money in short-term Treasury securities. Do not buy medium-term Treasury notes or long-term Treasury bonds at this stage. This way, you will not be negatively affected by rising interest rates. Quite to the contrary, when interest rates rise, you will be among the first to reap the reward, promptly rolling over your short-term Treasuries at higher and higher yields.

Step 2. Wait for the conditions I describe in Chapter 14 or for my signal by e-mail. Be patient.

Step 3. Switch a big chunk of your money to long-term Treasury bonds to lock in high, guaranteed yields. (For more detailed instructions and timing updates on when to switch to long-term bonds, go to www.moneyandmarkets.com/bonds.)

Step 4. Allocate a modest portion of your savings to high-grade corporate bonds.

Step 5. If Wall Street rating agencies capitulate to public pressure to revamp their rating models and scales, effectively downgrading most of the bonds they cover in one broad sweep, that will give you a second opportunity to buy long-term corporate bonds. Wait for bond prices to stabilize. Then buy more, continuing to focus on the highest-grade issues.

Step 6. Look seriously at buying stocks with a solid dividend-paying history, the subject of the next chapter.

CHAPTER 16

DIVIDENDS: YOUR SECOND GREAT INCOME OPPORTUNITY

Whan the country is struggling to lift itself out of a recession or depression, you don't want to take big chances with stocks that are small, unproven, and high risk.

Nor will you have to. You should be able to have your cake and eat it, too: relatively conservative companies, at deep-discount prices, with solid dividends and good growth potential. As Dad explains, that's precisely what he sought to do in the final years of the Great Depression:

> Throughout the 1930s, my brother and I were continually looking for dividend-paying companies. We bought a few here and there. But the best single opportunity actually came as the Depression was ending, in a very conservative sector of the market.
>
> Practically all other sectors had hit their lows in 1932 and 1933. But there was one major group that failed to recover significantly and then hit a new low at the end of the decade: utility stocks. While industrial stocks recovered, the utilities were clobbered and clobbered again. A key reason: Wall Street was afraid FDR was going to nationalize all utilities.

I worked as an analyst and business manager for a stock research company at the time. So I went to my boss, and I said: "FDR is already contemplating a war overseas. He's not going to fight another war at home. Let's get a study up on utilities. They're way down and they look like fantastic values." We got our staff together and spent a whole year researching the utilities.

I was deeply interested in utilities for the same reason many investors became enamored with them years later: a stable, cash-cow business with nice, steady growth. And, perhaps best of all, the likelihood of reliable interest on their bonds and rising dividends on their stocks.

After much painstaking effort, we came to the conclusion that it was time to buy. We bought bonds that were going at 25 cents on the dollar, like Standard Gas and Electric. We bought stocks in Commonwealth and Southern, which were trading on the Big Board at 10, 15, 16 cents a share.

It was another great buying opportunity: tremendous value, extremely low prices, virtually no buyers around except ourselves. The big speculators, the ones who had encouraged earlier price run-ups in utilities, were all gone, washed out. The more aggressive managers were also gone. The only ones left operating the utilities were engineers—solid, down-to-earth people who knew the technology and just wanted to provide a good service. It was a great time to buy.

Think about how different those times were from the recent stock market booms: In our era, few investors would research companies for more than a day or two—let alone a full year. Just that difference alone tells you a lot about the mind-set of investors in the Great Depression.

It's no wonder. The country had just endured a decade of choppy market ups and downs. So picking stocks by throwing darts at the wall was completely contrary to the investing culture that had evolved. Rather, investors studied each new opportunity in great depth and did not part with their money unless they were totally convinced it was the right choice. First, I recommend that you adhere to the same "I'm from Missouri" attitude. It's valid in good times, and it's especially valid when the country is trying to get back on its feet after a great recession or depression.

Second, income investments are not compatible with short-term trading. Look for companies you can comfortably hold for the long term.

Third, you need not feel rushed to buy. When Dad had all his ducks in a row—that's when he pulled the trigger. I recommend that you do the same.

In the future, however, the best bonds and dividend-paying stocks may not necessarily be in utilities. Weiss Research's dividend specialist, Nilus Mattive, has written extensively on this topic, and I've based the balance of this chapter on his research.

The Power of Dividends

Dividend-paying stocks offer a host of advantages that make them an ideal first choice when the economy is recovering from a depression.

Advantage 1: Relatively Resistant to Stock
Price Declines

If you run into some false bottoms and some false starts in a recovery, your risk of loss is significantly less than that of other stocks. Indeed, historically, companies that pay dividends have weathered bad markets far better than their peers that *don't* pay dividends. Example: In 2002, a very bad year for stocks, nondividend-paying stocks in the S&P 500 fell 30 percent. Dividend-paying stocks lost only 11 percent. Similarly, in 2008, an even worse year for stocks, paying stocks fell far less.

Advantage 2: Rising Yields

Even when nearly all other interest rates are falling, dividend stocks bought at the right time can be one of the few investments that provide rising yields.

Let's say you buy a stock for $10 a share and it's paying an annual dividend of $0.50. Your immediate yield is 5 percent, which is not bad. But watch what happens as the company boosts its dividend by $0.05 per share every year: 10 years later, the stock will pay an annual dividend of $1 a share. And since your cost for the stock is locked in at $10 per share, your effective yield (based on the original cost) is now 10 percent. If this pattern continues over time, your effective yield could grow to 15 percent or even 20 percent.

Thus, with a prudent selection and patience, buying and holding stocks that steadily raise their dividends can produce levels of income that are virtually impossible to find from other investments.

Consider Procter & Gamble (P&G), said to be "a dull investment." Although its circumstances could certainly change in another great recession or depression, its past experience illustrates the power of dividends in a growing economy: *P&G's shareholders have received larger and larger dividend checks every year for 52 consecutive years.*

Moreover, you wouldn't have to go back 52 years to see the benefits: If you had bought P&G just 15 years earlier, by 2007 you would be earning an effective dividend yield of 11.3 percent, more than twice what you could get on a Treasury bond at that time. If you had bought Procter & Gamble 20 or 30 years earlier, your effective dividend yield would be even higher.

Johnson & Johnson (J&J), another supposedly stodgy and boring company, delivered even better results: Investors who bought its shares 15 years earlier received an effective dividend yield of nearly 17 percent. And investors who bought Altria (the tobacco company formerly known as Phillip Morris) were receiving an 18.6 percent annual yield.

While other investors were busy chasing fast profits during the dot-com boom—only to see them go up in smoke—investors in companies with steadily rising dividends like P&G, J&J, and Altria made out like silent bandits. As long as they bought companies that continued to boost their dividends, their effective yields kept going up, and there was no limit to how high their dividend payments could rise.

Anheuser-Busch, one of America's leading beverage makers, raised its dividends nonstop for 30 years; Kimberly-Clark, a major U.S. producer of consumer and health care products, raised its dividends for 36 straight years; and Gannett, the publisher of some of the nation's best-selling newspapers, raised its dividend nonstop for 39 years.

Even solid companies like these may be forced to cut their dividends in a future great recession or depression. But this history illustrates how well they can do when the economy hits rock bottom and begins to recover.

Advantage 3: Strong Evidence of Performance

When a company sends you a dividend check, it's putting its money where its mouth is. Unlike earnings or sales, a dividend is not an accounting construct. It represents decisive and definitive evidence of the company's earnings performance and cash. So it should come as no surprise that companies paying consistent dividends also happen to be those that typically boast the most consistent pattern of rising share prices.

Advantage 4: The Potential for
High-Powered Total Returns

In addition to the dividend yield, let's not forget the real potential for the stock to rise in value.

The formula: Your total return = Yield + Gains

In other words, the total amount you make each year is the combination of *both* your dividend checks *and* the rise in the price of your shares. In a rising market with rising dividends, that can be a very powerful combination.

In the next chapter, Dad illustrates this vividly with dividend-paying gold mining shares he and his colleagues bought in the early 1930s. But here's a more modern example:

It's March 26, 1990. You visit a local McDonald's. You see a long line of customers in front of the register, wallets and purses in hand. You go home and call your broker. "Buy me 100 shares of McDonald's," you say. That day, the stock closes at about $29 a share. Its dividend yield is a hair better than 1 percent.

Your choice of McDonald's does not require massive due diligence and research: By 1990, McDonald's restaurants are everywhere—it's the fast food company by which all others are judged. Its business model is so tried and tested, and its name so well known, the stock is anything but a "fresh, hot stock." But fast forward to March 27, 2006. McDonald's stock closes at $34.55 a share. During the 16 years that you've owned it, the stock has split 2-for-1 on two occasions. Adjusting for these splits, your purchase price is equal to $6.20 a share. Meanwhile, the dividend is $0.67 a share, and your effective yield is 10.8 percent.

That would have been very attractive, as is. But there's more. Since you bought it, the stock has appreciated at an average annual rate of 17.8 percent per year. Your total return: the 10.8 percent yield *plus* the 17.8 percent yearly gains = 28.6 percent per year. At that rate, if sustained, you could double your money in less than four years. If you started with $10,000, after just seven years, you'd have over $45,000.

Advantage 5: Bargain Prices Can Help Deliver Even Higher Immediate Yields

After a major market decline, when you can pick up the shares at a fraction of their peak prices, dividend yields can be even higher. The key is to wait for the market to decline and to pick companies with the best likelihood of maintaining their dividend payments. If you do, even some of the stodgiest, dullest dividend-paying companies can boost your income nicely.

Without waiting for years of recovery, you could soon begin to earn high, double-digit yields.

Advantage 6: A Lot More Than Just a Promise to Deliver

Dividends are not guaranteed. Most companies can choose to suspend or lower their dividends any time they choose.

However, dividends still represent far more than a company's promise or forecast of future earnings; they are hard cash payments and nonrefundable. Never forget: Your paper profits can disappear if a stock falls. But the moment a dividend is deposited into your account, it's yours to keep regardless of any future decline in the share price.

Advantage 7: Get Paid While You Wait

In the wake of a great recession or depression, stocks could bounce back quickly. Or they could linger near the bottom, while the country cleans up its debts and the economy consolidates, building a firmer foundation for a recovery.

If the recovery is slow, a stock that does *not* pay dividends could have you sitting with a dead-in-the-water investment with no return. In contrast, with a dividend-paying stock, the *company pays you to wait*. Whether the stock rises or not, you can continue to collect your quarterly dividend checks.

Advantage 8: The Power of Compounding

As you probably know, compounding is one of the most powerful tools for building wealth. For example, if you put $10,000 into a savings account with a 6 percent annual interest rate, you'll have $10,600 after one year. Next year, you'll be earning 6 percent on the $10,600 rather than just the original $10,000. It might not seem like a big deal at first, but the effects over time can really add up. Ten years later, you'd have almost $18,000.

With dividends, the idea is the same. If you don't need the income from your dividend checks on a regular basis, you can use your regular payments to buy more shares. By doing so, you'll be steadily increasing your holdings of that company over time. More importantly, you'll also be setting yourself up for additional dividends on the new shares. When combined, these two simple forces become a very powerful form of compounding.

To document its power, Standard & Poor's looked at monthly data for its benchmark S&P 500 Index over a 50-year period, comparing simple price appreciation to the gains made by reinvesting any dividends paid. The results were astounding: The S&P 500's capital appreciation was 381.9 percent; its "dividends reinvested" gains were 905.1 percent!

Advantage 9: Reinvestment Plans

Many companies are more than glad to help long-term investors buy additional shares this way, so they've created dividend reinvestment plans (DRIPs) to make the process easier. In some cases, the company runs the plan itself. Most times, however, the plan is run by an independent agent. You sign up for the plan (either by phone or online). Then, the company itself or its plan agent will automatically reinvest your dividends in additional shares. (To find stocks with rising dividends, see page 217.)

Two Disadvantages of Dividend Stocks

When comparing corporate bonds to dividend-paying stocks, please don't ignore the two disadvantages:

1. *Dividends can be cut.* In the earnings crunch, some companies may cut or cancel their dividends. However, as long as they continue to be viable companies with relatively strong balance sheets, their past history of consistent dividend payments should be a good indication of what to expect in a future recovery.

2. *Stock price declines.* Dividend stocks can fall in price like any other stock, and the resulting loss could be larger than the dividends you receive during that period.

Bottom line: With all these pluses (and only two minuses), you'd think Wall Street would have been recommending dividend-paying stocks more actively. Unfortunately, however, throughout the 2000s, Wall Street seemed preprogrammed to talk up stock market *profits*. They rarely stressed the importance of dividends. I hope that will change, because high yields can make a vital difference in the lifestyle of millions of investors for many years following a depression.

HOW TO FIND STOCKS WITH STEADILY RISING DIVIDENDS

Many income investors have an overly simple approach—they blindly buy the stocks with the highest possible yields. But looking exclusively at a stock's yield could be a big mistake. If anything, a yield that is far above average is often a warning sign of a weak company.

If the stock's weakness is temporary, you could have a great investment on your hands; and in a great recession or depression, the market is bound to provide many such gifts. However, do not underestimate the possibility that the unusually high yield is a symptom of a very negative outlook.

Bottom line: It pays to do your homework. Here are the tools:

Both Standard & Poor's and Mergent regularly publish lists of stocks with steadily rising dividends (S&P's "Dividend Aristocrats" and Mergent's "Dividend Achievers"). Each company uses slightly different criteria, but the overall theme is the same. Mergent has a dedicated site for its lists. It's fairly easy to navigate, but here's a quick step-by-step guide:

Step 1. Go to www.dividendachievers.com.

Step 2. In the left-hand navigation bar, click on the tab labeled "Dividend Achievers Indices."

(Continued)

Step 3. You will see a list of various dividend-related indexes, each providing a link for additional information about the index.

Step 4. You can also select "Constituents" for a list of the individual components and also download a list of recent index changes.

To get S&P's lists:

Step 1. Go to www.standardandpoors.com.

Step 2. Click on "Indices" in the top navigation bar.

Step 3. On the left-hand bar, you'll now see an expanded list under "Browse by Index."

Step 4. In that expanded list, click on "S&P Dividend Aristocrats Indices."

Step 5. Scroll down the page to get information on each of these groups, including "Methodology" and "Constituents."

Step 6. For more specific instructions on dividend-paying stocks, visit www.moneyandmarkets/dividends.

Note: Web sites frequently change their layouts. These directions were accurate when we wrote them, but if the sites change, you may have to adjust your steps accordingly.

CHAPTER 17

THE GREAT FORK IN THE ROAD: INFLATION OR DEFLATION?

The crisis soon brings us to a great fork in the road: Will the government, in its zeal to end it at all costs, bring about *unbridled inflation,* driving nearly all prices sharply higher? Or will austerity and the sinking economy bring *deep deflation,* driving nearly all prices sharply lower? Before I answer that question, let me first show you the true consequences of each scenario.

The true consequences of unbridled inflation:

Inflation may ease the pain of debtors temporarily, help provide the semblance of a recovery, and even give the illusion that "the crisis is over." But such benefits are almost invariably short lived. They are limited to a privileged few. And even if they're more widespread or last a bit longer, they almost inevitably backfire in the form of new bubbles, new busts and, ultimately, an even deeper recession with more financial losses, more bankruptcies, and more layoffs. In a nutshell, unbridled inflation brings:

- *Still more bad debts.* Individuals and companies are once again encouraged to borrow, spend, and speculate, adding a new layer of burdensome debts to an already-overburdened economy.
- *The ultimate moral hazard:* Speculators, among the primary culprits of the boom and bust, are rewarded with even more cheap money and credit; while savers, essential to help finance a true recovery, are punished. After deducting inflation, they earn less than nothing for their money. Or worse, the value of their money is quickly eroded.
- *The destruction of the dollar.* Savings and retirement nest eggs are eroded. People have little incentive to work hard and every incentive to find alternative schemes for making money. The inflation corrupts society and sabotages efforts to bring about an economic recovery.

The true consequences of deep deflation:
Deflation comes with deep financial losses, more corporate bankruptcies, and much higher unemployment. But *those consequences are largely unavoidable anyway.* Moreover, there are major, lasting benefits that accrue with deflation:

- *A much-needed reduction of burdensome debts.* With deflation, debts are paid off or liquidated in bankruptcies. Bad debts are cleansed from the economic body, creating a clean slate for future growth.
- *Just desserts:* Speculators who took the most risk during the bubble suffer the biggest losses, while those who had the foresight and prudence to save their money benefit from the best real returns. Thus, deflation naturally delivers the most punishment to those who *caused* the crisis while delivering the greatest rewards to those most capable of *ending* the crisis.
- *A strong dollar:* The U.S. dollar gains in purchasing power, giving every American a bedrock of value to strive for, to save, and to invest prudently. This lays the foundation for shared sacrifice by families, local communities, and the country as a whole.

Clearly, despite the near-term pain, *deflation* is the lesser of the evils.

But at this stage of the crisis, there's no assurance that deflation will prevail. Yes, in 2008, U.S. commodity prices, wholesale prices, and consumer prices plunged; mortgage debts, corporate debts, and other forms of debt were liquidated at the fastest pace since the 1930s; and the U.S. dollar enjoyed the most rapid surge overseas since the mid-1980s.

But it was because of that deflation that government officials thought they had the leeway to bail out failing companies without restraint, cut interest rates to zero, print money to their heart's content, and pump up the economy with the largest stimulus packages of all time. "Who cares how much inflation that might create?" they reason. "Right now, as long as we have deflation, we can afford some inflationary consequences."

Plus, it was also due to that line of thinking that, in 2010, the Federal Reserve officially declared that one of its key goals was to actually *create inflation*. They viewed deflation as a vicious plague. They figured a "little inflation" is okay or even healthy. So they actually ran the money printing presses to make it happen. What they didn't realize is having "a little inflation" is as difficult to achieve as becoming "a little pregnant."

Moreover, recent history shows that their rationale is gravely shortsighted. The government's efforts to end the tech bust of 2000–2002 produced the housing bubble of 2003–2005; its efforts to end the subsequent housing bust produced the energy and commodity bubble of 2006–2007; and its most recent, desperate struggle to end the resulting economic disasters may harbor even greater dangers.

Indeed, looking back at these bubbles and busts in the first decade of the twenty-first century, it's clear that, despite some near-term successes, nearly everyone has lost: Millions of Americans were denied access to affordable homes, lured into unpayable debts, and then thrown on to the street with foreclosures. They were squeezed by surging fuel prices, squeezed again by vanishing credit, and then punched below the belt by job losses.

In the final tally, even the initial beneficiaries of the booms— the technology industry and the housing industry—were smashed. Investors in those industries experienced massive losses. And the federal government itself was severely weakened as its debt and deficits exploded in size.

Each time, just as soon as consumers resumed buying and business resumed expanding, most of the extra money and credit pumped into the economy merely reignited more borrowing and speculation. With each new cycle, America's finances, competitive ability, and recuperative power were weakened further. Instead of real growth, we got more bouts of inflation. Instead of lasting recoveries, we got more bubbles, more busts, and, ultimately, more tough times.

Here's the fundamental fallacy of the theories prevailing in our government today: Contrary to their view, *inflation does not cure deflation; and deflation in itself does not cure inflation.* Rather, inflationary forces are akin to the human diseases that produce high blood pressure. A weak heart or clogged arteries do not magically disappear just because the patient's pressure has fallen to dangerously low levels. Likewise, the fundamental causes of inflation do not disappear just because prices have recently plunged to new lows.

The causes of inflation are rooted in technological and cultural aspects of the economy that do not change quickly—sinking productivity, a bad work ethic, excessive greed, weak management, burdensome taxation, and more. Like the causes of high blood pressure, they remain embedded in the economic body, lurking behind the scenes, ready to wreak havoc. Even in the midst of an economic decline, even after an initial bout of deflation, they do not go away.

And, as my father described earlier, even while the economy is still tanking and most prices are still falling, the *fear* of inflation can suddenly rear its ugly head, sweep through financial markets, help drive interest rates sharply higher, and, ultimately, make the crisis worse.

My main point: The danger of inflation remains, raising several key questions for you right now.

In the Next Stage, Which Is Most Likely to Prevail—Deflation or Inflation?

The true pessimists of our time believe that government leaders will succeed in bailing out nearly every failing institution in the world, printing money indiscriminately to finance their folly; that we will somehow muddle through the worst financial crisis since the Great Depression without ever addressing its causes; that we will forever remain shackled by the heaviest debts of all time, with little hope of restoring what made our nation great; that government will overcome deflation simply by creating inflation. What they don't admit is that, once unleashed, inflation cannot easily be tamed—it could render paper currencies worthless, destroy the fabric of our society, and even undermine the capitalist system.

By comparison, my outlook is optimistic: Yes, political pressures will drive some of our leaders to make big blunders. However, I do not agree that this trend will prevail. I am confident that Washington will:

- Fail to reverse the long-overdue liquidation of bad debts.
- Fail to stop a much-needed reduction in the cost of living.
- Fail to create hyperinflation or kill the U.S. dollar.
- Fail to kill the incentive for Americans to work hard and make needed sacrifices.
- Fail to stop America from restoring its ability to compete globally.
- Fail to sabotage our capitalist free market system.
- Fail to ruin our chances for a prosperous recovery.

What Is Your Best Protection from Inflation?

To the degree that my optimism is well founded, the investments I have recommended in earlier chapters should give you nearly all of the protection you need. But to the degree that the inflation scenario prevails, you will need at least one more investment in your portfolio—gold. My recommendation is to consider gold in two phases:

Phase 1: Now, before we have confirmed evidence of price inflation. Own gold in moderate amounts—less than 10 percent of your liquid assets. Buy it as *insurance* against economic policy makers run amok.

Phase 2: Later, if we see a confirmation of price inflation. Expand your gold and related investments.

When Will Be the Best Time to Buy More Gold?

Dad's experience in the early 1930s, albeit in different circumstances, gives us some valuable clues:

> The first gold bugs of the twentieth century were friends of mine—men like Bernard Baruch, William Baxter, Thomas Bragg, and Ben Smith.
>
> Bernard Baruch was an adviser to several presidents and is famous for having made a fortune during the crash. William Baxter was the founder of the International Economic Research Bureau. Tom Bragg and Ben Smith were floor traders specializing in gold stocks. I was working for a Wall Street firm at the time, while writing freelance reports on inflation and gold for Baxter.
>
> The five of us had been accumulating gold coins in a small way. In those days, very few people were buying the gold pieces. They were being used mostly for gifts and weren't circulating. But we bought quite a few.
>
> The main reason we liked gold was that its price had been artificially held down at $20.35 an ounce. So the downside risk for us was strictly limited.
>
> But at the time, the average person did not view gold as an investment, as something that might go up or down in value. Instead, most still believed in holding cash in banks. The prevailing mood was that, if your money was in a bank, especially a large, well-known bank, it was safe no matter what. That's why I had such a hard time getting people to pull their money out of their banks.
>
> I had an even harder time getting them to buy gold, which was ironic because we could buy it so easily—just by walking up to bank tellers and asking for $20 gold pieces. They'd give you as many as you wanted, no questions asked. It was just like asking for $20 bills because all currency notes were exchangeable into gold.
>
> Then we started buying gold shares—this time, investing in bigger amounts. The shares were grossly undervalued and consistently snubbed by most traders.
>
> Gold and gold shares had a bad reputation. Earlier in the century, a bunch of shady characters used to roam the countryside peddling shares in mining ventures that soon went belly up.

So by the 1930s, most investors gave mining companies a wide berth. But we thought that was about to change. Besides, we didn't give a darn about what most people thought or said. We figured we couldn't go wrong if we concentrated on the biggest companies like Homestake and a couple of big Canadian companies. We knew we were on the right track because our gold stocks started to move up nicely.

We soon had very respectable gains. So some of the boys were itching to get out. With the '29 stock market crash still fresh in their minds, you couldn't blame them for being nervous. One worried about "some big selling which could hit at almost any time." Baruch said he was hanging on.

Our immediate question was: "Who's going to do the selling and how much?" I suggested we get the facts with a survey. I got a hold of the stockholder lists of some of the big mining companies and had our staff call about 400 people at random, asking a simple series of questions—"When did you buy your gold shares?" . . . "How much do you own?" . . . "What do you plan to do with them?"

Boy, were we surprised when we saw the results! We rarely got past the first question! About half the stockholders in mining companies didn't even know they owned the shares. The rest said they had the shares stashed away—in their attic or in a vault somewhere. None of the people had plans to sell the shares.

So I called another meeting and told the boys: "The only big source of selling would have to be from someone right here in this room." They all breathed a sigh of relief. We held on to our shares and doubled our profits.

We believed the president was going to raise the price of gold and *devalue the dollar*. We bought as much as we could, while we still could—gold coins, shares, bullion, you name it.

Then it happened. FDR announced that he was not only raising the price of gold and devaluing the dollar, he was going *confiscate gold from the public*. He was going to require ordinary people to turn in the gold they owned. We were ready, but we were also stunned. We had no idea FDR was going to be that tough.

The devaluation changed everything. It was the watershed event we were waiting for to help end the deflation. And most investors today have no idea how huge the profits were in gold shares after the devaluation. Homestake, for instance, went from a bottom of $65 per share after the crash to $130 and change in 1931. From there, it doubled again to more than $350 a share by 1933. By the time it peaked in 1936, it had climbed to $540 a share—an astronomical gain of more than $470 per share. That was a sevenfold increase.

In the meantime, the dividends also doubled, redoubled, and doubled again—reaching $56 per share in 1935. Think about it. The dividends earned in one year alone almost paid back the entire purchase price of the stock.

Homestake was not the only one. Dome, another great gold producer, did even better. You could have bought Dome for as little as $6 a share after the crash. But in the next seven years, it paid $16.60 per share in dividends. The dividends alone were equal to more than 2.5 times the cost of the stock. Meanwhile, the price of Dome rose to $61 a share. A person who put $10,000 into Dome could have walked away with more than $100,000—while nearly everything else remained depressed.

Cash was king back then. This was the Great Depression. Prices of everything were extraordinarily cheap. You just needed a modest portion of that to build real wealth. It didn't pay to get greedy.

What Are the Differences between Gold Investing in the 1930s and in the 2000s?

The differences between then and now are significant:

Difference 1. In the early 1930s, gold and the dollar were virtually interchangeable: The dollar was backed by gold, and gold's price was fixed in dollars. So gold was viewed merely as another way to save, an alternative to money in the bank. In the modern era, however, that's no longer the case. Instead, it can actually be said that gold is like the "anti-dollar." Thus,

- If gold soars to the stratosphere, it will probably mean our dollar has sunk dramatically.
- If gold prices do not surge, it will probably mean that the U.S. dollar is getting stronger.

Difference 2. In the early 1930s, the risk of loss was greatly reduced because *gold's price was already fixed at a very low level.* Gold investors of that era could buy gold with limited fear of loss. In contrast, gold investors in modern times have to contend with more downside risk. So no matter when you buy gold, watch the downside. Do not assume gold can go only up.

Difference 3. By the time Dad and his friends began buying gold, the United States had already experienced massive price deflation—not only in commodities, but in manufactured goods, services, and even the cost of labor. As of this writing, however, any deflation has been mostly shallow and sporadic.

Difference 4. In the early 1930s, the shares of gold mining companies were severely depressed. They had been hammered so often that savvy investors who owned them were anxious to dump them for a quick profit at the very first opportunity. Only after carefully surveying shareholders were they persuaded to hold on for a while longer. In contrast, in the 2000s, gold shares have been widely promoted, widely owned, and subject to some of the same crowd psychology that drove the booms and busts in other major investments. So beware of sharp corrections. Buy mining shares using the same prudence and tactics you would with other shares. Just because the companies mine gold doesn't mean your profits are guaranteed.

Why Can't Governments Just *Create* Inflation?

You might ask: *When confronted with the choice of either (a) depression and deflation or (b) inflation and growth, won't governments always prefer inflation? Why can't they just create inflation by printing money at will?*

They will certainly try, and the best evidence is the quantitative easing pursued by the Federal Reserve during the late 2000s and early 2010s. But what governments want is not always what governments get. And ultimately, their efforts to pump up the economy could fail. We may see government-created inflation for a while. But it's too soon to say that inflation will take off.

What about a Global Devaluation of the World's Major Currencies?

Why can't the major governments of the world agree to a global devaluation of all major currencies? Wouldn't that end the deflation and drive the price of gold through the roof?

A global devaluation would be a windfall for nations with huge debts to foreign countries, such as the United States. But it would largely wipe out the wealth accumulated by nations with big loans to the United States, especially Japan and China. So reaching a global agreement at this stage could be extremely difficult. Anything is possible in the future, though. As Bernard Baruch said to my father in another context, "Wait till you can see the whites of their eyes."

What about the Possibility of Massive Hyperinflation?

You ask: *In Germany after World War I, the government ran the money printing presses like crazy. The currency became so worthless, you needed three trillion real marks to buy one dollar, with often extreme consequences: When a wheelbarrow of money was stolen, the thief took only the wheelbarrow, leaving the money behind. When they needed something to start a bonfire, paper money was a prime choice. It was hyperinflation.*

Today, with such a large debt crisis, why won't the same thing happen to the U.S. dollar? Even if it's not nearly as bad, couldn't that drive the price of gold to thousands of dollars per ounce?

Anything is possible, but I believe this is unlikely for two reasons:

1. Because of the world's capacity to produce and ship goods in massive quantities, we have an unprecedented abundance of supplies, driving prices lower. After World War I, the conditions in Germany were precisely the opposite. Factories were destroyed and railroads were in shambles, creating an acute scarcity of goods that naturally drove their prices higher.

2. Because of today's highly active and fluid markets for government securities. This makes it possible for investors to dump their government bonds, creating hyperinflation. This means that, ultimately, the *power* to make inflation-deflation decisions has been transferred from politicians to bond investors. Since they will always prefer to be paid back in more valuable dollars, they represent a powerful force helping to avoid hyperinflation and turning the nation back toward deflation. I explain in the next chapter precisely how this can happen.

How to Invest in Gold

Gold can be an excellent investment at the right time. It can also be a high-risk investment at the wrong time. I suggest you follow these basic guidelines:

1. Don't become too fixated on the glitter of gold as a monetary metal or a safe haven. Although those qualities can help support gold prices, history proves that they are no match for falling demand, abundant supplies, and deflation. Therefore, you should not accumulate large amounts of gold as a be-all-end-all substitute for cash or savings.

2. Regardless of some theories to the contrary, the hard-nosed reality is that gold is generally a good investment in inflationary times but a bad investment in deflationary times. As long as inflation is not confirmed, invest up to 10 percent of your liquid assets in gold. Later, following government measures and watershed events to end deflation, it may be a time to expand your holdings.

3. If inflationary forces heat up there should be a larger opportunity for gold investors. As an additional signal, remain on the lookout for deliberate efforts by the authorities to cheapen the dollar and push prices higher.

(Continued)

Weiss Research's gold expert, Larry Edelson, recommends several alternative vehicles for investing in gold:

1. *Gold-based exchange-traded funds (ETFs).* These are the handiest and most flexible vehicles. http://goldeconomy.com/reports/etf1.htm. A gold ETF invests strictly in gold bullion. They are liquid, require no maintenance by the investor, and are traded on the major stock exchanges. Best of all, gold bullion ETFs do not require you to take delivery of physical gold and store it. Two prime examples:

   ■ The SPDR Gold Trust (GLD). Each share represents one-tenth of an ounce of pure gold.

   ■ The iShares Comex Gold Trust (IAU). Almost identical to GLD, though it generally trades with lesser volume.

2. *Physical gold.* You can buy ingots, gold bars in many sizes, and gold bullion coins. I generally do not recommend rare gold coins. It's highly complex, and more like investing in art.

   For physical gold, your best choice is gold ingots and bars. Gold bullion coins, like the American Eagle, are nice to look at, but dealers charge a premium of 4, 7, or even 8 percent for their purchase. The premium includes the cost of the U.S. Mint's charges to make the coin, plus the dealer's commission. As a rule, it's not worth it.

   You can get more gold for your money every time you buy ingots or bars than when you buy gold bullion coins. If you were to buy, say, 10 ounces of gold at $800 per ounce, it would run you just a tad over $8,000. But if you were to buy 100 one-ounce gold American Eagles, you'd pay over $8,500 for the same amount of gold. The same applies to Canadian Maple Leafs, Mexican Peso gold bullion coins, and the South African Krugerrand.

   That's why, at the right time, we prefer ingots and bars, especially the 1- and 10-ounce ingots, and for larger purchases, the 32.15-ounce kilo bars. They're relatively easy to buy and easy to store. Just make sure you are buying what's called "four nines fine" gold, meaning 99.99 percent pure gold. The most common hallmarks are Johnson Matthey, Engelhard, Credit Suisse, and Pamp. Most reputable dealers carry these ingots and bars in these hallmarks or can readily acquire them for you.

From whom do you buy? Choose a dealer based primarily on the quality of the service. Then establish a long-term relationship with one or two. (For some examples, visit www.moneyandmarkets.com/gold.)

3. *Gold mining shares.* Favor gold mining mutual funds over picking individual gold shares. The reasons are obvious: you get diversification and a professional manager. Picking individual gold mining shares can offer greater returns, but also more risk.

CHAPTER

THE DEMISE OF
THE DOLLAR?

This brings us to the final question, the most important for us all: Will the United States survive this crisis? Can it thrive in the years that follow?

My answer is yes, but with one unambiguous admonition: Our strength as a nation is ultimately predicated on the viability of the U.S. dollar. To the degree that we let inflation return and fail to protect its value, our survival will be less certain and our recovery more elusive. This is not a new revelation for me. I have fought for a stable dollar all my life, and my father did the same before me. So before I tell you what we can do about this today, let me defer to him—to tell you what his vision was, how he acted upon it, and why he ultimately failed.

Despite the Great Depression, there was one all-important investment that not only survived, but actually thrived: The U.S. dollar. Thanks to deflation, prices fell on virtually everything. And because of fear, investors shunned risk and sought the safety of cash. Result: The dollar's purchasing power and value surged.

That was the saving grace of hard times. A strong dollar gave people something to work for. It was the essential foundation for a recovery.

But after World War II, I saw signs that the dollar was weakening. Corporate America was starting to build up debts. So was the federal government. I was not against debt per se, but I felt debts should be added in moderation, with plenty of capital and cash to back it up.

When President Eisenhower entered his last two years in office, the federal budget was going haywire. The estimates for the deficit were running close to $13 billion. In those days, that was huge.

Eisenhower didn't have to wait until 2009 to learn that debts and deficits would lead to trouble. He knew it all too well back in 1959.

In the first days of January, I turned on the radio to listen to Eisenhower's State of the Union Address. Ike complained about the excessive costs of military hardware. He insisted that "we must avoid extremes of waste and inflation which could reduce job opportunities, take us out of world markets, shrink the value of savings." Most important, he announced that he would submit a balanced budget to Congress.

The next day, I ran down to check the papers. I looked for a headline such as "*Ike Proposes Balanced Budget.*" But I couldn't find it anywhere. The story was buried on the inside pages. "The most conspicuous reaction to Eisenhower's speech," it said, "came in the form of an unrestrained yawn by the Senate Democratic leader, Lyndon B. Johnson."

I was outraged. And I made up my mind to do something about it.

I organized the Sound Dollar Committee, choosing former president Herbert Hoover as Republican co-chairman and presidential adviser Bernard Baruch as Democratic co-chairman. The Committee would lobby and advertise for a balanced budget and against inflation.

Herbert Hoover was eager to participate. But Bernard Baruch, despite his sympathies, was skeptical. Toward the end of February, I decided to make a final attempt to win his support. So I gave him a call.

"It's the wrong time," Baruch said. "We really can't do anything until we see the whites of their eyes."

"But we're already doing it," I said. "We've started the campaign with a full-page ad in the *Wall Street Journal.* We sent you a copy. Did you receive it?"

"Fine, fine!" he said. "But I've tried time and time again to give them that advice, to keep the budget balanced, to protect the dollar. Truman wouldn't listen. Eisenhower wouldn't listen. So now he's changed his mind. Even if your campaign succeeds, I question whether they'll follow through. But go ahead and see what you can do. You have my blessing."

Top: The author's father, J. Irving Weiss (left) and presidential adviser Bernard Baruch (right) were among the few Americans who correctly anticipated the deep stock market decline of the early 1930s, using it as a major opportunity to build wealth. Weiss and Baruch later invested in gold mining shares, among the best performing stocks of that decade.

Bottom: In the years before he passed away in 1997, J. Irving Weiss transferred to the author his knowledge and personal experiences of the Great Depression, seeking to provide a virtual road map of how future bubbles and busts might unfold. They often debated the similarities and differences between the two eras (left) and studied Weiss Sr.'s charts on various interest rates from the early 1930s to the present (right).

We went ahead without him or Hoover, and instead, I got others to join: Leonard Spacek, a fiercely outspoken champion of shareholder rights who became the second managing partner of Arthur Andersen; Leslie R. Groves, a major force in the construction of the Pentagon and a leader of the Manhattan Project, where the first atom bomb was made; plus many others.

The first ad in the *Wall Street Journal* merely set off the first sparks and was followed by an ad in the *Chicago Tribune*. Then *Chicago Tribune* owner McCormick called and said: "I believe in what you are doing. I'd like to put in a two-page spread on my own at my own expense." The *Los Angeles Times* and the *New York Daily News* followed suit.

Soon, scores of newspapers and magazines joined the Sound Dollar Committee in its nationwide campaign to fight inflation, balance the budget, and protect the dollar.

Congressmen would walk into their offices on a Monday morning and be struck immediately with the clutter of mailbags. They'd ask their clerks: "What the hell is this? Where did all this mail come from?"

"They're protests, sir."

"Protests against what?"

"They're coupons protesting inflation–cut out from the newspapers, sir. They're running big ads against inflation."

It was an avalanche! According to a survey by the *Chicago Tribune* on the Hill, the total response was 12 million postcards, coupons, letters, and telegrams.

By mid-March, the public's attitude had switched from apathy to intense interest. According to *BusinessWeek:* "Just about anywhere you go these days, the talk will turn to inflation. The subject comes up with friends at cocktails, in the brokers' boardrooms, and among businessmen who feel a responsibility to avoid price increases."

All of a sudden, Washington was a "city full of inflation fighters. For an explanation," wrote *BusinessWeek,* "leaders in Congress began the session talking like big spenders; now they are talking about cutting Eisenhower's budget."

Senator Proxmire, who had been steadfastly in favor of the deficit spending, changed his mind and voted for the balanced budget. One congressman after another shifted his vote to support the Eisenhower budget. The budget was balanced. Unfortunately, however, it was the last real balanced budget.

I believe I was right in my debate with Bernard Baruch: We did not have to wait to be effective. But in a more lasting sense, he was right. After Eisenhower left office, the country was led in precisely the opposite direction from the one we had hoped for. It flew off into a new orbit of debt. And someday, I feared, it would all wind up in collapse.

The Next Great Battle

Today, I am chairman of the Sound Dollar Committee, a nonprofit, nonpartisan 501(c)(3) organization that remains as devoted as before to the same philosophy of moderation. I have maintained its registrations in nearly all 50 states. I pay the annual fees and taxes religiously.

But in the half-century since Eisenhower's 1960 balanced budget, too many budget-busting events have occurred, and too few opportunities for meaningful change have emerged. Given the 2008 debt crisis and the government's response so far, it is unrealistic to expect a balanced budget for years to come.

Moreover, over the years, Washington, Wall Street, and Main Street have progressively built up a greater and greater pool of debts and bets, while continually diminishing the savings typically required by modern economies to underpin such debts.

Fannie Mae expanded the secondary market for home mortgages. Freddie Mac was founded to expand it even further. Credit cards boomed. The federal debt mushroomed. The government's future obligations for Medicare ballooned. Each successive American president inherited, enlarged, and passed on bigger debts to the next, always seeking to erect—with guarantees, bailouts, and backstops—a taller and taller dike to hold back the periodic tides of financial crisis.

With each new economic cycle, however, the debt collapses became more threatening—first, just a few corporations like Penn Central Railroad and Chrysler in 1970; then entire financial industries like savings and loans in the 1980s and life insurers in the 1990s. Each time, the causes of the crisis were papered over with more easy money and more debt.

But now, in the twenty-first century, we've come to the end of the line. In the 2008 debt crisis, the quantity of debt was so big and the quality so toxic, great plumes of black sludge overflowed into the economy as a whole, prompting investors to dump the shares of even the best of companies. And in the 2010 sovereign debt crisis, governments who had sought to absorb that toxic matter into their own balance sheets were themselves the targets of investor attacks.

Our leaders try to plug every leak with more money—first in subprime mortgages, then all mortgages; first short-term credit markets, then all credit markets; first Bear Stearns, then Lehman, AIG, Fannie Mae, Freddie Mac, Washington Mutual, Wachovia, GM, Chrysler, and Citigroup; each bigger than the previous, each bringing us closer to the threshold of the absurd.

When brokers went broke, the government funneled money into brokers. When asset-backed securities went bad, the government pledged $700 billion to buy up asset-backed securities. When commercial paper went bad, the government pledged to guarantee commercial paper. When credit cards, consumer loans, and other debt sank, they did the same. Ditto for entire countries on the brink of bankruptcy. Each time the question was asked: How much further can they go? When will they have to stop?

At this juncture, the Sound Dollar Committee is no match for this tidal wave. Even the government itself is being tossed in its swells. There is only one group of people that can steer our country in the right direction: *You, me, and other like-minded individuals.*

We are not a class. We do not belong to one single political party. And we don't hire corporate lobbyists.

We are investors.

Simply by fighting for our own individual safety and future well-being, we can help put our country on a better path. And we can do it all thanks to some amazing weapons at our disposal.

Our first weapon is cash. At the right time, we can vote with our dollars—with the cash we have accumulated in anticipation of tough times. To cast our votes, we don't have to wait for the next election. Nor must we travel to Washington to beg before some faceless bureaucrat. All we have to do is make the right investment decisions—to withhold our cash and refrain from buying as long as we're displeased, or to deploy our cash and begin buying as soon as our demands are met. We make these decisions to maximize our own personal financial safety and future growth. But our decisions also advance our cause—to promote safety and the opportunity for growth as a nation.

Our second weapon is the market. Thankfully, despite all the government's failed promises—and even after some of its worst blunders—the market survives. We have a viable stock market not only for industrial companies, but also for banks and insurance companies. We have a market not only for corporate securities, but also for *government* securities. We can buy or sell virtually anything at any time.

Third, we have great strength in numbers. My company, Weiss Research, has over 600,000 readers. The members of our Financial Publisher's Association reach 14 million investors. And *hundreds* of millions of investors around the world share similar desires and goals: To protect their savings, boost their income, and grow wealth.

This is why I know we can win the battle for sanity and moderation. *And this is why I invite you to join me now.*

No membership dues. No obligation. No master plan. We are strictly a group of rational, well-intentioned investors, doing what we feel is right for ourselves and for our loved ones. We have *investor power,* and our impact can be far-reaching.

Investor Power on Wall Street

Let's say you, I, and like-minded investors decide to stand up against Wall Street.

We're sick of CEOs who trash company earnings and walk off with millions. We're tired of brokers who want *us* to buy the bad stocks they're trying to *sell.* We're fed up with analysts who give out *buys* and *holds* for pay but treat *sell* like a dirty, four-letter word. We're disgusted with triple-A bonds that are really *junk* in disguise.

We demand change—not out of political fervor, but because we want to *protect our capital.* Until we get the needed changes to satisfy our right to safety, we go on a buyer's strike. Or we sell.

That message doesn't take long to reach the CEOs, the brokers, and the Wall Street analysts. It's reflected immediately in the price of the stocks and bonds they own, issue, or recommend. It sends an instant signal that they cannot ignore.

Far-fetched? Quite to the contrary, we've seen investor power drive recent events time and again.

Investors declared a buyer's strike on securities backed by sub-prime mortgages; and they virtually shut that market down.

Next, investors turned to securities backed by any mortgage or loan, shutting most of those markets down as well.

They declared buyer's strikes on the shares of Bear Stearns and Lehman Brothers; Fannie Mae and Freddie Mac; Washington Mutual, Wachovia, and Citigroup. These companies' stock prices plunged 80 percent, 90 percent, 95 percent, even 99 percent. Their market capitalization was wiped out. One after another, these Goliaths were felled by investor power.

Episode after episode, we saw the same pattern. Investors saw a bubble about to burst, they ran for cover, and the bubble burst. They didn't create the bubble. Nor was there a plot to bring a company down. Investors merely sought to protect their own capital and stopped buying or started selling. And that was the beginning of the end for each company caught in their crosshairs.

Rest assured, few investors do this on a whim or out of malice. They need proof. Indeed, in 2008, it was only after the largest giants of each financial sector revealed gross misdeeds or mistakes that they became directly vulnerable to investor wrath—Countrywide, the biggest U.S. mortgage lender; Fannie Mae, the biggest U.S. government-sponsored enterprise; Merrill Lynch, the largest American investment bank; Washington Mutual, the largest U.S. savings and loan; American International Group, the largest U.S. insurance company; and Citigroup, the richest banking conglomerate.

No matter how tall and powerful these Goliaths might have been, they were no match for Davids like you and me. They had committed unforgivable financial sins. They delivered unforgettable losses. Their day of reckoning arrived. Investors rendered their verdict. And that was it.

Was there a rush to judgment? Did investors fire indiscriminately or in panic? Rarely. The verdicts were invariably based on hard evidence of ailing assets and public confessions of financial faults.

Investor Power in Washington

In a saner time or place, each of these giant companies would have to pay the penalty—reorganize or go out of business; shape up or ship out. But they did neither.

Why? Because another, even larger Goliath stepped into the fray, shielded their managers, and commuted their final sentence: Uncle Sam, the government of the United States of America.

One by one, Uncle Sam picked up the failed companies, injected capital, force-fed loans, sucked out bad assets, and swore to protect them with blanket guarantees. Uncle Sam's goal was to calm the public and make the pain in the market go away. But the real result has been a pact with the devil that could return to haunt us for several reasons.

First, Uncle Sam had to *borrow* the bailout money. But he already had a pile-up of debts: at the end of 2007, the U.S. Treasury owed $5.1 trillion, while U.S. government-related entities owed another $7.4 trillion. Total federal debt, not including obligations for Social Security and Medicare, was $12.5 trillion. That was bad enough. But two and a half years later, by mid-year 2010, even though some private sectors had been forced to cut *down* their debts, government debts had continued to grow by leaps and bounds: $8.6 trillion owed by the Treasury plus $7.7 trillion owed by government-related entities, for a total of $16.3 trillion.

Second, Uncle Sam's only viable mechanism for borrowing all that money is by selling bonds and other government securities to guess who! *Investors!*

Much like Bear Stearns, Fannie Mae, Washington Mutual, or Citigroup, Uncle Sam must get his money from investors by selling them securities; and these investors are not obligated to buy them. Worse, they're free to dump previously bought securities at any time in any amount. Uncle Sam has no way of twisting their arm to buy. Nor can he stop them from selling if that's their aim. Ultimately, he has no special powers over investors that Wall Street companies lack.

Third, the investors who financed Uncle Sam can be just as tough and demanding as the investors who owned companies like Bear Stearns or Washington Mutual. The biggest single group of these investors is overseas. Many are U.S. banks, pension funds, insurance companies, cities, and states. Also among them are individuals like you and me, holding over $1 trillion in government-related securities. Combined, we have more firepower in Washington than any other entity in the country or on the planet.

The reason: Uncle Sam needs us. He needs us to *hold* the U.S. government bonds we've already bought from him. And he needs us to buy more *new* bonds to finance his new spending and deficits.

We are his lender, his creditor, his benefactor. He must keep us happy. He cannot afford to do anything that will make us angry or turn us away. Yes, we will seriously consider buying and holding his bonds. They have the potential to pay us solid, guaranteed interest. But only on our terms! Only when we say it's the right time!

If Uncle Sam hints at violating our trust in any fashion, we have the power to say, "No deal." We can rebel if he's spending our money wantonly. We can pull away if he's threatening to pay us back with a devalued currency. Or we can snap shut our wallet simply because we foresee some such shenanigans in the future. That's precisely what global investors did to Greece, Ireland, and other countries that committed similar financial sins. It's what they could do to the United States as well.

How do we rebel against Uncle Sam, and what happens if we do? The sequence of events is no different from what we've already seen with each investor rebellion against corporate America and Wall Street: We go on a buyer's strike. Or we sell. And the ultimate result will be a sea change in Uncle Sam's attitude, policy, and behavior.

We rebel. And we can change history.

I know what you're thinking: We're too small and the government is too big. Yet this is precisely what U.S. and global bond investors did in 1980 and what they could do *again* in the future. To understand exactly how, let's go back to that critical time in history.

Investor Power in Washington: A 1980 Case Study

The time is late 1979; the place, back-office trading rooms of Salomon Brothers, Merrill Lynch, and dozens of other companies in downtown Manhattan. This is where most U.S. government securities are traded, bought, and sold on the market like any corporate bond or municipal bond.

Inflation is approaching double digits. The federal deficit is out of control. Russia invades Afghanistan, raising fears of a hotter Cold War; there is more deficit spending and inflation.

Bond investors fear that their money will be practically worthless by the time their bonds mature. So they go on a buyer's strike. No matter what Wall Street or Washington says, they refuse to buy long-term Treasury bonds.

Here's my diary of the events that ensue:

New York, February 5, 1980. Yields on longest-term U.S. government securities have just broken through the 11 percent level–the all-time peak reached during the Civil War. "Faced with a prolonged buyer's strike," one seasoned pro tells the *Wall Street Journal,* "we decided to throw in the towel and get yields up to a level where some cash buyers might be shocked off the sidelines." But even at 11 percent, most investors aren't interested.

Some analysts believe that inflation fears are the sole cause of the collapse. Why should investors buy bonds yielding 12 or even 13 percent, they say, if they expect inflation to be at 18 or 20 percent? But also weighing on the market is an avalanche of new bond supplies coming from the government to finance a bulging deficit. Like any commodity, the more abundant the supplies relative to demand, the more the price falls.

New York, February 6. Some panicky bondholders are unloading at any price, but there are few takers. According to the *Wall Street Journal,* the flood of sell orders has prompted all except two of the largest, best-capitalized bond houses to effectively abandon their market-making role. This is no longer merely a case of a price collapse. It's a *market* collapse in the literal sense of the word; the dealers themselves are packing up and going home!

New York, February 11. The pressure on Uncle Sam to do something drastic is mounting by the minute. By some estimates, investors have losses totaling 25 percent of the market value of their bond holdings, or more than $400 billion. A source at one sizable bank in the East says that, if he has to liquidate his Treasury notes, the loss will amount to more than $225 million, wiping out the bank's capital.

New York, February 19. The collapse continues to gather momentum. According to the *Journal,* the Treasury bond market is reeling through "an even blacker Tuesday as inflation and interest rate fears send prices lower." Yesterday alone, Treasury bonds lost over 5 percent of their face value, double the 2.5 percent drop that caused traders to refer to February 5 as "Black Tuesday."

New York, February 24. Pessimism in the bond market is off the charts. The bond market collapse is now about three times worse than its worst collapse last year.

Actual Meeting in 1980, Fictional Dialogue

The scene shifts from New York to Camp David, the second week of April 1980. A previously scheduled meeting between President Jimmy Carter and the recently appointed Federal Reserve Chairman Paul Volcker is expanded to include chief executives from two leading Wall Street firms, Salomon Brothers and Merrill Lynch.

I wasn't there, and I don't know what was said. But based on various accounts of those present as well as the outcome of the meeting, I have created the fictional dialogue that follows to help you better understand the actual, urgent issues that were on the table. Bear in mind that, in the future, the United States may face a dilemma that's similar in many ways.

Chairman: Gentlemen, we have come to a dangerous fork in the road, a desperate situation for our government and a dangerous one for our country. Investors are on strike, and it has become almost impossible to sell our government bonds at any price. We're facing a calamity in which we will not be able to raise the funds we urgently need to meet government payroll and fund day-to-day government operations. We must make every sacrifice to satisfy the demands of bond investors.

President: I understand why people are reluctant to buy bonds. They are afraid of inflation. They're afraid that when their bonds mature, the government will pay them back with money that's worth less. But that's happened before, and all we had to do was pay a higher interest rate. Why isn't that possible now?

Chairman:	Because there's a buyer's strike, and what's—
President:	I understand, but . . .
Chairman:	What's worse is that the bond market mechanism itself is collapsing.
President:	What precisely does that involve?
Salomon:	The U.S. government sells its bonds like an auto manufacturer sells its cars. Take General Motors, for example. GM rarely sells its cars directly to the public. Instead, it has a network of dealers all over the country. The dealers buy the cars at auction, paying a wholesale price. They hold the cars on their lots. They mark up the price. And then they sell them retail. The government does the same with its bonds. You, the issuer, sell them at auction to a nationwide network of bond dealers like us. We, the dealers, buy the bonds wholesale; we put 'em on our shelves; we mark 'em up; then we sell 'em retail.
Merrill:	We are one of the two largest government bond dealers.
Salomon:	We're the other. And we can tell you flatly: Under these conditions, *we cannot be your bond dealers anymore.* Three-month Treasury bills are okay. Investors trust you for three months. But medium-term Treasury notes and long-term Treasury bonds? Impossible! You see, as long as bond prices were relatively stable, we could afford to hold your bonds in inventory. Between the time we bought them at auction and the time we placed them with investors, if the price went up, we made a small profit; if the price went down, we took a small loss. We could handle that. We could even hedge against it.
President:	And now?
Salomon:	Now, bond prices aren't just falling; they're collapsing. In fact, bond prices have fallen so far so quickly, and bond dealers have lost so much money so suddenly, their capital is being wiped out. So they've

packed up and gone home. Nearly the entire dealer network for U.S. government securities is shut down. We and Merrill are practically the only ones still open for business in government bonds.

Merrill: Yeah, we're open all right. But we're not doing business. The buyer's strike is so severe, we can't even find buyers for $100 million in U.S. government bonds. Typically, we could place a small lot like that in a heartbeat. Now we can't find a buyer for that amount, let alone for the billions you need us to place. We call Salomon and try to sell the government bonds to them. They call us and try to sell the bonds to us. We're like the last two kids on the street corner trying to trade the same marbles.

President: So why can't the U.S. government merely pay a higher yield?

Salomon: We've been there and done that. Yields have already skyrocketed. But it's not making any difference. You must not underestimate the power of investors. They are rebelling against U.S. government bonds, against the U.S. government itself. It doesn't matter how much yield they get. They're not buying. Unless the government takes action—urgent and radical action—the game is over.

President: Explain, please.

Chairman: By *game,* they mean borrowing from Peter to pay Paul. That's the game the U.S. government has been playing for many years now. How do we pay off our debts coming due? We count on lenders—investors—to renew their loans to us. But ultimately, we're no different from any other borrower. As soon as the lender pulls out, as soon as they refuse to roll over our debts, it's *game over.*

President: Then what?

Chairman: It's hard for me to actually put this into words, but it's true. At that point, we may as well shut down and start a new republic. And I'm not saying that just as a metaphor. It's the real, natural consequence of being so dependent on debt and so dependent on the open market for bonds. Forget about the election in November! We would not have enough money for payroll *this week*. Our own paychecks would bounce.

President: What do you propose?

Chairman: We must kill the inflation monster. We must drive a dagger into its heart. I have already clamped down on the money supply. But that wasn't enough. I've already switched from the irrational policy of fixing the price of money—interest rates—to the rational policy of controlling the *supply* of money and letting the market drive interest rates where it may. But that wasn't enough either. Now we've got to also clamp down on credit. It's the abundance of credit that's fueling the inflation.

President: How do you clamp down on credit?

Chairman: What I propose is a package of measures that we call *credit controls*. Credit cards are a driver behind the borrow-and-spend behavior of consumers, and that's driving up prices. We must restrict the use of credit cards. Commercial paper is a major source of corporate spending, also driving prices higher; and money market funds are the biggest buyers of commercial paper. So we slap a freeze on money market funds; we don't let them accept any new money from investors. There's more. But this should give you a sense of how drastic the measures must be.

President: What will that do to the economy?

Chairman: It will most likely cause a sharp contraction of consumer spending. There's no avoiding that. But what would you prefer—a decline in the economy tomorrow or instant death due to a U.S. government default today?

President: You're saying we have no choice.

Chairman: No, we don't. Investors are on strike. They are very powerful. We're at their mercy.

Washington, D.C., April 15, 1980. Shortly after the Camp David meeting, on April 15, 1980, the White House announces an unprecedented package of credit controls, clamping down on virtually all forms of credit. It is seen as the only way to kill the inflation monster; the only way to revive the moribund government bond market. The economy plunges, and President Carter loses the election. But the bond market recovers.

The Government's Last Rescue

We saw a similar pattern in the sovereign debt crisis of 2010, and in both cases, the moral of the story was clear: Investors, large and small, acting in their own self-interest, were able to force a major reversal in the policies of the most powerful governments in the world.

In Greece, Ireland, and other weak European countries, austerity was their only choice. And in the United States of 1980, for the first time in history, a president in the White House, in a presidential election year, took actions to severely restrict credit and kill inflation. It demonstrated the ultimate power of investors like you to overcome even the strongest of political agendas.

In the not-too-distant future, could investor power strike Washington again? Could they declare a buyer's strike on U.S. government bonds and threaten to shut down the U.S. government like they did in 1980?

Most observers think not. They see no inflation on the horizon. They see investors flocking to U.S. government bonds for safety. Most important, they blindly assume that the U.S. government bond market is immune to the crisis of confidence that has struck nearly every other market. What they're not seeing is the similarities between 1980 and today:

- A vast abundance of already-issued U.S. government bonds all over the globe—huge supplies ready to be dumped on the market at a moment's notice.
- A flood of *new* bond supplies that will soon be issued—to finance the government's trillion-dollar deficits.
- A strong reason for dumping bonds. In 1980, it was the fear of inflation; in the current era, it is the fear of a government gone wild, printing money indiscriminately to bail out the world.

■ As occurred in the early 1930s, if there is a double-dip recession, another powerful motivating force could be the urgent need to *raise cash!* Remember: In hard times, investors sell not only because they've turned sour on an investment; they also sell because *they need the money.*

In 1980, President Carter learned that the only thing that would satisfy investors and bring them back into the circle of buyers was action to kill inflation.

And in early 2010, several countries in Europe learned the same lesson during the sovereign debt crisis. Unless they implemented austerity measures to cut spending—despite mass public protests—they would be unable to borrow money to roll over their maturing debts; they'd have to default; and their entire economy would be sunk into a far deeper ditch than anything their self-imposed austerity could conceivably cause.

The same could happen in the United States. And the most urgent demand by investors could be to scale back, freeze or even reverse government bailouts, stimulus, and money printing.

To understand how, let's say we're among the countless investors around the world who own long-term U.S. government bonds.

Our message to Uncle Sam is simple:

Uncle Sam, we own your government securities because we trusted you. We lent you the money for the purpose of running your government. But now you've taken our money and passed it along to a third party, to bail out bankrupt companies. That's a deal breaker. If we wanted to lend our money to those companies, we would have done so directly, in the first place. We didn't because we don't trust those companies. We trusted you. Now maybe we can't trust you anymore, either. Now it looks like you're just one of them.

We're not asking for anything out of the ordinary. All we're asking is that our money be used primarily for the purpose for which it was originally intended—to finance the government's operations and to cover a deficit that retains a modicum of sanity. That's the only way to guarantee that we'll get our money back 30 years from now and that we'll get paid in dollars that are still solid.

If Uncle Sam refuses, we declare a buyer's strike. Bond prices collapse. Yields surge. And the ghosts of 1980—close cousins of the demons that struck Europe in 2010—return.

But it's not entirely a bad thing. It forces the government to be more careful with our money. It drives bond prices down and interest rates up, giving us the opportunity to lock in some of the highest real yields of all time (as explained in Chapter 15).

A sea change sweeps through Washington.

Until that moment, the theory of government bailouts is that Uncle Sam is *lifting up* companies from the quagmire of bad debts. Now, it is suddenly realized that the old theory is upside down: In reality, it's the bankrupt companies that are dragging the U.S. government down.

Instead of bailing out the world, the government must save itself. *It is the government's last rescue.*

Despite the hardship, my hope—and my forecast—is that there will be one outstanding benefit: *the recovery of the dollar.*

Our money's purchasing power goes up, not down; the U.S. dollar is worth more, not less. To earn that valuable dollar, all Americans have an incentive to work harder and sacrifice more. Most important, the recovery of the dollar gives us the opportunity—albeit not the certainty—to restore America's strength. But first, much needs to be repaired, and a new foundation must be laid.

CHAPTER 19

THE FOUNDATION FOR RECOVERY

With the return of inflation, any recovery will be labored and shaky. Without inflation, it can be vigorous and stable. Here are the two possible scenarios that ensue.

The greater-of-the-evils inflation scenario: Bad debts are shuffled around to larger companies, and larger companies are nationalized by the government. The day of reckoning is forever postponed; debt burdens, forever enlarged; a real recovery of America's strength, always beyond reach.

The lesser-of-the-evils deflation scenario: Recovery from debt addiction is not an easy process. It takes introspection, courage, and great moral fortitude. It requires personal sacrifice and collective support. But as a nation, we've overcome tougher obstacles before. We can overcome this one as well. The recovery, even if delayed, is sustainable and restores America's greatness.

I am an optimist. So let's begin by talking about the lesser-of-the-evils scenario. If you have avoided debt and built up a nice nest egg of cash, you are among the minority of investors ready to lead the recovery and benefit handsomely in the process. And I am there with you.

But the majority is not that far behind us. One sunny morning, despite the bankruptcies, the unemployment, and the hardships they bring, most Americans wake up to the realization that the nation's cup is half full: The buildings are still standing. The highways are still intact. The phones are working, and the lights are still on. The Internet is running; the nation's pool of knowledge and know-how is mostly intact; the world has not come to an end.

Factories and farms are ready and able to produce goods and supplies in abundance. In almost every home, citizens own durables that can meet their needs for quite some time—vehicles, appliances, equipment, and a vast accumulation of household goods. There are few critical shortages.

In Washington and on Wall Street, there are no tools, weapons, or devices available to compel people to make the wrong economic or investment decisions. Instead, there are countless markets in which they can readily dispose of any goods they don't need and acquire any they want. Cheaply!

The foundation for a recovery, however, must still be built, phase by phase, slowly and deliberately through three processes—acceptance, admission, and action.

Phase 1: Acceptance

Throughout my lifetime—and probably yours as well—the controlling economic theory has always been that the Great Depression was an anomaly, a single, unique accident that could have been prevented.

The belief has been that, in the 1930s, the government's hands-off approach is what caused and prolonged the economic suffering. And from that belief, it was concluded that "*the* Depression," as it's been called, was a monumental blunder that must not be repeated; that any future depression could easily be prevented.

The greater-of-the-evils inflation scenario: This belief persists. It drives Washington and Wall Street into ever-greater bailouts to rescue prior bailouts; more money printing to cover up prior money printing excesses; ever greater blunders; and ever bigger deceptions to cover up earlier blunders.

The lesser-of-the-evils deflation scenario: As America begins to experience another bust, it does not take economic policy makers long to realize that the 1930s Great Depression was *not* a unique phenomenon after all.

Like Mark Twain, who was shocked at the age of 21 to realize how much his father had suddenly learned, our leaders see that their 1930s predecessors may not have been that ignorant after all.

Our leaders recognize that, despite the trillions spent, lent, invested, or guaranteed, the government is not able to prevent a devastating economic decline. They finally understand that it was actually their own zeal to create a perpetual boom that set up the conditions for the subsequent bust.

Before this critical moment of acceptance, our leaders think they can buck the vicious cycle of debt and deflation. They feel compelled to get banks to resume lending, consumers to resume borrowing, and investors to take more risk again.

After this moment of acceptance, however, they realize that approach was upside down or, at best, premature. They accept not only the fact that they're losing the war against deflation, but also that it may be the wrong war to fight in the first place. They begin to view deflation in an entirely new light—as a cleansing process, which can help reduce debts, bring down prices, and restore balance.

Finally, they make a monumental policy shift. They say, simply: *Since we can't beat it, we may as well lead it.*

Their new challenge is no longer to *stop* the cleansing. Rather, it is to proactively manage the process to avoid its most harmful social and political consequences.

Phase 2: Public Admission

The greater-of-the-evils inflation scenario: Washington and Wall Street become obsessed with "proper messaging." Their first priority is to create special commissions and fine-tune their choice of words in order to filter the facts and shroud the truth. Addressing the true causes of the crisis is the *last* priority, always relegated to a future day that never comes.

The lesser-of-the-evils deflation scenario: Our leaders—or a new crop of leaders that come to power—publicly admit earlier errors and confess to the real constraints to their power. They announce, perhaps bluntly, perhaps subtly, that Uncle Sam is no longer the nation's lender, spender, investor, and guarantor of last resort; that each citizen must step up and make the needed sacrifices to restore the nation's economic health.

Phase 3: Action!

The greater-of-the-evils inflation scenario: Little is done to change harmful trends already in place in the early stages of the crisis.

For example, in the U.S. housing market between 2006 and 2010, many attempts were made to stem the tidal wave of home foreclosures. But consistently, the message transmitted to indebted homeowners was: "To qualify for government debt relief, you have to fall behind in your payments. You must be delinquent. If you're cutting your food budget, if you're pawning your wedding rings, and if you're doing all that to stay current with your mortgage payments, you don't qualify. Sorry, no mortgage relief for you!"

In this scenario, the carrot-for-the-delinquent, stick-for-the-worthy approach persists. Millions more abandon their homes or are driven into foreclosure. And, ironically, among the first to join that mass movement are some of the very same groups that, in an earlier stage of their payment history, were identified as the categories *most* qualified for mortgage relief. Even more surprising—millions who can afford to make their monthly payments, decide to default strictly as a tactic for living in a home rent free while they await eviction, saving their money, or even spending it elsewhere. As a society, instead of lightening our debt burdens, we merely prolong them; instead of countering the culture of default, we merely enhance it.

The lesser-of-the-evils deflation scenario: With public admission of past errors, the upside-down policies of recent years are replaced and reversed.

Households that are current with their mortgage reap the rewards that naturally come with home ownership; those that are delinquent declare bankruptcy and forfeit other assets.

Banking and government officials treat debts as debts, charity as charity. Instead of pouring good money after bad to rescue delinquent borrowers, they encourage lenders to liquidate bad debts.

Instead of neglecting the victims of past foreclosures, they support organizations that house the homeless, feed the hungry, and help recovering debt addicts—with prompt penalties for those that abuse the government's largesse. Instead of bailouts in the trillions, they need only budgets in the billions or millions. Instead of promoting delinquency, they foster an environment of responsibility.

This transformation is not driven by some miraculous return of morality. It is driven mostly by the hard reality that *the government simply does not have the money to do more.* With its financing drying up, it cannot afford the giant bailouts for failed companies. They cost too much. Volunteerism, education, prevention, emergency care, tender loving care, and a dose of tough love are far less expensive.

In Washington, the Federal Reserve and the U.S. Treasury also change their ways. Earlier, they sought easy, flip-the-switch shortcuts to resolve the crisis: Rate cuts and money printing by the Federal Reserve; fast-track bailout, stimulus, and tax packages passed by Congress; instant gratification for all. But in this scenario, that, too, is reversed.

In a policy shift reminiscent of the Fed's shift under Chairman Paul Volcker in 1979, instead of controlling the price of money and credit (interest rates), the Federal Reserve seeks to moderate the *supply* of money and credit, allowing interest rates to find their own level. Interest rates skyrocket initially. But then they come down naturally—settling at more normal levels.

Instead of sweeping bad debts under the rug, banks and government examiners knuckle down to the painstaking process of sorting through each mortgage and loan on the books, tracking down the parties in each debt obligation, documenting the detail of every derivative contract. Then, with good databases in place, they perform the needed triage to liquidate the bad, segregate the good, and send the balance to rehab.

Instead of propping up bad banks, they proactively shut them down. Instead of shotgun mergers to shuffle toxic paper from weak to strong hands, they compel each bank to dispose of its own waste, sometimes under federal supervision, sometimes on their own recognizance.

Much as in a vote recount after a disputed election, no stone is left unturned, no debt blindly repudiated, no lender compelled to refinance.

Earlier, they fought against the debt liquidation and against the price deflation. Now, they realize they were fighting the wrong war. They were holding back a tide that could solve problems already obvious to nearly everyone: excess debt, unaffordable housing, sick schools, and the country's inability to compete globally.

Earlier, bankrupt banks and rich CEOs were the first in line for government handouts. Now, those priorities also change dramatically. Hospitals, fire departments, and police forces—hurt severely by city and state budget cuts—are first in line; public schools, a close second.

Hospitals, in particular, are a classic example of misplaced priorities. Earlier, even while politicians debated the fine points of national health care programs, hospitals were going broke. Their revenues from paid elective procedures were drying up. Their outlays for unpaid emergency care were surging. Their losses were so large, they were firing staff, shutting down facilities, and turning away emergency patients. Now, however, that changes too. Rather than trillions to rescue banks, a small fraction of that money is spent to bail out hospitals. Before reforming a health care system that's floundering, they focus on saving people who are dying.

Earlier, some observers feared that the U.S. government might default on its own debts. But now those fears begin to fade.

The U.S. Treasury honors, at all costs, its direct obligations. No matter where you live or who you are, if you're an investor or saver who has bought U.S. Treasury securities, you get your money back, promptly and on time. No matter how you bought your Treasuries—through a money market mutual fund, a broker, a bank, or through the Treasury Direct program—you are guaranteed equal treatment.

If the government does not have the cash, it borrows more. If the government cannot borrow more, it raises the rate it pays. If higher rates are still not enough to overcome investor fears, deeper spending cuts are made, more deflation ensues, an even stronger dollar is encouraged.

No more tricks and gimmicks are accepted; no more government smoke and mirrors are possible. In their place is tough love for everyone, especially Uncle Sam himself.

Tough Consequences

The inflation scenario: America sinks into a prolonged period of malaise punctuated by bouts of chaos. The many speculative bubbles produce few winners; the ensuing busts, many losers.

America suffers a second Great Depression that drags out for so long, it ultimately becomes more severe than the first. Unemployment, although lower than the 1930s initially, eventually surges to the highest level in American history. We witness periods of on-again-off-again industrial shutdowns and work stoppages. In some hard-hit regions, there are times when more people are out of work than on the job. Tent cities are belatedly erected to house the homeless, but they're overcrowded. Portable kitchens are set up to feed the hungry, but they're overwhelmed.

We witness mass internal migrations among the middle class, starvation among the poor, pandemics of diseases that are eminently curable. A financial Katrina in every major city of America.

The deflation scenario: The economic decline is severe but less so than the 1930s experience. Moreover, to achieve this outcome, the government does not have to create a second New Deal. It merely updates, funds, and staffs institutions still in place from the first New Deal. Even the most ambitious emergency relief effort is less expensive than some of the *least* ambitious bank bailout efforts.

The surpluses, technology, and logistic know-how are readily available. The U.S. government simply shifts its priorities from the war on deflation that it cannot win to the war on human suffering that it must not lose.

These efforts do not create a welfare state or lead the economy to a socialist dead end. Much like protecting New Orleans from a second Katrina or defending the homeland from another 9/11, it is basic emergency preparedness.

Nor do these efforts preclude pursuing the battle for a recovery. Once most of the bad debts are liquidated, and once federal deficits are under control, *then* the government invests in helping to stimulate a recovery. Like any investor, the government learns that taxpayer money buys a lot more benefits for citizens in deflation than it possibly could with inflation.

Despite some wrong turns and missed opportunities, the right choices are made. And despite continuing conflicts that are part of our nature, we have the opportunity to embark on the most moderate—and enduring—era of prosperity in the history of mankind.

CHAPTER 20

FUTURE FORTUNES

In the wake of bubbles, busts, recession, and depression, many old fortunes die, and many new ones are born. Out of poverty and suffering come good times and new wealth. Dad explains it in the context of his childhood:

Growing up in New York City in the early 1900s, the differences between the haves and have-nots were vividly clear to me, even as a child. We lived on the East Side of Central Park, which was tough and poor. The rich lived mostly on the West Side of Central Park, which was lavishly elegant.

But tough is not bad. My heroes were world-famous boxing champions that grew up in my neighborhood, and I ran errands for them. I learned how to fight, too. I had no choice. If you couldn't fight, you didn't have friends; and if you didn't travel with friends, you could never cross the line into other neighborhoods without getting beaten up.

Before I was seven, my brother and I began to invest in matches. We'd buy a case. Then we'd spend the whole day selling them on the busiest street corner we could find. We tried not to go home until the last box was sold. But keeping that money for ourselves was a no-no. Every single dime had to go back to my mother.

We used to practice gymnastics on the roof of our building, and I once found an injured bird there. I began nursing it back to health. But it happened to be a particularly tough month for my parents. One afternoon, I came home from school and learned we had "chicken soup" for dinner. I also learned it was not made from chicken. I lost my appetite, but I never forgot just how precious the family savings really was.

When the war began, most people called it the "Great War." Others said it was "The War to End All Wars." No one called it the First World War until the Second World War; they never believed we'd have another one. Ironically, it was the war that first got me interested in investments. Plus, it reinforced my awareness of rich and poor.

It happened when our elementary school teacher asked us to sell Liberty Bonds to raise money to support the war effort. So one Saturday, my friends and I decided to walk over to the West Side to sell some bonds. I figured I'd be lucky if I sold $20 worth.

But just as we were walking through the Central Park tunnel, we saw a nicely dressed woman walking in the opposite direction. I stopped her and said: "Ma'am, would you be interested in buying a Liberty Bond?"

She smiled broadly and answered: "You're selling Liberty Bonds? Well, young man, I just happen to be going to the bank on Fifth Avenue to buy some Liberty Bonds. So I might as well buy them from you."

She bought $200 worth! In just a few moments I had raised many times what I had hoped to raise for the entire month. I was a hero in my class and was proud of every moment. This type of experience left me with a feeling of patriotism and a desire to help my country that stayed with me for the rest of my life. It also taught me we were all in the same struggle together, rich or poor.

Later, in the 1930s, that lesson served me well. I never felt one ounce of loathing for the rich. Most lost their fortunes and suffered like everyone else. I certainly had no disdain for the poor. They had all the talent and ability to build new fortunes.

When I think of fortunes, Joseph Kennedy, the father of JFK, comes to mind. He had a better head start than most, of course. But it was in 1933 that he started building his biggest fortunes. He was one of our clients, and I visited him in Palm Beach. I tried to get him to buy silver when it was trading at about 17 cents an ounce. His other advisers talked him out of it, though. Too bad. If he had invested a meager $4,000, he could have bought 22 1,000-ounce silver bars. Then, years later, the Kennedy family could have sold them for $50,000 each, netting more than a million for each $4,000 invested.

Growing up, my experience was not altogether different, but in a very different place and time.

Dad believed not only in saving money but also in saving trees. So when I was six, he decided to start an experimental organic tree farm in Brazil. He figured the family could live there, while he'd commute to and from Wall Street every couple of months. My Mom, even more adventurous than Dad, loved the idea.

Dad's in-laws, especially my grandmother, thought he had lost his marbles. They were wrong except in one respect: The commute was 40 hours, one way.

For me, though, it was the experience of a lifetime. The year was 1952. We were in the center of Brazil, far from cities, paved roads, electricity, or phones. My friends were even poorer than kids growing up in the immigrant neighborhoods of New York City a half-century earlier.

That didn't surprise me. What I found amazing, though, is that, on anything that mattered, they always seemed to know a lot more than I did. That's when I came to understand that the United States is not alone in the world. Till this day, the United States is my favorite country, and that's why I live here. But I also love Brazil, where I was raised, Japan, where I did my doctoral fieldwork, and Russia, where my maternal grandparents were raised.

I have traveled to every continent except Antarctica. I have studied every major world language except Arabic. And I can assure you, the poor and middle-class individuals who get rich after this roller-coaster crisis will not be strictly in the United States. New fortunes will be made everywhere on the planet, opening up vast global opportunities for you.

Before I tell you more about those, let me remind you that your first major investment opportunities will be right here in the United States. You'll feel like a kid in a candy shop. You'll have your pick of tremendous bargains—many more than you could possibly scoop up even with the greatest of cash hoards.

I want to guide you step by step so you can build up your investment portfolio steadily. Here's the scenario I see unfolding and how we can respond:

First and foremost, when long-term interest rates soar temporarily, we shift a good portion of our cash from short- to longer-term Treasuries. As an intermediate step, we also buy 5- and 10-year

Treasury notes. And we make the shifts one step at a time, in modest amounts at first, adding as we go. (Please review Chapter 15.)

Second, as the tide of corporate bankruptcies subsides, we look more seriously at high-grade corporate bonds. Hopefully, the Wall Street rating agencies thoroughly revamp their grades, bringing them into sync with reality. If not, we find independent ratings or indicators to guide us. The payoff is yields that are as much as double the best yields we can get on Treasuries—not to mention triple-digit capital gains as beaten-down corporate bonds bounce back sharply in price.

Third, dividend-paying stocks. No, not all of the established, name-brand companies survive. But most do. Weiss Ratings gives us a list of the most stable among them; Weiss dividend specialist Nilus Mattive picks them out as the cream of the crop; and we buy them for a good discount from their peak prices. We also include some with dividend yields and capital gain potential that put the best corporate bonds to shame (Chapter 16).

Fourth, real estate. You pick your favorite location, your favorite property, and your dream price. Then we compare them to hundreds of other prime properties, also selling for a song.

Mike Larson, who first warned us about the housing bust in 2005, helps us time the next long-term boom. It's not a superboom, but we don't want it to be. Those don't last very long anyway.

Specifically, I have been eyeing choice beachfront properties in southeast Brazil, northeast Australia, plus several locations closer to home. As they hit rock bottom, they become unbelievably cheap, within easy grasp of average Americans who may never have dreamed of owning a beautiful home so close to the ocean.

But before buying these or similar gems, wait for my e-mail alerts. (Just don't forget to get on my list at www.moneyandmarkets .com/guide.)

Fifth, gold and silver. We start with exchange-traded funds (ETFs) that are dedicated to each of these metals. Plus, it's also time to travel. We put together a tour group. We hit the road, and Larry Edelson, Weiss Research's precious metals expert, is our first guide. He takes us to North American mining companies with abundant cash, virtually no debts, and the most efficient production facilities.

FIVE GOLDEN RULES FOR BUILDING NEW FORTUNES

As the world economy recovers and you pursue the opportunity to build new fortunes, it's vital that you do so without missing a beat or suffering a major setback. Here are the guidelines to follow:

Golden Rule 1: **Keep Your Priorities Straight**

Aim *first* for savings and capital preservation, *second* for growth, and last for speculative profits.

Golden Rule 2: **Controlling Risk Is Just as Important as Maximizing Gains**

Profit potential can be an important driver of your ultimate success. However, controlling your risk is actually *more* important.

For investments that expose you to large potential losses, use stop-loss orders. If the value of your stock or ETF falls, there is no guarantee that you will get a price that corresponds exactly to the stop-loss level you specify. But it should help protect your capital—either to prevent a larger loss or to protect an open profit.

Diversify beyond the stock market by investing in various asset classes—including a large allocation to Treasury bonds at the right time, plus, as economic prospects improve, high grade corporate bonds, solid dividend-paying stocks, precious metals, real estate, and even commodities or foreign currencies.

Golden Rule 3: **If You Speculate, Use Only Money You Can Afford to Lose**

Far too many investors speculate with the keep-safe portion of their nest egg. They fail to realize that speculation can ruin them just as easily as it can pay off big rewards.

(Continued)

Do not use funds that you'll need for emergencies, your children's or grandchildren's education, basic necessities, retirement living expenses, or long-term health care. If you find yourself *counting* on the expected gains so as to make your financial plan a success, you have probably exceeded your limits. Even if you do have enough capital, do not speculate if you find yourself losing sleep over it.

Golden Rule 4: Keep Your Emotions in Check

Treat investing as a business. It's not a game. Consider your income as revenues. Categorize and keep track of your expenses, including broker commissions and fees, as you would in any business. The more you do so, the more objective you will be about every aspect of your money.

Review your financial position monthly. This is especially important in tough times. Do it much like you would review your business's monthly financial statements.

Don't hesitate to change your strategy as needed. If the investment is not working for you, seriously consider moving on. Don't get stuck in an investment rut.

Golden Rule 5: Especially if You Trade Actively, Reduce Your Commission Costs to the Bone

Consider this scenario: You're not a buy-and-hold investor. But you're not an active trader, either. Starting with $100,000 in your brokerage account, you buy 20 different securities, with an average initial value of $5,000 each. Then, you buy and sell each one only twice a year, with an average profit of 5 percent per trade before commissions. With consistent profits like those, you'll retire rich, right? Not necessarily.

According to a survey of broker commissions we conducted, if you're paying top-dollar commissions (actually charged by 27 percent of the firms in our survey), your entire $100,000 will be totally wiped out by commissions by the end of year nine.

You can avoid disaster simply by using a broker who charges you the average commission rate among the brokers we surveyed. But, assuming the same preceding scenario, the results are *still* disappointing. All you'd make is a meager $21,675 in profits after 10 long years with no losses.

The *only* way to make good money trading semi actively in the stock market is to find brokers with commissions on the low end of the scale. In the preceding scenario, instead of just $21,675, you'd have $108,374 in profits *after* commissions. In other words, just by switching from average commissions to low commissions, you'd multiply your profits by nearly *five* times. Bottom line: Either trade *less* actively, or shop *more* proactively for low commissions.

In a temporary setback or bust, the price of the gold, silver, zinc, and other metals dip below production costs at many mines. That's one reason the mining shares are so cheap. But as soon as metal prices rise above production costs, the mines ramp up production and their share prices double and triple in short order. That's essentially the same reason Homestake and Dome Mining made so much money for my father's colleagues in the early 1930s. If we see similar opportunities, we grab them. But we don't wait for that scenario.

Sixth, Weiss Research's globetrotting Sean Brodrick guides the tour from here. He loves to go off the beaten track—deep underground in seventeenth-century Mexican silver mines, up to Canada in 10-degree weather far beyond the last northern road, or to the jungle of the Haitian-Dominican border. Just like my grandmother thought my father was crazy for going to Brazil in 1952, most people think Sean's crazy to go to these places now. But that's how he finds some of the best investment opportunities in what promises to be a brand new bull market for the world's scarcest natural resources.

Seventh, foreign blue chips, including those paying steady, high dividends. In the aftermath of a second depression, many Americans give up on foreign stock markets, especially in countries like Japan. They say those economies will be "forever mired in the doldrums" or that "their aging population can never get off the ground."

Fortunately, we know at least one American, Weiss Research's Tony Sagami, who disagrees and puts his money where his mouth is. But it's not simply because he was born in Japan. His own words:

> Hardship breeds success. That's true for individuals, companies, even entire nations. It's why the United States sprang forward after the Great Depression. It's why China, Japan, and even formerly dirt-poor India can spring forward, too. It's a fundamental principle that can unlock great investment opportunities for you.
>
> I know this from personal experience. After World War II, my mother fell in love with an American GI in Tokyo, and I was born nine months later. But he soon left us and went home to the U.S. Later, mom and I crossed the ocean to find him, but then wound up spending our first two months in America living under a bridge.
>
> Today, I own two technology companies. But my best times are traveling back to my native Japan, discovering the roots of Japanese culture in China, and exploring the rest of Asia to find wealth-building wonders for investors.
>
> Despite bad times, don't believe folks who tell you Japan is a has-been country. It has a close, capital-intensive partnership with China. Its new generation of leaders learned some major lessons about depressions and deflation in the 1990s. And I think they know how to avoid most of the blunders and extravagances. Indeed, modern Japan still reminds me—to a large degree—of the spirit that my parents brought me up with: Debt avoidance, hard work, and few luxuries.
>
> That helps explain why Japan has a lot more savings than we do. China is very different in most respects, but when it comes to savings, they have a lot in common.

As China and Japan recover, so does energy demand. Oil and gas prices climb back nicely.

Eighth, alternative energy. At first, it's dead in the water. "As long as traditional energy sources are so cheap," people say, "Why worry about alternatives?" But earlier energy shortages are blamed as one of the factors that triggered the great recession, and there's a widespread determination to avoid repeating the mistakes of the past. Renewable energy sources begin to attract new capital.

My personal favorite is ethanol made from sugarcane. Slowly and silently, the global demand for ethanol begins to rise, creating new industries that makes early investors wealthy.

It's about time! Ever since I married Elisabeth in 1969, and ever since I began visiting her family farm in Brazil, we have been talking about a future in which millions of cars would run on ethanol made from sugarcane. The concept is simple: a renewable energy source that's not subject to oil embargoes or Mideast conflicts, producing cleaner fuel, more jobs, and less pollution.

By 2010, Brazil's economy was already there—all new cars running with flex fuel engines and all fuel stations offering a choice of ethanol or gasoline. Now, continuing in our future scenario, as the global economy recovers, Brazil exports high-tech ethanol mills to Florida, Louisiana, Mississippi, and our close allies in the Caribbean. The Caribbean countries supply the United States with all the sugarcane–based ethanol we can't produce ourselves. And the industry takes off.

Earlier, investors focused on the fact that corn-based ethanol is inefficient. They failed to make the distinction between corn and sugarcane. Now they do. Previously, some investors didn't believe global warming, whether natural or man-made, would make a difference, and Detroit didn't want to let go of gasoline. Now, they recognize that their stubborness was a big blunder. Moreover, ethanol and other alternate fuels reduce our dependence on petroleum imports and give us firmer control over our own destiny.

With time, every country on the planet switches to automobiles running on renewable fuels. With a shift from 600 million gasoline- or diesel-burning cars and trucks on the road, we witness the most massive transformation since the industrial revolution.

Ninth, that's one reason global stock markets recover dramatically, and back in 2007, we got a sneak preview of the profit potential. Investors in the U.S. stock market made 6.4 percent for the year, which was not bad. But among all the stock markets in the world, the U.S. market ranked 65th.

If you had invested in France's stock market index instead, you would have done nearly twice as well—with an 11.9 percent gain. Canada's stock market index could have made you more than four times more money—with a 25.1 percent gain. Hong Kong would have given you eight times more, with a 55.5 percent gain. Brazil did 11 times better, with a 72.4 percent gain, and China's blue chips could have made you 28 times more, with a 179.8 percent gain.

Thus, while a $10,000 investment in the United States would have handed you a paltry $643 profit in 2007, the same investment in Brazil could have made you $7,244 richer, and if you had invested in the average Chinese blue chip, your $10,000 investment would have made you $17,975 richer.

Yes, in 2008, some of those gains were reversed as most foreign stocks suffered a severe correction in response to the debt crisis. But in 2009 and 2010, we saw a pattern similar to 2007's, as illustrated by the picks made by Weiss Research's ETF specialist Ron Rowland in his July 16, 2009, column of our *Money and Markets*: After just one year, his readers had seen a 23.3 percent gain in the South Africa ETF (EZA), a 27.7 percent gain in the Brazil ETF (EWZ), 33.5 percent gain in the Malaysia ETF (EWM), 33.6 gain percent in the India ETF (INP), plus a 63.8 gain percent in the Russia ETF (RSX), all despite buying late and selling late.

Or consider the longer-term performance of foreign markets, *including* the big 2008 dip: From January 1, 2003, through August 13, 2010, South Korea's major market index rose 194 percent, Singapore's rose 274 percent, Mexico's was up 363 percent, and Brazil's jumped 972 percent—not to mention some more exotic markets with even better performance. If you had simply bought and held Brazil's blue chips, $100,000 invested in 2003 would have been worth $1,072,000 by mid-year 2010. Amazingly, that was 41 times more than the rise in the Dow during the same period.

In a global recession, don't expect foreign markets to be immune from sharp declines. But in a long-term, sustainable recovery, these kinds of gains could be multiplied over many years. Indeed, some of the world's regions that were among the poorest may be among the quickest to catch up, including sub-Saharan Africa, Northeast Brazil, and South Asia, just to name a few. The resource in greatest demand: water, opening up major opportunities in companies that can dig wells cheaply.

But we don't have to go far afield to invest. As Ron Rowland illustrated with his 2009 picks, with a country-specific ETF in a regular U.S. brokerage account, we can own a portfolio of the most actively traded stocks in our choice of South Africa, Brazil, Malaysia, India, Russia, Singapore, and many other emerging markets. We can use a single ETF to diversify among several countries within a broader region, such as Latin America, Europe, or Asia. And we can diversify even further with ETFs that cover multiple regions of the world. Or, if we prefer not to venture too far, opportunities in the United States are also abundant. Hundreds of ETFs are dedicated to specific industry sectors.

No matter what, when, or where, just be sure to invest cautiously, following our five golden rules of investing.

As Dad first learned growing up in Harlem, our success is not measured strictly by how much we can make in one year or even five. It reflects what we can do for future generations as well. That is the essence of savings, the only way to truly survive bubbles, busts, recession, or depression—and thrive in the decades that follow.

NOTES

Chapter 1. Why the Tough Times Are Just Beginning!

1. The materials from J. Irving Weiss (1908–1987) are based on his extensive writings, including titles such as *The Money Squeeze, Too Many Hands in Your Pockets, The Third Crash,* various unpublished manuscripts, and the author's notes from extensive life history interviews.

2. I completely reject the argument that cultural and structural differences between the Japanese and U.S. economies justify Washington's view that it can repeat Japan's mistakes and somehow achieve a better result. My fieldwork in Japan for my doctorate focused on precisely this issue; and if anything, I found that the evidence supports the opposite thesis: The close cooperation between the private and public sectors in Japan—compared to the continuing conflicts between Wall Street and Washington—actually make it *less* likely that the U.S. government can succeed where Japan failed. See also Chalmers Johnson, *MITI and the Japanese Miracle,* Stanford University Press, 1982; and Edward J. Lincoln, *Japan's Industrial Policies,* Economic Institute of America, 1984.

3. See "Barack Obama-san," *Wall Street Journal,* December 16, 2008, A22.

4. The ruling Liberal Democratic Party (LDP) had lost its majority in the past, but except for a very short period, no other party had ever been strong enough to form a government until the 2009 elections. That's when the LDP was roundly defeated and Japan saw the first real transfer of political power in the postwar era—all largely due to the government's steps that inadvertently prolonged Japan's 20-year depression.

5. Former chairman Alan Greenspan, in testimony before the House Committee on Oversight and Reform hearings of October 22, 2008, opens with the statement, "We are in the midst of a once-in-a-century credit tsunami," and then went on to admit that the Fed had erred in allowing the housing bubble to evolve. A few weeks earlier, Treasury Secretary Henry M. Paulson Jr. literally

bent down on one knee as he pleaded with House Speaker Nancy Pelosi not to blow up the financial system by withdrawing her party's support for the Troubled Asset Relief Program (TARP).

6. "Proposed $700 Billion Bailout Is Too Little, Too Late to End the Debt Crisis; Too Much, Too Soon for the U.S. Bond Market," www.moneyandmarkets. com/files/documents/Final-Bailout-White-Paper.pdf.

7. *Quarterly Report to Congress,* Office of the Special Inspector General for the Troubled Asset Relief Program (SIGTAR), 8, www.sigtarp.gov/reports/ congress/2010/July2010_Quarterly_Report_to_Congress.pdf.

8. While the Federal Reserve feared that deflation (falling prices) would depress consumer demand and sink the economy, the average American family feared that further inflation would pinch their already-stressed household budgets. Indeed, on November 3, 2010, even as the Federal Reserve announced it was again running the nation's money printing presses to "create inflation," prices were already rising sharply for commodities, groceries, energy, health care, and tuition.

Chapter 2. The Government Declares War on the Financial Crisis

1. Before the Lehman failure, it took 5,012 days for the monetary base to double—from $426.6 billion on December 21, 1994, to $849.9 billion on September 10, 2008. However, subsequent to the Lehman Brothers failure, because of the Fed's quantitative easing (money printing), this measure doubled in just 112 days, jumping to $1.7 trillion by December 31, 2008. This 112-day doubling of the monetary base represented a growth rate that was 44.8 times greater than during the preceding 5,012 days. In contrast, in preparation for a feared Y2K crisis, the Fed accelerated the growth in the monetary base by a far smaller amount—$73 billion, from $557.2 billion on October 6, 1999, to $630.2 billion on January 12, 2000. And in response to the 9/11 terrorist attacks, the Fed accelerated the growth by only $39.7 billion, from the $625.1 billion reported for September 5, 2001, to $664.8 billion on September 19, 2001. Data: Federal Reserve—Aggregate Reserves of Depository Institutions and the monetary base, not adjusted for changes in reserve requirements, average daily figures, not seasonally adjusted. For the author's tabulation of the data, go to http://images.moneyandmarkets. com/1514/monetary-reserves-PDF.pdf.

2. See *Too Big Has Failed,* Thomas M. Hoenig, www.kansascityfed.org/SpeechBio/ HoenigPDF/Omaha.03.06.09.pdf.

3. "U.S. 'Creative Accounting' Could Repeat Greek Tragedy," CNBC interview, February 16, 2010.

4. *United States Monetary Policy,* Columbia University Press, 1958.

5. Investigation of the Financial Condition of the United States: Hearings before the Committee on Finance, United States Senate, U.S. Government Printing Office, 1957.

6. Quoted in "Can You Keep Going Much Longer?" Sound Dollar Committee political advertisements, *Wall Street Journal,* January–March 1959.

7. "Federal Debt and the Risk of Fiscal Crisis," Congressional Budget Office, July 27, 2010, www.cbo.gov/ftpdocs/116xx/doc11659/07-27_Debt_FiscalCrisis_Brief.pdf.

8. Data source: Federal Reserve and Office of the Comptroller of the Currency.

9. Data source: "Summary of Receipts, Outlays, and Surpluses or Deficits: 1789–2015," Office of Management and Budget, Table 1.1, www.whitehouse.gov/omb/budget/Historicals.

10. For more details, see "Election's impact on stocks, gold, oil, currencies and more!" by Martin D. Weiss, *Money and Markets,* October 10, 2010, www.moneyandmarkets.com/elections-impact-on-stocks-gold-oil-currencies-and-more-2-40346.

11. For more on this topic, see "Glimpses of the End Game," by Martin D. Weiss, *Money and Markets,* June 14, 2010, www.moneyandmarkets.com/glimpses-of-the-end-game-39381.

Chapter 3. Wall Street Deceptions, Cover-Ups, and Lies

1. In the 1980s and early 1990s, Weiss Ratings was a division of Weiss Research, Inc., and was subsequently spun off as a separate subsidiary of Weiss Group, Inc. For more on Weiss corporate history, see "History of Weiss Research, Inc." at www.moneyandmarkets.com/content/history.html. For more on its public service, see "Weiss Research, Inc. Chronology of Public Service Activities," www.moneyandmarkets.com/topic/services/public-service/.

2. According to the U.S. Government Accountability Office (GAO), for the large insurance companies that failed in the early 1990s, the leading insurance rating agency, A.M. Best Co., assigned a "vulnerable" rating before failure in only one of the six cases; in one case, Best stopped rating the insurer and never warned its customers; and in the remaining four cases, it issued its warnings only after the companies had already failed. S&P and Moody's also issued warnings only *after* failures. In contrast, the GAO reported that Weiss was the only one that issued its warnings far ahead of time in all six cases. Comparing a larger universe of 30 failed companies, the GAO found that Weiss beat Best by a factor of three to one. Weiss was also the only one to correctly identify the truly secure companies: Among Weiss's top-rated firms, there were no failures; among S&P's and Best's top-rated firms, there were several. Sources: GAO, *Insurance Ratings: Comparison of Private Agency Ratings for Life/Health Insurers,* September 1994, and Weiss, *Performance Review of Insurance Ratings Agencies,* March 1995.

3. Wall Street rating agencies rarely publish ratings without the consent of the rated company and most will remove them from circulation if requested. A.M. Best and Company, for example, defines its NA-9 rating as "assigned to companies eligible for ratings, but which request that their rating not be published *because they disagree* with our rating." [Italics added.] The GAO found

that, in 4 out of 30 insurers that failed in the early 1990s, "Best never actually assigned a 'vulnerable' rating. Instead, Best changed these ratings from 'secure' to one of its 'not assigned' categories." In each case, Best's standard operating procedure was to cooperate with the companies, remove the bad ratings from circulation, and hide the financial weaknesses from the public. And in each case, the companies failed, causing severe hardships to consumers. Ibid., GAO, 1994.

4. *The Insurance Forum* reports that Standard & Poor's charged from $10,000 to $50,000 per company per year, Moody's charged from $15,000 to $45,000, and Best's fees were similar to those of Standard & Poor's and Moody's. In contrast, Weiss never accepts compensation of any kind from the companies it covers, deriving its revenues exclusively from the sale of its research to consumers and investors. *Esquire* wrote "only Weiss [is] free of any possible conflict of interest."

5. Martin D. Weiss, "Toward a Full Disclosure Environment in the Insurance Industry," testimony before the U.S. Senate Committee on Banking, Housing, and Urban Affairs.

6. Before the global settlement, in December 2000, Zachs Investment Research reported that 99 percent of the stock ratings issued by Wall Street brokers and banks were *buy* or *hold,* with only 1 percent *sell* ratings, implying widespread bias favoring positive ratings. After the global settlement, sell ratings were more common and performance improved, but independent firms still vastly outperformed Wall Street in correctly identifying the best and worst stocks for investors: In 2005, the *Wall Street Journal* reported that, among 23 stock research providers, four of the five top performers were independent firms— Weiss (ranked number 1 in performance), Columbine Capital (number 2), Ford Equity Research (number 4), and Channel Trend (number 5). These four firms greatly outperformed the Wall Street firms Merrill Lynch, J.P. Morgan, Goldman Sachs, Piper Jaffray, Lehman Brothers, UBS Investment Research, Credit Suisse First Boston, Smith Barney, Morgan Stanley, Thomas Weisel Partners, and Bear Stearns. Continuing bias and conflicts of interest on Wall Street were the primary cause. Despite their performance success, however, independent firms were not able to gain market share. See Jane J. Kim, "Stock Research Gets More Reliable," *Wall Street Journal,* June 7, 2005.

7. Martin D. Weiss, "Dangerously Close to a Money Panic," *Money and Markets,* December 3, 2007, www.moneyandmarkets.com/dangerously-close-to-a-money-panic-9299.

8. Ibid., and Martin D. Weiss, "Closer to a Financial Meltdown," *Money and Markets,* March 17, 2008, www.moneyandmarkets.com/closer-to-a-financial-meltdown-4-9608. Separately, Richard Bove of Punk Ziegel & Company downgraded virtually all of the Wall Street banks, saying the Bear Stearns funds' collapse does not reflect a problem at the firm itself, but rather reveals troubles with the entire system.

9. Martin D. Weiss warned of an outright failure of Fannie Mae in *Safe Money Report,* September 18, 2000. Plus, in the fall of 1999, Treasury Secretary

Lawrence Summers warned "Debates about systemic risk should also now include government-sponsored enterprises, which are large and growing rapidly," and in 2005, Business & Media Institute warned that "Fannie Mae was a looming taxpayer-backed disaster."

10. Martin D. Weiss, *Safe Money Report,* April 2005. Weiss warned that, due to massive losses and financial failures, investors should not touch the following companies with a "ten-foot pole": Aames Investment, Accredited Home Lenders, Beazer Homes USA, Countrywide Financial, DR Horton, Fannie Mae, Freddie Mac, Fidelity National Financial, Fremont General, General Motors, Golden West Financial, H&R Block, KB Home, MDC Holdings, MGIC Investment, New Century Financial, Novastar Financial, PHH Corp, PMI Group, Pulte Homes, Radian Group, Ryland Group, Toll Brothers, Washington Mutual, and Wells Fargo & Company. By year's end 2008, 11 of the 25 companies had filed for bankruptcy or been bailed out or bought out. All had suffered severe stock declines, with average declines of 81.3 percent.

Chapter 4. Housing: How to Escape the Greatest Bust of All Time

1. Testimony to the House Financial Services Subcommittee on Financial Institutions and Consumer Credit, March 30, 2004; Susan Finch, "An Offer to Refuse," *Times-Picayune,* New Orleans, August 22, 2004.
2. Appraiser complaints. See "Appraisers Petition against 'Make the Deal'" at www.ired.com/news/2001/0102/appraiser.htm.

Chapter 6. How Safe Is Your Bank?

1. Readers can view the 1-hour video at www.moneyandmarkets.com/x-list-webinar, or refer to the partial transcripts at www.moneyandmarkets.com/x-list-transcript-1, and www.moneyandmarkets.com/x-list-transcript-2.
2. For data on U.S. derivatives, visit www.occ.treas.gov/deriv/deriv.htm; for global derivatives, go to www.bis.org/statistics/derstats.htm.

Chapter 7. How to Find Safe Insurance Companies

1. GAO, *Insurance Ratings: Comparison of Private Agency Ratings for Life/Health Insurers,* September 1994.
2. Eric N. Berg wrote extensively on this topic in "New Ratings for Insurers are Disputed," *New York Times,* January 10, 1992, www.nytimes.com/1992/01/10/business/new-ratings-for-insurers-are-disputed.html; and in "The Bad Boy of Insurance Ratings," *New York Times,* January 5, 1992, www.nytimes.com/1992/01/05/business/the-bad-boy-of-insurance-ratings.html.

Chapter 8. How to Shop for the Best Life Insurance

1. "Statement of Martin D. Weiss, President," Hearings before the Committee on Commerce, Science, and Transportation, February 27 and May 7, 9, and 23, 1991, 158–207. Also available online at www.moneyandmarkets.com/files/documents/Congressional-Hearing-Martin_Weiss_Testimony_1991.pdf.

Chapter 11. All-Weather Investments for the Best and the Worst of Times

1. For regular e-mail updates on ETFs from Weiss Research editor Ron Rowland, sign up at www.moneyandmarkets/alert.

ACKNOWLEDGMENTS

In some ways, I have been writing various bits and pieces of this book since 1974, when the first major economic crisis of my generation struck the country and ripped through New York City's finances. Therefore, to properly acknowledge those who have contributed to this effort, I must span the 36-year time horizon between then and now.

My father, J. Irving Weiss—probably the only person to make a fortune in the Crash of 1929 and live to do it *again* in the Crash of 1987—left behind 70 years of rich experience. Before he passed away, he patiently endured the seemingly endless life-history interviews that I conducted. My loving wife, Elisabeth, persistently questioned as I read her the entire manuscript, start to finish. My older brother, Joseph Weiss, provided the input of a PhD economist. And my son, Anthony, despite the pressures of daily life in Tokyo, closed the loop by reviewing the final draft, still finding conceptual disconnects that no one else noticed.

A great fallacy of most economic analysis is its focus on measuring continuous, linear processes like growth and its relative *lack* of attention to discontinuous processes, such as stock market crashes, financial collapses, and historic reversals in government policy, when structural changes are the most intense. Thus, beyond the many years of training I got at home in economic theory, I am especially grateful to the great scientists in the fields of cultural anthropology, sociology, political science, and economics who gave me a more holistic understanding of economic systems and structural change: Colin Turnbull, George Bond, Allen Johnson, Myron Cohen, Morton Fried, Marvin Harris, James Hsu, Herbert Passin, and Philip Stanniford. I thank them immensely for the analytical tools without which this book would have been impossible.

The most current contributions, however, come from the independent-thinking experts who give me so many valuable ideas on a daily basis at the Weiss Group, including Amber Dakar (personal finance), Bryan Rich (foreign currencies), Claus Vogt (economic theory), Gavin Magor (insurance company solvency), Gene Kirsch (bank solvency), Larry Edelson (silver and gold), Michael Larson (real estate, interest rates, and financial companies), Melissa Gannon (ratings), Monty Agarwal (portfolio theory), Rudy Martin (Latin America), Nilus Mattive (dividends and income), Ron Rowland (ETFs), Sean Brodrick (natural resources), and Tony Sagami (Asia). Dorianne Perucci and Maryellen Murphy made very significant contributions. Amber was especially helpful providing in-depth research, and I also used research provided by John Burke and Mandeep Ray. Ellen Lehrer provided valuable insights regarding real estate and mortgages. David Lackey, Clayton Makepeace, Peter DeSanctis, and Bentley Radcliff gave me important critiques. I am also indebted to Dan Rosenthal and Dr. Kurt Richebächer for their many years of friendship and teachings.

Among the 50,000 investors who receive our *Safe Money Report* and the half million who get our *Money and Markets,* it never ceases to amaze me how many send me questions and feedback or how insightful those comments are. Their contributions to this book were among the most helpful of all.

ABOUT THE AUTHOR

Among the nation's leading experts who can help you through bubbles, busts, recession, or depression, Martin D. Weiss, the founder and chairman of Weiss Ratings, Inc. is easily one of the most qualified.

During the stock market and housing bubbles of recent years, he consistently steered investors away from the dangers before the busts. And for the past two decades, he has specifically named—and publicly warned about—nearly every large financial failure in the United States, giving millions of Americans the opportunity to get their money to safety well ahead of time.

The *New York Times* wrote that Weiss was "the first to warn of the dangers and say so unambiguously." Separately, a study by the U.S. Government Accountability Office (GAO) concluded that Weiss far outperformed all of the nation's major rating agencies, including Standard & Poor's, Moody's, and A.M. Best, in warning of future life and health insurance company failures.

Separately, the *Wall Street Journal* reported that his company's stock ratings outperformed those issued by all brokers and independent research firms they covered, including JPMorgan Chase, Merrill Lynch, Goldman Sachs, Piper Jaffray, Credit Suisse First Boston, Smith Barney, S&P Equity Research, Morgan Stanley, and 14 others.

A key factor in Dr. Weiss's success is his devotion to empirical research and zero tolerance for bias, the reason *Forbes* named him "Mr. Independence" and *Esquire* wrote that he is one of the few who is "free of any possible conflict of interest."

Throughout his career, the author has been an advocate for consumers and investors, providing congressional testimony and proposals for better risk disclosure by financial institutions, sounder accounting by corporations, and more prudent fiscal policies by government.

Dr. Weiss is the CEO and founder of the Weiss Group, Inc., which includes not only Weiss Ratings, but also Weiss Research, Inc., a think tank and publishing firm; and Weiss Capital Management, Inc., an SEC-registered firm managing money for investors since 1980. The Weiss School, a pre-K elementary and middle school for gifted children in Palm Beach Gardens, Florida, was also a subsidiary of the Weiss Group until 2010, when the Weiss family donated the school to the community by converting it into a not-for-profit 501(c)3 corporation.

The author is also co-founder of the Financial Publishers Association, whose members reach 14 million investors, and chairman of the Sound Dollar Committee, a nonprofit organization founded by his father, which helped President Dwight D. Eisenhower balance the federal budget in 1959.

Martin Weiss's publications include *The Ultimate Safe Money Guide,* a *New York Times* and *Wall Street Journal* best seller, and *Crash Profits.* He holds a PhD in cultural anthropology from Columbia University and is fluent in 11 European, Asian, and African languages. After living many years in Latin America and Asia, he currently resides with his wife of 41 years in Palm Beach Gardens, Florida.

To contact the author, e-mail martin@weissinc.com or sign up for his alerts at www.moneyandmarkets.com/guide. If you do not have e-mail, and would like to receive one of the free reports mentioned in this book, call 800-814-3029, or mail your request to Martin D. Weiss, c/o The Ultimate Money Guide, 15430 Endeavour Drive, Jupiter, FL 33478.

INDEX